The Book of Mormon: The Foundation of Our Faith

Sidney B. Sperry

Other volumes in the Sperry Symposium Series
from Deseret Book Company:

The Testimony of John the Beloved
Voices of Old Testament Prophets
The Doctrine and Covenants, a Book of Answers
Nurturing Faith through the Book of Mormon
The Apostle Paul: His Life and His Testimony
Thy People Shall Be My People
The Heavens Are Open
Doctrines of the Book of Mormon
The Lord of the Gospels
A Witness of Jesus Christ
Doctrines for Exaltation

The Book of Mormon: The Foundation of Our Faith

*The 28th Annual
Sidney B. Sperry Symposium*

Deseret Book Company
Salt Lake City, Utah

© 1999 Deseret Book Company

All rights reserved. No part of this book may be reproduced in any form or by any means without permission in writing from the publisher, Deseret Book Company, P. O. Box 30178, Salt Lake City, Utah 84130. This work is not an official publication of The Church of Jesus Christ of Latter-day Saints. The views expressed herein are the responsibility of the authors and do not necessarily represent the position of the Church or of Deseret Book Company.

Deseret Book is a registered trademark of Deseret Book Company.

Library of Congress Cataloging-in-Publication Data
Sperry Symposium (28th : 1999 : Brigham Young University)
  The Book of Mormon : the foundation of our faith / 1999 Sperry Symposium.
    p.   cm.
  Includes bibliographical references.
  ISBN 1-57345-599-7
  1. Book of Mormon—Criticism, interpretation, etc.—Congresses.   I. Title.
BX8627.S772   1999
289.3'2221—dc21
                                                                99-043430

Printed in the United States of America   72082-6551
     10   9   8   7   6   5   4   3   2

Contents

Preface vii

1. The Power of the Book of Mormon
   Robert J. Matthews 1

2. The Doctrine of Faith
   Robert L. Millet 13

3. Alma to Corianton:
   A Pattern for Modern Parents
   Philip Allred 24

4. The Book of Mosiah:
   A Primer for the Restoration
   Richard E. Bennett 37

5. A Perfect Formula for Knowing Right from Wrong
   Randy L. Bott 49

6. The Salvation of Children: A Case
   for Restoration and Revelation by Translation
   Guy L. Dorius 62

7. The First Coming of the Lord to the Jews:
   A Book of Mormon Perspective
   Richard D. Draper 73

8. A Banner Is Unfurled: The Doctrine
   of the Gathering in the Book of Mormon
   Timothy W. Durkin 87

9. Thy Walls Are Continually before Me:
   The Indispensable Role of Zion in the
   Plan of Salvation
   Steve Fotheringham 101

10. FOREORDINATION IN THE BOOK OF MORMON
    Brian M. Hauglid 117

11. SHOWING, KNOWING, AND CONVINCING:
    THREE WAYS THE BOOK OF MORMON RESTORES
    HOPE FOR THE LATTER-DAY SAINT FAMILY
    Richard D. Hawks 134

12. THE RIGHTEOUSNESS OF THE REDEEMER
    Daniel K Judd 148

13. SICKLE OR SWORD? CONVERSION VERSUS
    COMPULSION IN THE BOOK OF ALMA
    Michael L. King 162

14. CONFLICT IN THE BOOK OF MORMON:
    TYPES AND SHADOWS OF SPIRITUAL BATTLE TODAY
    John P. Livingstone 174

15. REPENTANCE IN THE BOOK OF MORMON
    Robert L. Marrott 187

16. ABINADI, MOSES, ISAIAH, AND CHRIST:
    "O HOW BEAUTIFUL UPON
    THE MOUNTAINS ARE THEIR FEET"
    David Rolph Seely 201

17. THE DOCTRINE OF GOD THE FATHER
    IN THE BOOK OF MORMON
    Andrew C. Skinner 217

18. LOST AND FOUND:
    THE PLAIN AND PRECIOUS THINGS
    Brian L. Smith 232

19. THE DOCTRINE OF AGENCY IN THE BOOK OF MORMON
    Blair G. Van Dyke 244

20. THE RESTORATION OF THE DOCTRINE OF ANGELS
    AS FOUND IN THE BOOK OF MORMON
    Mary Jane Woodger 257

    INDEX 271

Preface

Nearly a year before the publication of the Book of Mormon, the Lord told Oliver Cowdery, the Prophet's principal scribe in recording the translation, "The things which you have written are true" (D&C 18:2). Thus Oliver had the testimony of the Creator himself that the book was true. To say that the book is true is to say that it is real and that its characters and events actually took place; it is to say that its teachings are reliable, that they constitute the gospel of Jesus Christ, and that they are a faithful witness of that which men of God in times past—having seen our day—directed to us.

Oliver was reminded that "in many instances" the Spirit of the Lord had testified to him that what he had written was true, and therefore he was commanded to "rely upon" that which he had written. "In them," the Lord said, "are all things written concerning the foundation of my church, my gospel, and my rock" (D&C 18:3–4). This revelation had come at Oliver's request when he sought direction in the assignment the Prophet had given him to draft a founding document for the Church which was about to be organized. There was no question in the minds of the two men, who would be sustained as the first and second elders in the Church (D&C 20:2), that the truthfulness of the Book of Mormon was the foundation upon which it was to rest.

That foundational document, known to us as Doctrine and Covenants 20, announces that the Book of Mormon contains "the fulness of the gospel of Jesus Christ" as it is to go both to the Gentiles and to the Jews (v. 9). It identifies three singular purposes of the Book of Mormon: first, to prove that the Bible is true; second, to prove that Joseph Smith is a prophet; and third, to prove that God is the same yesterday, today, and forever (vv. 11–12). It then declares that the world will be judged by these three evidences. Moreover, it promises a crown of eternal life to those who receive the Book of Mormon in faith and work righteousness, whereas those who harden their hearts in unbelief against it are promised that it will "turn to their own condemnation" (v. 15). Having so declared, this revelation then states, "By these things"—that is, in and through the truths restored to us in the Book of Mormon—"we know that there is a God in heaven." That God is described as the infinite, eternal, unchangeable God who framed both the "heaven and earth, and all things which are in them" (v. 17).

The declaration thus made to all the world is that we as Latter-day Saints believe in God because of our faith in the Book of Mormon and, further, that it is the foundation of our faith. Our testimony does not and cannot rest in either the traditions or the doctrines of historical Christianity. It is a new dispensation of which we testify. Our testimony is that the God of heaven has dispensed anew all the truths of salvation, chief among them that God is the Father of our spirits and that Jesus of Nazareth was begotten of him in the flesh. We have not built the house of our faith out of the theological rubble of the past. Nor have we built on the shifting sands of philosophical speculation. Of such we stand independent. Our communication is with God and angels; our founding scripture has been preserved for us as it came from the pens of its original writers. It is here that our faith is founded.

It is the purpose of this volume to center the attention of the reader on distinctive truths restored to us in the Book of Mormon and to shine the light of inspiration and good scholarship on gospel truths that would not be ours were it not for the testimony of the ancient prophets whose writings were, by the providence of God, preserved for us in the Nephite record. Meaningful insight is given on a broad range of doctrinal topics. This has been accomplished in such a way as to find practical application in the daily experiences of those who believe in it and accord their lives with its teachings. It is

Preface

the hope of all who participated in the 1999 Sperry Symposium that this volume will stand as a meaningful evidence that the Book of Mormon is indeed the foundation of our faith.

>   Joseph Fielding McConkie
>   David M. Whitchurch
>   Fred E. Woods
>   Patty A. Smith
>
>   THE 1999 SIDNEY B. SPERRY
>   SYMPOSIUM COMMITTEE

CHAPTER ONE

THE POWER OF THE BOOK OF MORMON

ROBERT J. MATTHEWS

The best thing about the Book of Mormon is that it is true. It is a true record and it is true doctrine, and the truth has a certain power all its own. The Book of Mormon is a source of eternal gospel truth.

I first obtained a conviction in my soul about the Book of Mormon when I was eighteen years old and was reading it every day. I didn't know about the promise of Moroni 10:4—to pray about whether or not it was true—but long before I got that far into the book, I had an intense feeling that I was reading sacred truth. I did not know anything about archaeological evidences, styles or patterns of writing, Hebrew language or customs, biblical prophecies, or geographical locations. I have never doubted the Book of Mormon, and when I seriously began reading it I felt something good working inside me that told me the Book of Mormon was right, and was not just another book. That experience began about fifty-five years ago. I have never forgotten it, nor lost the feeling, and have felt it repeated many times. Learning of external evidences and internal complexities, while very interesting, has increased my knowledge, but not measurably increased my testimony.

THE NATURE OF THE BOOK OF MORMON

Following are three statements that emphasize the distinctive message of the Book of Mormon and show why it has such a strong influence upon those who study it. The first is from the Prophet

---

Robert J. Matthews is professor emeritus of ancient scripture at Brigham Young University.

Joseph Smith: "I told the brethren that the Book of Mormon was the most correct of any book on earth, and the keystone of our religion, and a man would get nearer to God by abiding by its precepts, than by any other book."[1]

The second is from Elder Orson Pratt:

"The Book of Mormon claims to be a divinely inspired record, written by a succession of prophets who inhabited ancient America. . . .

"This book must be either *true* or *false*. If true, it is one of the most important messages ever sent from God to man, affecting both the temporal and eternal interests of every people under heaven to the same extent and in the same degree that the message of Noah affected the inhabitants of the old world. If false, it is one of the most cunning, wicked, bold, deep-laid impositions ever palmed upon the world, calculated to deceive and ruin millions who will sincerely receive it as the word of God. . . .

"The nature of the message in the Book of Mormon is such, that if true, no one can possibly be saved and reject it; if false, no one can possibly be saved and receive it."[2]

The third statement is from Elder Bruce R. McConkie. He observed that people generally seem to be able to read the Holy Bible and either believe it or reject it without severely reacting toward other people. He noted that those who do not believe the Bible generally do not feel an urge to make war upon those who do believe it. Their differences are usually intellectual rather than emotional. He noted, however, that when it comes to the Book of Mormon the situation is quite different. These are his words:

"There is, however, one great difference between the Bible and the Book of Mormon that shows why some people can disbelieve the Bible and let the matter drop, but disbelieving the Book of Mormon, they find themselves compelled to arise in wrath and defame the Nephite record. It is that people who believe the Bible, as they suppose, can also believe any creed of their choice and belong to any church that suits them. But belief in the Book of Mormon presupposes the acceptance of Joseph Smith as a prophet as well as membership in the church organized by him. . . .

"Further, the Bible is difficult to interpret and understand, and reasonable men, approaching it wholly from an intellectual standpoint, can reach divergent conclusions on almost all doctrines—hence, the many contending sects in Christendom. The Bible is indeed the perfect tool to support every conceivable doctrinal view. But the Book of Mormon is otherwise; this American scripture sets forth the doctrines of salvation in simplicity and plainness so that reasonable men, even from an intellectual standpoint, can scarcely disagree. This leaves religionists in the position where they must freely accept or openly oppose the Nephite scripture. There is no middle ground, no readily available gray area, no room for compromise."[3]

This is a principal reason the Book of Mormon is the "keystone." Its doctrinal teachings are so well defined that it holds in place all doctrinal interpretation.

We will now examine a few distinctive teachings of the Book of Mormon—some things that we would not know at all without it and some things that are alluded to in the Bible but not understood without the Book of Mormon.

JESUS VISITED ANCIENT AMERICA

Without the Book of Mormon we would not know that Jesus, after his resurrection from the dead, visited and taught a branch of the house of Israel in the Western Hemisphere, particularly showing them his resurrected immortal body. That is a basic message of the Book of Mormon, which also provides a summation of his teachings (see 3 Nephi 11:28).

We also learn from the Book of Mormon that after Jesus visited the ancient Nephites in the Americas and showed them his resurrected body, he spoke of his intention to visit the lost tribes of Israel for the same purpose—showing them his resurrected body. Jesus said the Father had commanded him to make this appearance to the lost tribes. We have no reason to doubt that this was accomplished. The Book of Mormon does not tell us where the lost tribes were located geographically, but it does affirm that such a visit was to be made (see 3 Nephi 16:1–3).

We read in the New Testament that after Jesus was resurrected from the tomb in the Holy Land, he showed his body to the Twelve at Jerusalem and commanded them to feel the nail prints in his hands and his feet, and the wound in his side (see Luke 24:36–40;

John 20:20, 27). He also showed himself, after his resurrection, to more than five hundred brethren in Galilee (see 1 Corinthians 15:4–8).

It was later that same year when he visited the Nephites, and commanded them to feel the nail prints and the side wound. The purpose of this experience was so that they would know he was their Redeemer, and had been crucified, died, and rose from the grave with the same body. We may thus confidently conclude that Jesus' visit to the lost tribes included a similar occurrence of seeing and touching, especially since Jesus himself said that the purpose of his visit to the lost tribes was to show himself to them (see 3 Nephi 17:4). We would not have known of Jesus' visit to the Nephites, nor the purpose of it, if we did not have the Book of Mormon. We can be sure that when the ancient record of the lost tribes of Israel is revealed, it will likewise contain a detailed account of Jesus' visit to them for the precise purpose of affirming that he is the Son of God, the Messiah, that he was crucified, died, and rose from the tomb, all of this as an atonement for man's sins. Thus the Bible, Book of Mormon, and the record of the lost tribes will all agree as to who Jesus is, because the Lord speaks "the same words unto one nation like unto another" (2 Nephi 29:8).

Jesus Visits Only Israelite Nations

There are other significant dimensions to the extra-biblical visits of the resurrected Jesus to the Nephites and the lost tribes of Israel. We learn from the Book of Mormon that such an explicit and profoundly real visit of Jesus—to show his resurrected body—is an event that occurs only to those who are of the house of Israel, and that he does not visit non-Israelite groups in such manner.

There is a hint of this in Matthew 15:24, when Jesus stated, "I am not sent but unto the lost sheep of the house of Israel." This passage alone, however, is not sufficient to clearly reveal the principle. There is also the statement of Jesus to the Jews that "other sheep I have which are not of this [Jewish] fold: them also I must bring, and they shall hear my voice" (John 10:16). But even this is not enough to establish the doctrine beyond doubt, and most readers today, and even the Jews to whom Jesus said it (including the disciples; see 3 Nephi 16:4) think that the "other sheep" were the Gentiles (see

3 Nephi 15:22). The Book of Mormon leaves no doubt as to the meaning, removing all ambiguity—Jesus personally visits only the house of Israel. The explanation, in Jesus' own words to the Nephites reads:

"And verily I say unto you, that ye are they of whom I said: Other sheep I have which are not of this fold; them also I must bring, and they shall hear my voice; and there shall be one fold, and one shepherd.

"And they understood me not, for they supposed it had been the Gentiles; for they understood not that the Gentiles should be converted through their preaching.

"And they [the Jews] understood me not that I said they shall hear my voice; and they understood me not that the Gentiles should not at any time hear my voice—that I should not manifest myself unto them save it were by the Holy Ghost.

"But behold, ye have both heard my voice, and seen me; and ye are my sheep" (3 Nephi 15:21–24).

THE DEPTH AND INTENSITY OF THE FALL OF ADAM

The fall of Adam and Eve (and of all mankind) is taught in the Bible, but not with the detail, clarity, depth, repetition, severity, and intensity as is in the Book of Mormon. The Fall is introduced in Genesis 3, and is described by Paul in Romans, chapters 3, 4, and 5, and in 1 Corinthians, chapter 15. Even so, it is only from the Book of Mormon that we learn the doctrine concerning the Fall, its precise beneficial consequences, and how extensively and severely it has touched every human being. Furthermore, the Book of Mormon provides the clearest declaration of what would have been the fate of every person if there had not been an atonement by Jesus Christ.

Time and space will not permit an extensive discussion in this treatise; however, let us examine two aspects. From Lehi we learn that without the Fall, Adam and Eve would have had no children; hence, no human family upon the earth (see 2 Nephi 2:22–25). Thus, the Fall is beneficent to us all, and very necessary.

From Jacob, the son of Lehi, we obtain what might be the most penetrating observation about the effects of the Fall on mankind. Jacob explains what would become of every soul if it were not for the redemptive power of Jesus Christ. He spoke of two conditions that have come upon all mankind because of the fall of Adam. These are (1) the death of the body and (2) being cut off from the presence of the Lord, or what is called "spiritual death." Jacob says that these two conditions came on mankind "by reason of the fall; and the fall came by reason of transgression" (2 Nephi 9:6). He then states: "Wherefore, it must needs be an infinite atonement—save it should be an infinite atonement this corruption could not put on incorruption. Wherefore, the first judgment which came upon man must needs have remained to an endless duration. And if so, this flesh must have laid down to rot and to crumble to its mother earth, to rise no more" (v. 7).

The effects of the Fall are so widespread and so deeply entrenched in each human soul that an infinite atonement is required to overcome them. What is "the first judgment that came upon man" that Jacob speaks of? It is the Lord's pronouncement: "Thou shalt surely die" if you partake of the fruit of the tree of knowledge of good and evil (Genesis 2:17). Jacob notes that the judgment (death) would be of an endless duration if it were not for the infinite atonement. That is, man's body would die, rot, crumble, and return to mother earth, and never rise again.

But the Fall also brought spiritual death. In fact, Adam, Eve, and all mankind experience the spiritual death before the physical death. Because all mankind experience the spiritual death, what would be the consequences to the spirit of man if there were a fall but no infinite atonement? Jacob says:

"O the wisdom of God, his mercy and grace! For behold, if the flesh should rise no more our spirits must become subject to that angel who fell from before the presence of the Eternal God, and became the devil, to rise no more.

"And our spirits must have become like unto him, and we become devils, angels to a devil, to be shut out from the presence of our God, and to remain with the father of lies, in misery, like unto himself" (2 Nephi 9:8–9).

What does that mean? It means that every person would become a devil. Even little children, who because of the Atonement are innocent before God, could not be saved (see Mosiah 3:16). All mankind, unable to save itself, and without a savior, would be without hope.

The Power of the Book of Mormon

Truly Jacob calls this death an "awful monster" (2 Nephi 9:10, 19). Jacob continues his discourse explaining that only Christ has the power to deliver mankind from these two deaths (see 2 Nephi 9:11–27).

Nothing in the Bible expresses the power and consequences of the Fall as vividly as does the Book of Mormon, and no prophet in the Book of Mormon does it any better than Jacob does. Having learned the crucial doctrine from the language of Jacob, we then appreciate the same doctrine couched in less vivid words taught by Lehi (see 2 Nephi 2:5–10), by Nephi (see 2 Nephi 11:6), by King Benjamin (see Mosiah 3:16–17), by Abinadi (see Mosiah 16:4–9), by Amulek (see Alma 34:9–12), by Alma (see Alma 42:9–15), and by Moroni (see Mormon 9:12–14). I feel it is safe to say that without the Book of Mormon we would not understand how severe, and yet how beneficial and necessary, the fall of Adam is. Nor would we see how totally dependent mankind is on the infinite atonement of Jesus Christ.

THE "VERY POINTS" OF DOCTRINE

The Book of Mormon contains the "very points" of Christ's doctrine (1 Nephi 15:14). But we can't use these points if we don't know what they are and where they are located, as the following experience illustrates.

Over thirty years ago, while discussing the Fall and the Atonement with friends, the notion came up as to the possibility of an alternate plan and even an alternate or backup savior. I revolted at the suggestion and felt that such an idea lacked faith and lacked the trust we ought to have in both the Father and the Son. Most of the others in the group felt that since Jesus had agency there was a possibility of him failing. The consequences to mankind of such a failure were so crucial that a backup was needed, and so forth. After we haggled over these items, Peter's well-known statement of Acts 4:12 came to my mind. This passage, spoken to the Jewish ruling council in Jerusalem, declares that Jesus Christ is the Savior. Furthermore: "Neither is there salvation in any other: for there is none other name under heaven given among men, whereby we must be saved." I thought that this passage touched upon every part of the controversy—no other person, no other name, and so on.

Much to my surprise, Peter's words were not convincing to the group because, said they, Peter spoke after Jesus had already made the Atonement, therefore by then he had become the only Savior. They felt Peter's statement did not negate the possibility that previous to the actual accomplishment, a backup had been needed. I was perplexed. Although I knew that what they were saying was not good doctrine, I couldn't think of any scriptures that categorically stated what they required as proof.

As a result of that experience, my awareness was sharpened, and I began to notice every passage that could be applied. I found several in the Book of Mormon. For example, Nephi, nearly 600 B.C., while speaking of Christ, proclaimed: "There is none other way nor name given under heaven whereby man can be saved" (2 Nephi 31:21). King Benjamin, in 124 B.C., was more explicit: "There shall be no other name given or any other way nor means whereby salvation can come . . . only in and through the name of Christ" (Mosiah 3:17). Benjamin later declared: "There is none other salvation save this which hath been spoken of; neither are there any conditions . . . except the conditions which I have told you" (Mosiah 4:8; see also 5:8). Since all of these were spoken before Christ accomplished the Atonement, they verify beyond reasonable argument that there never was an alternate plan nor a backup savior.

A corollary is found in 2 Nephi 2:24, wherein Lehi states: "All things have been done in the wisdom of him [God] who knoweth all things." Such a statement does not permit an experimental plan. Furthermore, we learn from Moses 4:1–4, that an alternate plan and another savior were included in Lucifer's proposal, which, of course, was rejected.

Having found these points of doctrine, I determined that never again would I be placed in such a situation. I knew the doctrine; I just hadn't focused on the best passages in order to teach it. It proved Elder McConkie's point that the Bible is sufficiently vague to support many doctrinal views. Even though Peter's statement is correct, it is not definitive enough to prevent speculation.

What about the group of friends that sparked the controversy? I do not even remember who they were. But they have probably since found these passages themselves and have self-corrected.

THE LAW OF RESURRECTION

As previously noted, the Book of Mormon declares emphatically that Jesus was resurrected from the dead with the same body he lived in while on earth. It likewise declares that all mankind will be similarly resurrected. We not only receive our same body, but once resurrected, we cannot die a physical death again. Amulek testified to what I call the law of resurrection. After explaining that every human being will be resurrected from the dead with every limb and joint in place, and not even a hair missing (see Alma 11:42–44), Amulek said: "Now, behold, I have spoken unto you concerning the death of the mortal body, and also concerning the resurrection of the mortal body. I say unto you that this mortal body is raised to an immortal body, that is from death, even from the first death unto life, that they can die no more; their spirits uniting with their bodies, never to be divided; thus the whole becoming spiritual and immortal, that they can no more see corruption" (Alma 11:45).

Note that Amulek, standing before a live audience, refers to "this mortal body," evidently meaning the body which they beheld—his live mortal body—is the one that will become immortal.

The prophet Mormon also makes it clear that he believed that all will be resurrected in the self-same, identical bodies they lived in as mortals. As he lamented the loss of his people who were slain in the last great battle at Cumorah, and as he had stood among their dead bodies, he reflected that "their flesh, and bones, and blood lay upon the face of the earth, being left by the hands of those who slew them to molder upon the land, and to crumble and to return to their mother earth.

"And my soul was rent with anguish, because of the slain of my people, and I cried:

" . . . Ye are gone, and my sorrows cannot bring your return.

"And the day soon cometh that your mortal must put on immortality, and these bodies which are now moldering in corruption must soon become incorruptible bodies; and then ye must stand before the judgment-seat of Christ" (Mormon 6:15–16, 20–21).

THE LAW OF RESTORATION

Book of Mormon prophets speak of an all-encompassing law of restoration, which is the underlying principle that governs the

Resurrection, the return of each person to the presence of God for the Judgment (see Alma 11:43–44; 42:23), and also the verdict of the Judgment. Some form of the word *restoration* (restored, restore, etc.) occurs at least sixty times in the Book of Mormon in a theological context.

The terms *resurrection* and *restoration* are often found together in the same passage, because resurrection is part of the larger plan of restoration. *Restoration* is actually the more definitive term, because it requires that in the Resurrection a person receives the *same* body that was his or her mortal body—otherwise what had taken place would have been only a *replacement,* not a *restoration.*

Since the law of restoration could occupy an entire essay by itself, only a few key verses will have to suffice in this treatise:

"The plan of restoration is requisite with the justice of God; for it is requisite that all things should be restored to their proper order. Behold, it is requisite and just, according to the power and resurrection of Christ, that the soul of man should be restored to its body, and that every part of the body should be restored to itself.

"And it is requisite with the justice of God that men should be judged according to their works; and if their works were good in this life, and the desires of their hearts were good, that they should also, at the last day, be restored unto that which is good.

"And if their works are evil they shall be restored unto them for evil. Therefore, all things shall be restored to their proper order, every thing to its natural frame.

"And now behold, is the meaning of the word restoration to take a thing of a natural state and place it in an unnatural state, or to place it in a state opposite to its nature?

"O, my son, this is not the case;

"For that which ye do send out shall return unto you again, and be restored; therefore, the word restoration more fully condemneth the sinner, and justifieth him not at all" (Alma 41:2–4, 12–13, 15).

When understood, the law of restoration can be a guide to us and gives additional meaning to gospel concepts, such as the first shall be last, the restoration of all things, the gathering of scattered Israel, the coming together of the continents, and the earth being renewed to receive its paradisiacal glory.

A Specific Plan of God

The Book of Mormon repeatedly tells that God has a plan for the salvation of the human family. It also states that Satan has a cunning plan calculated for man's destruction and misery.

Although it might be surmised from the Bible that God has a plan, the Bible in its present form and content does not categorically so state, whereas the Book of Mormon has at least twenty-seven such instances, and also at least five statements about Satan's plan.

Concerning God's Plan

- Merciful plan of the great Creator (see 2 Nephi 9:6)
- Plan of our God (see 2 Nephi 9:13)
- Plan of deliverance (see 2 Nephi 11:5)
- Great plan of redemption (see Jacob 6:8; Alma 34:31)
- Plan of salvation (see Jarom 1:2; Alma 24:14; 42:5)
- Plan of redemption (see Alma 12:25–26, 30, 32–33; 17:16; 18:39; 22:13–14; 29:2; 39:18; 42:11, 13)
- Plan of the Eternal God (see Alma 34:9)
- Great and eternal plan (see Alma 34:16)
- Plan of restoration (see Alma 41:2)
- Great plan of happiness (see Alma 42:8)
- Plan of mercy (see Alma 42:15, 31)

The Plan of Satan

- The cunning plan of the evil one (see 2 Nephi 9:28; Alma 28:13)
- Plan of thine adversary (see Alma 12:4–6)
- Secret plan of awful wickedness, originated by the devil and given to Cain (see Helaman 6:22–30; Ether 8:8–26)

It is important to note that the plan of God for the salvation of mankind is complete and comprehensive, from premortal life to final destiny. All parts of the plan are essential, none are optional—it is a package, and must be followed in its entirety.

Additional Significant Items

Several others items dealt with in the Book of Mormon are either unique to it, or were at least first made known by it and were later amplified by subsequent revelation. Among these are:

1. The New Jerusalem will be in the Western Hemisphere (see 3 Nephi 20:22; 21:23; Ether 13:2–10). The New Jerusalem is

mentioned in Revelation 21, but since no hint is given as to its location, one is led to suppose it is in the Middle East.

2. Mulek, son of King Zedekiah, came to America. The Bible gives the impression that all of Zedekiah's sons were slain by the Babylonians (see 2 Kings 25:7). The Book of Mormon tells us that one son, Mulek, came to the Western Hemisphere, was alive and well, and produced a posterity in America (see Helaman 6:10; 8:21).

3. Melchizedek was a great king and prophet. Although the Bible speaks well of Melchizedek, it offers very little detail, and confuses the record by saying he is without father or mother (see Genesis 14:18–20; Hebrews 7:1–4). Fortunately Alma 13:14–19 presents otherwise unknown events in Melchizedek's ministry. The Joseph Smith Translation of the biblical passages referred to above gives additional knowledge, and corrects the misstatement about his parentage.

Conclusion

The foregoing pages contain but a token presentation of what the Book of Mormon offers by way of divine, revealed, necessary gospel truth.

Notes

1. Joseph Smith, *Teachings of the Prophet Joseph Smith,* sel. Joseph Fielding Smith (Salt Lake City: Deseret Book, 1976), 194.

2. Orson Pratt, *Orson Pratt's Works on the Doctrines of the Gospel* (Salt Lake City: Deseret News Press, 1945), 107.

3. Bruce R. McConkie, *A New Witness for the Articles of Faith* (Salt Lake City: Deseret Book, 1985), 460–61.

CHAPTER TWO

THE DOCTRINE OF FAITH

ROBERT L. MILLET

The Book of Mormon is a singular scriptural record. It is a gift of God, given to the people of our dispensation to bear witness of the divine Sonship of Christ and to restore plain and precious truths that have been taken away or kept back from the Bible (see 1 Nephi 13:20–42).

Faith is the complete trust, confidence in, and reliance upon the merits, mercy, and grace of Jesus Christ for salvation. It is a gift of the Spirit (see Moroni 10:11), a divine endowment that affirms to the human heart the identity and redemptive mission of the Savior. Though one might speak of faith in a broad sense as the underlying reason why people live and move and go about their daily activities, the faith of which the scriptures speak, especially the Book of Mormon, is faith in the Lord Jesus Christ.

THE NEED FOR FAITH

The fall of Adam and Eve, though an essential part of the eternal plan of the Father (see 2 Nephi 2:25; Moses 6:48), brought dramatic changes to man and to all forms of life on earth. Because of the Fall, man is alienated from the Father and from things of righteousness; he is subject to spiritual death (see Alma 12:16, 32; 42:9). As Aaron taught the father of King Lamoni, "Since man had fallen he could not merit anything of himself" (Alma 22:14). No matter how noble his own efforts to overcome spiritual death, to love and serve others, or to keep the commandments of God, man will forevermore fall short of the divine standard. His works, though acceptable to God, will always be insufficient to save him (see 2 Nephi 25:23).

Robert L. Millet is dean of religious education and a professor of ancient scripture at Brigham Young University.

In short, had there been no means of bridging the chasm between sinful man and a sinless God, nothing that man could do would make up for the loss. Thus, there is a need for an atonement, a means of reconciling finite man with an infinite Deity, of repairing the breech between earth and the heavens. Man cannot save himself or rely upon his own merits. Truly, by the works of the law, no flesh is justified (see 2 Nephi 2:5). Because "all have sinned, and come short of the glory of God" (Romans 3:23), man cannot be justified—pronounced innocent or free from sin—by law or by works. Man's only option is to be justified by faith, to lean upon one who did in fact keep the law of God perfectly. It is only through the name of Jesus Christ—meaning his power or authority, his atoning mission and work—that salvation comes to the children of men (see 2 Nephi 9:24; Mosiah 3:17; 26:22; Alma 22:13; Helaman 14:13; Acts 4:12). In the words of Amulek, the atonement of Christ "bringeth about means unto men that they may have faith unto repentance" (Alma 34:15).

ELEMENTS OF FAITH

God the Father is the ultimate object of our worship (see 2 Nephi 25:16; Jacob 4:5; D&C 18:40; 20:19; JST John 4:25–26). Jesus worshiped the Father, and so must we. Our faith is therefore in the Father, just as it is in the Son. To have faith in the Son of God is to have faith in God, and so it is that many references in the Book of Mormon to faith or belief or trust or reliance mention God as often as they do Christ. Thus "as Christ is the way to the Father, faith centers in him and in his redeeming sacrifice and goes thereby to the Father, who is the Creator."[1]

The apostle Paul wrote that "faith is the substance [assurance, JST] of things hoped for, the evidence [or proof] of things not seen" (Hebrews 11:1). Our faith must be in something substantial, something of worth. "All belief is founded on evidence," Elder Orson Pratt explained. "A true faith is founded on true evidence; a false faith on false evidence. And in no case can a man have faith, either true or false, unless it is the result of true or false evidence. The greater the evidence, the greater will be the faith resulting from that evidence."[2]

Korihor had every reason to have faith in God; as Alma pointed out, he had evidence from the prophets and the scriptures, as well as the order of the cosmos (see Alma 30:44; D&C 88:45–47). But he chose not to receive and incorporate those evidences into the construction of his house of faith, and he thereby laid the foundation for his own demise. Near the end of the Nephite saga, Mormon prayed with all his heart for the deliverance of his people, but his prayers were "without faith, because of the hardness of their hearts" (Mormon 3:12). That is, Mormon was unable to exercise faith in their behalf because his people offered no evidence of repentance whatsoever.

Alma declared to the Zoramites that to have faith is "not to have a perfect knowledge of things; therefore if ye have faith ye hope for things which are not seen, which are true" (Alma 32:21; compare Ether 12:6; Hebrews 11:1). Sincerity and devotion to a cause are not sufficient; saving faith can only be exercised in that which is true. Thus, no matter how committed the Zoramites were to their unusual liturgy atop the Rameumptom (see Alma 31), their false beliefs concerning God could not result in faith unto life and salvation. Their refusal to believe in the coming condescension of God the Son precluded salvation, no matter how consistently they cried out to their deity in their weekly ritual.

We see also from this passage that faith is intimately connected with hope: to have true faith in Christ is to have hope in Christ. When we come to know who Jesus is, how great and marvelous are his powers and his knowledge, and the nature of his sacrificial offering—when we gain faith in Christ—then we gain a hope in Christ. No one can attain unto faith except he shall then have hope. We need not speak of faith as something one either has in its fulness or does not have. Gaining faith is a process. And so it is with hope. Individuals like the Zoramites begin with the simple hope that there is a Savior (see Alma 32:27). On the other end of the continuum are those who know their Lord, have treasured up his word, and have been valiant in their witness. Their hope is for eternal life, for exaltation in the celestial kingdom.

"And what is it that ye shall hope for?" Mormon asked. "Behold I say unto you that ye shall have hope through the atonement of Christ and the power of his resurrection, to be raised unto life eternal, and this because of your faith in him according to the promise. Wherefore, if a man have faith he must needs have hope; for without faith there cannot be any hope" (Moroni 7:40–42). The disciple of Christ has hope, not in the worldly sense (wishing or yearning), but rather in the sense of anticipation, expectation, and assurance that through the Divine Redeemer he will be saved in the highest heaven. He is motivated and directed, not by self-confidence, but by his confidence or hope in Christ.

BELIEF, TRUST, AND RELIANCE

In the scriptures there is no distinction made between true faith and true belief; belief is a synonym for faith. To have faith in Christ is to believe in Christ, to "believe that he is, and that he created all things, both in heaven and in earth; [to] believe that he has all wisdom, and all power, both in heaven and in earth" (Mosiah 4:9). The Nephite prophets labored diligently to invite their people "to believe in Christ, and to be reconciled to God" (2 Nephi 25:23), "for the Lord covenanteth with none save it be with them that repent and believe in his Son, who is the Holy One of Israel" (2 Nephi 30:2). The Nephites were called upon to "believe in Christ, and view his death, and suffer his cross and bear the shame of the world" (Jacob 1:8). Truly, "whosoever shall believe on the Son of God, the same shall have everlasting life" (Helaman 14:8).

In summarizing the first principles and ordinances of the gospel, Mormon wrote: "And if it so be that ye believe in Christ, and are baptized, first with water, then with fire and with the Holy Ghost, following the example of our Savior, . . . it shall be well with you in the day of judgment" (Mormon 7:10).

Trust and reliance are likewise synonyms for faith. To have faith in Christ is to trust in him, to rely completely upon him. The Lord Jesus extends his arm of mercy toward those who trust in him (see Mosiah 29:20). Those who come unto Christ trust in his arm, meaning his power, rather than the arm of flesh (see 2 Nephi 4:34), for "whosoever putteth his trust in him the same shall be lifted up at the last day" (Mosiah 23:22). Of the 2,000 stripling warriors, Helaman noted: "Now this was the faith of these of whom I have spoken; they are young, and their minds are firm, and they do put their trust in God continually" (Alma 57:27).

Nephi explained that the Saints of God were able to come unto Christ through "relying wholly upon the merits of him who is

The Doctrine of Faith

mighty to save" (2 Nephi 31:19). Moroni likewise wrote that people are nourished by the good word of God, "to keep them in the right way, . . . relying alone upon the merits of Christ, who was the author and the finisher of their faith" (Moroni 6:4). Jacob added the sobering conclusion to the matter: only those who have "perfect faith in the Holy One of Israel"—meaning, presumably, a wholehearted belief in, a complete trust in, and a total reliance upon, his redeeming blood—can be saved in the kingdom of God (2 Nephi 9:23). Again, because we cannot save ourselves, our absolute dependence must be, not in ourselves, no matter how impressive our accomplishments, but in him who bought us with his blood. Like Jacob, we are redeemed "because of the righteousness of [our] Redeemer" (2 Nephi 2:3).

A Principle of Power

Faith is more than a tenet, more than a doctrine. It was the Prophet Joseph Smith who taught that faith is a principle of power, the power by which gods and men bring to pass divine purposes.[3] When the former-day Saints, especially those in the Book of Mormon, operated by faith, they operated according to the mind and will of God.[4] Faith is not merely the power of suggestion, the power of positive thinking. The faithful, though filled with hope in Christ, are not just more optimistic than the world. People do not exercise faith by wishing and willing something to be. Men and women operate by faith when they first seek to know the mind of God on a matter and then proceed confidently; they first obtain their "errand from the Lord" (Jacob 1:17) and then move forward with a quiet but dynamic assurance that God will work his wonders through them.

For example, Nephi was "led by the Spirit, not knowing beforehand the things which [he] should do" (1 Nephi 4:6). He could move into otherwise frightening circumstances, including life-threatening situations, without knowing the details of his assignment. Why? Because he knew what was most important; though he did not know the how, he knew why he was to proceed. Nephi knew what God wanted him to do, and so his confidence was centered in God. He demonstrated faith in going and doing the things that God had commanded, knowing in his heart that he would not be asked to do so unless the Almighty would open the way (see 1 Nephi 3:7).

Abinadi evidenced his faith in the Savior when he sealed his messianic witness with his life's blood (see Mosiah 11:20–17:20), just as Zenos (see Helaman 8:19) and Zenock (see Alma 33:17) had done many years before. Ammon, Aaron, Omner, and Himni exercised their faith in the redemption of Christ, volunteered for missionary service, and were able to be instruments in the hands of God in leading many thousands of Lamanites to the covenant gospel (see Mosiah 28:1–9; Alma 17–23). Alma and Amulek were delivered from captivity through their faith (see Alma 14:27; Ether 12:13), while Nephi and Lehi, sons of Helaman, both men of profound faith and spiritual maturity (see Helaman 3:21; 11:19), participated in the spiritual rebirth of a large number of Lamanites (see Helaman 5; Ether 12:14). Because of the faith of the brother of Jared, he was able to remove a mountain. In addition, the brother of Jared "could not be kept from beholding within the veil" (Ether 3:19); indeed, "the Lord could not withhold anything from him, for he knew that the Lord could show him all things" (Ether 3:26; see also Ether 3:19; 12:20, 30).

Fruits of Faith

There are numerous fruits of faith—attitudes and actions that derive from believing, trusting, and relying upon Christ. We have already mentioned hope, and it is through faith that forgiveness comes, by which the soul is cleansed and sanctified (see 1 Nephi 12:10–11), and by which people are made alive in Christ (see 2 Nephi 25:25). Faith leads to joy and peace of conscience (see Mosiah 4:3; Helaman 5:47). It is by faith that men and women undergo a mighty change of heart when they come into the gospel covenant (see Mosiah 5:7; Alma 5:12). People are made whole through their faith in Christ, through their reliance upon One they have never before seen or heard (see Enos 1:8).

Faith and patience generally result in deliverance (see 1 Nephi 1:20; 7:17; Mosiah 24:16; Alma 14:26–28). Jacob encouraged his people to "look unto God with firmness of mind, and pray unto him with exceeding faith, and he will console you in your afflictions, and he will plead your cause, and send down justice upon those who seek your destruction" (Jacob 3:1). Helaman wrote how "the Lord our God did visit us with assurances that he would deliver us; yea, insomuch that he did speak peace to our souls, and did grant unto us great faith, and did cause us that we should hope for our deliverance in him" (Alma 58:11). So often the One in whom we trust does not remove the burden from our backs; rather, he lifts and lightens the burdens, so that we do not feel them (see Mosiah 24:11–14). Through faith, deliverance comes not only from physical bondage but also from temptation and from Satan's grasp. Alma instructed his son Helaman to teach the people "to humble themselves and to be meek and lowly in heart; teach them to withstand every temptation of the devil, with their faith on the Lord Jesus Christ" (Alma 37:33).

Further, true faith always manifests itself in faithfulness, in sustained obedience and endurance to the end (see 1 Nephi 7:12; Alma 44:4; 48:15). The Risen Lord declared that "no unclean thing can enter into [God's] kingdom; therefore nothing entereth into his rest save it be those who have washed their garments in my blood, because of their faith, and the repentance of all their sins, and their faithfulness unto the end" (3 Nephi 27:19). Ammon pointed out that "he that repenteth and exerciseth faith, and bringeth forth good works, and prayeth continually without ceasing—unto such it is given to know the mysteries of God" (Alma 26:22).

Spiritual gifts, signs, and wonders are also fruits of faith in Christ (see 2 Nephi 26:13; 27:23). Jesus announced to the Nephites that signs "follow them that believe" (Mormon 9:22–24). Mormon explained that "it is by faith that miracles are wrought; and it is by faith that angels appear and minister unto men" (Moroni 7:37; see also Mosiah 8:18; 3 Nephi 19:35). Before listing the various gifts of the Spirit, Moroni exhorted his readers to "deny not the power of God; for he worketh by power, according to the faith of the children of men, the same today and tomorrow, and forever" (Moroni 10:7).

Faith and Knowledge

Some have supposed that faith and knowledge are on opposite ends of a continuum, that once a person has knowledge he no longer has or needs faith. Actually, faith and knowledge build upon one another. A certain degree of knowledge is necessary in order to exercise faith, even "a particle of faith" (Alma 32:27). Then, after one has begun to develop faith, new and added knowledge comes—new feelings and desires, new insights, new perspectives. There is a sense in which one might speak, as Alma did to the Zoramites (see Alma 32:34; Ether 3:19), of one's faith being replaced by knowledge whenever a testimony of a particular principle has been obtained. In reality, however, faith has not disappeared, but instead has been added upon.

Faith is a principle of power and thus a divine attribute possessed by God in perfection;[5] God is the embodiment of faith, just as he is the embodiment of love and justice and judgment and mercy. And so mortals are not working toward that day when they will no longer live and act by faith, but rather toward that day, beyond the Resurrection, when they operate by perfect faith. "In the eternal sense," Elder Bruce R. McConkie has written, "because faith is the power of God himself, it embraces within its fold a knowledge of all things. This measure of faith, the faith by which the worlds are and were created and which sustains and upholds all things, is found only among resurrected persons. It is the faith of saved beings."[6]

Growing in Faith

The people of God work and labor and sacrifice and serve in order to build their faith and thus expand the power of God in their lives. The Book of Mormon teaches clearly how faith comes and, therefore, how it develops and is perfected. First of all, faith comes as one encounters the word of God, whether the spoken or written word. "Faith comes by hearing the word of God," Joseph Smith taught, "through the testimony of the servants of God; that testimony is always attended by the spirit of prophecy and revelation."[7] Nephi read the words of Isaiah to his people in order that he "might more fully persuade them to believe in the Lord their Redeemer" (1 Nephi 19:23).

Alma called upon the Zoramites to plant the word in their hearts—to ponder upon and pray over the idea that Christ should come to earth and offer salvation to all men (see Alma 32:26–31; 33:14–23; 34:4–5). In this famous sermon on faith, Alma described the process by which the faithless develop in time the saving faith in Christ that leads to life eternal. That process entailed belief, action, and spiritual confirmation or witness. One begins through demonstrating a willingness to experiment upon the idea of a Savior, to plant that idea in his heart. He then performs the actions appropriate to spiritual investigation, such as prayer, scripture study, association with the people of God, and meaningful service to fellowman. He then gains a confirmation, the peaceful but powerful assurance that the word is good, that in fact Jesus is the Christ and Redeemer of the world and that salvation comes through him. There also follows the corollary change of nature that flows from faith in the Lord. The believer begins over time to embody and exemplify Christlike attributes, for "every seed bringeth forth unto its own likeness" (Alma 32:31). This process of assurance and validation continue throughout one's life.

Mormon spoke of a time when the Nephites "did fast and pray oft, and did wax stronger and stronger in their humility, and firmer and firmer in the faith of Christ, unto the filling their souls with joy and consolation, yea, even to the purifying and the sanctification of their hearts, which sanctification cometh because of their yielding their hearts unto God" (Helaman 3:35). Nephi, son of Helaman, taught that faith comes as people repent and cry unto God, so that "the cloud of darkness [is] removed from overshadowing you" (Helaman 5:41). Further, Moroni set forth the mighty truth found also in the New Testament, the doctrine that we gain faith and come to know as we do (see John 7:16–17). He confirmed that "faith is things which are hoped for and not seen; wherefore, dispute not because ye see not, for ye receive no witness until after the trial of your faith" (Ether 12:6). President Harold B. Lee taught that we must be willing to "walk to the edge of the light, and perhaps a few steps into the darkness, and you will find that the light will appear and move ahead of you."[8]

The final great fruit of faith is eternal life. In the first estate, man walked by sight and by faith. Those who were valiant in the premortal existence demonstrated "exceeding faith and good works" there and were foreordained and foreappointed to significant assignments here (Alma 13:1–6). In this life, man walks by faith (see 2 Corinthians 5:7); that is, he proceeds through life with the Spirit-given assurance that his actions are approved of God and will result in the salvation of his soul. To see with an "eye of faith" (Alma 5:15; 32:40) is to act according to the witness of the Spirit, to act as though one had seen, and thus had, perfect knowledge. The Saints of God view things with an eye of faith in this life—until one day, because of their faithful endurance, they see "with their eyes the things which they had beheld with an eye of faith" (Ether 12:19).

"The very name of the kind of life [God] lives is eternal life, and thus eternal life consists in living and being as he is. In other words, eternal life is to gain the power of God, which power is faith, and thus to be able to do what he does and to live as he lives. And the great and eternal plan of salvation that he has ordained and established consists of those laws, ordinances, and powers whereby faith is acquired and perfected until it is possessed in the same degree and to the same extent that it exists in Deity. Faith will thus dwell independently in every person who gains eternal life."[9]

Conclusion

The Prophet Joseph Smith taught that "when men begin to live by faith they begin to draw near to God; and when faith is perfected they are like him; and because he is saved they are saved also; for they will be in the same situation he is in, because they have come to him; and when he appears they shall be like him, for they will see him as he is." In this sense, the plan of salvation is "a system of faith—it begins with faith, and continues by faith; and every blessing which is obtained in relation to it is the effect of faith, whether it pertains to this life or that which is to come. To this all the revelations of God bear witness."[10]

I feel a great surge of gratitude for the revelations of the Restoration, particularly the Book of Mormon. The Bible chronicles acts of faith and deeds of wonder in both the Old and New Testaments, and there are a few places wherein the principle of faith is discussed. But it is to the Book of Mormon that we turn if we are serious about gaining faith like the ancients. In the Book of Mormon, we have restored to us, first of all, the knowledge of the God of miracles, the God of revelation, the God of the ancients. Having established these fundamental truths, all other doctrinal matters are then revealed in their pristine purity and fitted into place in the grand scheme of restoration. We learn from the Book of Mormon what faith is, the objects upon which it rests, and the fruits that flow from it. The Book of Mormon is not just a book about faith. It is a book that describes the process of faith, illustrates that process, and invites us, by the power of the Holy Ghost, to be active participants, first, in

The Doctrine of Faith

the acquisition of faith unto life and salvation, and, second, in the dissemination and perpetuation of faith throughout the earth.

Alma taught that if we will nourish the word—especially the proposition concerning the redemptive reality of Jesus the Christ—that the fruits of faith will be forthcoming in our lives, that the seed of faith in Christ "shall take root; and behold it shall be a tree springing up unto everlasting life.

"And because of your diligence and your faith and your patience with the word in nourishing it, that it may take root in you, behold, by and by ye shall pluck the fruit thereof, which is most precious, which is sweet above all that is sweet, and which is white above all that is white, yea, and pure above all that is pure; and ye shall feast upon this fruit even until ye are filled, that ye hunger not, neither shall ye thirst" (Alma 32:41–42).

NOTES

1. Bruce R. McConkie, *A New Witness for the Articles of Faith* (Salt Lake City: Deseret Book, 1985), 185.

2. Orson Pratt, "The Kingdom of God," *Orson Pratt's Works on the Doctrines of the Gospel* (Salt Lake City: Deseret News Press, 1945), 48.

3. See Joseph Smith, *Lectures on Faith* (Salt Lake City: Deseret Book, 1985), 1:15–17; 7:6; compare Hebrews 11:3.

4. See McConkie, *A New Witness for the Articles of Faith*, 167, 191–92, 206.

5. See Smith, *Lectures on Faith*, 1:15–17; 7:6; Hebrews 11:3.

6. McConkie, *A New Witness for the Articles of Faith*, 209.

7. Joseph Smith, *Teachings of the Prophet Joseph Smith*, sel. Joseph Fielding Smith (Salt Lake City: Deseret Book, 1976), 148.

8. Cited in Boyd K. Packer, *The Holy Temple* (Salt Lake City: Bookcraft, 1980), 184.

9. McConkie, *A New Witness for the Articles of Faith*, 169.

10. Smith, *Lectures on Faith*, 7:8, 17.

CHAPTER THREE

ALMA TO CORIANTON: A PATTERN FOR MODERN PARENTS

PHILIP ALLRED

At the conclusion of Alma's Zoramite mission, he called his three sons together "that he might give unto them every one his charge, separately, concerning the things pertaining unto righteousness" (Alma 35:16). While other father-to-son talks are recorded elsewhere in scripture,[1] Alma's account is unique. In it we are given a detailed illustration of how a parent can help a wayward child who has committed serious moral transgressions. Four chapters[2] of Alma's instructions are directed toward his youngest son, Corianton, who had deserted his missionary duties and fallen into grievous sin while among the Zoramites (see Alma 39–42).

The specific counsel Alma gave Corianton offers timely insight for latter-day families with similar circumstances. His exhortation is an exceptionally practical yet profound mix of discipline and doctrine, suggesting even the proportion of time to spend between the two. The key to Alma's counsel is his remarkable explanation of the eternal consequences of mortal choices. This leads his son to recognize the necessity of the Savior and of his need to repent. Today's families can apply the technique of Alma's counsel to assust them.[3]

Alma's method and message[4] may be outlined under five headings: assess the behavior according to gospel standards (39:2–6), exhort

---

Philip Allred is an instructor of religion in the Idaho East Area of the Church Educational System.

sincere repentance (39:7–14; 41:9; 42:29–30), follow the Spirit (39:12, 17; 40:1; 41:1; 42:1), teach true doctrine (see scriptures below), and show greater love and trust (42:31). These five headings form a timeless template that parents and counselors may apply.

Assess the Behavior According to Gospel Standards

In his counsel to Corianton, Alma immediately tackles the problem of Corianton's behavior. Reminding him that he had the example of his brother and the words of his father to guide him, he lists three specific sins his son has committed: (1) he boasted in his own strength and wisdom, (2) he left his teaching of the gospel, and (3) he consorted with a prostitute (see Alma 39:2–3).

Pride, abandonment of missionary calling, and fornication are serious matters. Alma places the wickedness of the latter in context with the two most grievous sins a person can commit—murder and denying the Holy Ghost (see Alma 39:5–6). This clear conviction of Corianton's immorality has a double effect. First, it leaves Corianton with no question as to the seriousness of his sins. Here is a plain and unmistakable declaration of guilt that will help Corianton fully grasp the spiritual jeopardy that he has placed himself in. Second, the accompanying effect is optimistic. Alma's use of the word *unpardonable* when describing the denial of the Holy Ghost should reveal to Corianton that *his* sins—though terrible—are forgivable.[5] In this way, the guilt that Corianton should feel will also prompt him to repent.

In proportion to his entire counsel, Alma's discussion of Corianton's sins is direct and brief. In ninety-one verses, only five are used to define and rank Corianton's sins (see Alma 39:2–6) and just eleven more to exhort him to repent (see Alma 39:7–14; 41:9; 42:29–30). Elder Boyd K. Packer has warned, "Preoccupation with unworthy behavior can lead to unworthy behavior."[6] Lehi appears to have been similarly brief on discipline while counseling his wayward sons; he also spent the bulk of his time teaching and prophesying (see 1 Nephi 8:36–38).

Exhort Sincere Repentance

Corianton's pride and boasting may have calloused his conscience in the same way that Laman and Lemuel had become "past feeling" (1 Nephi 17:45). Recalling his own impenitent past, Alma explains to Corianton that "I would not dwell upon your crimes, to harrow up your soul, if it were not for your good" (Alma 39:7). Alma is explaining that guilt should lead to repentance. Unfortunately, guilt can be like a two-edged sword—functional or dysfunctional. Satan can pervert this divine tool by tempting the sinner to become discouraged rather than motivated.[7] Alma is inviting his son to become inspired by this functional "remorse of conscience" (Alma 42:18) in order to change his life. Guilt, as a divinely designed consequence of sin, is meant to impel individuals to come unto Christ and repent. In the closing moments of his counsel, Alma returns to the utility of guilt by encouraging Corianton to "only let your sins trouble you, with that trouble which shall bring you down unto repentance" (Alma 42:29). Alma firmly exhorts Corianton: "repent and forsake your sins," because "ye cannot hide your crimes from God and except ye repent they will stand as a testimony against you at the last day" (Alma 39:8–9; see also 41:9). This directs Corianton to consider the inevitable accounting he will make for his actions.

As part of his exhortation to repent, Alma *commands* Corianton to counsel with his elder brothers (see Alma 39:10). In our modern world the word *command* can carry a negative connotation—one suggesting force or compulsion. Indeed, coercion is in direct contradiction to the Lord's plan. Still, Alma uses this word twice more with Corianton. Alma explains why: "And now *the Spirit of the Lord doth say unto me:* Command thy children to do good, lest they lead away the hearts of many people to destruction; *therefore I command you,* my son, *in the fear of God,* that ye refrain from your iniquities" (Alma 39:12; italics added). He was following the Spirit's direction, to the very words he was given. Alma also recognized and was true to his position as a steward in the Lord's behalf for his children. Discomforts parents might feel at the direction to command, chastise, exhort, or preach to their children may be overcome by the Comforter when they heed his directions (see also Moroni 6:9).

Follow the Spirit

Alma was directed by the Spirit throughout his counsel to his son. After he had reproved Corianton and passionately urged his repentance, Alma indicates that he *perceives* that his son's mind is not yet at rest and because of this, there "is somewhat more I would say unto thee" (Alma 40:1). In fact, each of the following chapters begins with the same word, *perceive* (see Alma 41:1; 42:1).[8] The word *perceive* is instructive. Alma is in tune with the still small voice of the Holy Ghost. In each case, Alma discerns a doctrine that Corianton misunderstands and then begins a discourse on it. The significance of this pattern is crucial in gospel counseling. Consider Elder Boyd K. Packer's axiom: "True doctrine, understood, changes attitudes and behavior." He explains that "the study of the doctrines of the gospel will improve behavior quicker than a study of behavior will improve behavior.... That is why we stress so forcefully the study of the doctrines of the gospel."[9]

The sequence and content of the doctrines Alma taught were dictated by Corianton's circumstances. Appropriately fitting the doctrine to the dilemma will require both the guidance of the Holy Ghost and a measure of doctrinal literacy on the part of the mentor. There is likely no one-size-fits-all doctrinal approach. Jacob serves as an example of how the Spirit may direct differently under similar circumstances. His people, like Corianton, were prideful (see Jacob 2:13–22) and immoral (see Jacob 2:23–28), and Jacob, like Alma, acknowledged the Spirit's influence on his teachings (see Jacob 1:17; 2:11, 23; 4:15, 18). Yet, he spent relatively little time on the doctrines that Alma taught.[10] For his people's particular needs he was led to prophesy extensively about the destiny of Israel by quoting and explaining Zenos' allegory of the tame olive tree (see Jacob 4:15–18; 5:1–77; 6:1–4). Jacob's approach was apparently effective, as "some years had passed away" before Sherem began to strive to "overthrow the doctrine of Christ" (Jacob 7:1–2).

Just like these ancient prophets, Latter-day Saints also have the ability to apply the doctrine individually through the gifts of the Spirit. "To some it is given by the Holy Ghost to know the differences of administration, as it will be pleasing unto the same Lord, according as the Lord will, suiting his mercies according to the conditions of the children of men" (D&C 46:15; see also 1 Corinthians 12:4–6; Moroni 10:8). In this regard, the Prophet Joseph Smith taught that "this is the principle on which the government of heaven is conducted—by revelation adapted to the circumstances in which the children of the kingdom are placed."[11]

Teach True Doctrine

The Universal Role of Christ as the Savior (Alma 39:15–19)

Parents of struggling children like Corianton may be puzzled by Alma's doctrinal direction at first, yet Alma is forming a three-part gospel response to Corianton's rebellious behavior. First, he reminds Corianton that Christ "shall come to take away the sins of the world," regardless of the generation in which they live (Alma 39:15–19). This uncovers his son's doctrinal misunderstanding of Christ's role as Redeemer. Second, Alma appears to lay aside Corianton's immediate misconceptions about the Savior and begins a discourse on the Resurrection. That may seem surprising; however, Alma clarifies that it is only through Christ that the Resurrection is even possible (see Alma 40:3). Also, Corianton had evidently been puzzled about the timing of Christ's coming and the Resurrection (see Alma 39:17; 40:2, 16, 18), along with the law of restoration in general (see Alma 41:1). Third, Alma turns to the doctrine of Christ's atonement to show how the Savior provides a just redemption for those who repent (see Alma 42:26). Alma's teachings form the basis for Corianton's new understanding of two crucial gospel doctrines: accountability and atonement. These twin doctrines, when understood together, constitute a powerful combination against false belief and the sinful behavior that stems from it.

Accountability

Postmortal spirit world (Alma 40:6–15). Alma establishes that all individuals are accountable for their actions by demonstrating the future impact of temporal behavior on death, resurrection, and the Final Judgment. First, Alma teaches that there is a judgment at death. On the one hand, the "righteous are received into a state of happiness, which is called paradise, a state of rest, a state of peace, where they shall rest from all their troubles and from all care, and sorrow" (Alma 40:12). On the other hand, "the spirits of the wicked . . . shall be cast out into outer darkness; there shall be weeping, and wailing, and gnashing of teeth" (Alma 40:13). Alma's use of outer darkness as a temporary hell between death and the Resurrection is clearly different from the eternal residence of Satan and those who defect into perdition, spoken of in Doctrine and Covenants 76:32–38, 44–48. It is the latter that is so commonly called outer darkness in the Church today. Naturally, Corianton is thus led to consider his own inevitable placement at death in this spirit world—a solemn task for one who has committed the sins Corianton has.

The Resurrection (Alma 40:2–5, 16–23; 41:2). The Resurrection itself is the second event that mortal choices will influence. Alma defines the Resurrection as the reuniting of the "soul with the body," in distinction to the spirit's "consignation to happiness or misery" in the spirit world (Alma 40:16–20). This physical miracle—where "every limb and joint shall be restored to its body; yea, even a hair of the head shall not be lost; but all things shall be restored to their proper and perfect frame"—is categorized as part of "the restoration . . . of which has been spoken by the mouths of the prophets" (Alma 40:22, 24). *It is in this resurrected body,* Alma explains, that all will "be brought to stand before God, and be judged according to their works" (Alma 40:21). He continues, "The plan of restoration is requisite with the justice of God; for it is requisite that all things should be restored to their proper order. Behold, it is requisite and just, according to the power and resurrection of Christ, that the soul of man should be restored to its body, and that every part of the body should be restored to itself. . . . Therefore, all things shall be restored to their proper order, every thing to its natural frame" (Alma 41:2, 4).

Three modern leaders in the Church have elaborated on the nature of this physical restoration. President John Taylor taught that our mortal body is a "self-registering machine" by which "all the various senses of the body, are so many media whereby man lays up for himself a record which perhaps nobody else is acquainted with but himself." This will be significant later—"when the time comes for that record to be unfolded all men that have eyes to see, and ears to hear, will be able to read all things as God himself reads them and comprehends them, and all things, we are told, are naked and open before him with whom we have to do."[12]

Elder Bruce R. McConkie wrote that this physical accounting is one way to understand the "real through figurative sense" in which "the *book of life* is the record of the acts of men as such record is written in their own bodies." He explains that "it is the record engraven on the very bones, sinews, and flesh of the mortal body." This means that "every thought, word, and deed has an affect on the human body; all these leave their marks, marks which can be read by Him who is Eternal as easily as the words in a book can be read."[13]

President David O. McKay quoted a contemporary thinker with approval when he taught that "we are spinning our own fates good or evil. . . . Every smallest stroke of virtue or of vice leaves its ever so little scar. . . . Down among his nerve-cells and fibers the molecules are counting it, registering and storing it up."[14]

All this points to the absolute intertwining of physical and spiritual accountability inherent in the Resurrection. Elder Jeffrey R. Holland has written that the "impact of that doctrine of restoration is sobering for those who may have believed that Christ's atonement and their resurrection would somehow bring something more than was deserved."[15] Alma is inviting his son to recognize the future consequences that the law of restoration will have on his resurrected body (see Alma 41:11–15).[16] This is powerful doctrine for one so preoccupied with his physique (see Alma 39:2).

Final Judgment (Alma 40:22, 24–26; 41:3–15; 42:1, 23, 27–28). The third event affected by the Restoration is the Final Judgment. Alma points to the time when all "men should be judged according to their works" (Alma 41:3). He simplifies the mechanics of this moment for his son by teaching the simple, yet profound truth that all men "stand or fall; for behold, they are their own judges." This is so because people are in the process of making themselves either good or evil through their daily desires and actions. Thus they "judge" themselves in the here and now by "whether [they will] do good or do evil" (Alma 41:7).

Elder Holland continues: "Alma made it very clear that if our works are good in this life, and the desires of our hearts are good, then in the Resurrection we will be restored to that which is good. But, by the same token, if our works are evil, then our reward will be the restoration of evil in the Resurrection. To Corianton, who apparently was taking casually some of these 'points of doctrine,' Alma expressed strongly that no one should fallaciously assume that the restorative powers of the Resurrection could restore one 'from sin to happiness' [Alma 41:10]."[17]

The effect that the physical-spiritual restoration of the Resurrection will have on the Final Judgment is implied throughout the Book of Mormon. Jacob taught that "all those who die in their sins . . . shall return to God, and behold his face, and remain in their sins" (2 Nephi 9:38; see also vv. 46–48). Abinadi declared "the Lord redeemeth none such that rebel against him and die in their sins" (Mosiah 15:26). These will not come forth in the First Resurrection, but will remain in prison until the last, remaining filthy (see D&C 88:96–102). Helaman, when counseling with his two sons, noted the careful distinction that Amulek made with Zeezrom about salvation being not *in* our sins but rather *from* them (see Helaman 5:10; Alma 11:34–37; see also Alma 6:8). Moroni also warned that wicked resurrected persons will carry with them a "consciousness" of their "filthiness" and "nakedness" and will remain "filthy still," but the righteous will be "righteous" and "happy still" (Mormon 9:2–5, 13–14; see also 2 Nephi 9:13–16).

Atonement

President Ezra Taft Benson once observed that "no one adequately and properly knows why he needs Christ until he understands and accepts the doctrine of the Fall and its effect upon all mankind."[18] Alma has effectively caused his son to recognize his sins and their inevitable consequences. In fact, Corianton's new sensitivity to an impartial restoration worried his mind, and Alma perceived that his son was grappling with "the justice of God in the punishment of the sinner" (Alma 42:1). Apparently Corianton had bought into the false notion that in the end "God will beat us with a few stripes, and at last we shall be saved in the kingdom of God" (2 Nephi 28:8). Corianton is now primed to understand the Savior's merciful and just solution.

This life is a probation, a preparation (Alma 42:2–11). Alma begins with Adam and Eve, explaining that every soul that comes to mortality does so under conditions of probation. "A time [was] granted unto man to repent, yea, a probationary time, a time to repent and serve God." Through the Fall's effect of "[cutting us] off both temporally and spiritually from the presence of the Lord," all mankind "became subjects to follow after their own will." Alma continues to reason that if God had immediately "reclaimed" Adam and Eve from "this temporal death," it would have frustrated the "plan of happiness" (Alma 42:4, 7–8). This is ironic because in this "probationary state" every soul sins and becomes "carnal, sensual, and devilish, by nature" (v. 10). This is, however, just the point that Alma is making with his son—all are fallen, and all are lost; Corianton is no different from other mortals. God's justice allows for each person to make his or her own choices. Whereas each person sins (as Alma himself poignantly knew), God has mercifully provided a way out—a "means to reclaim men from this fallen state" (v. 12). Thereby this life becomes a "preparatory state" prior to returning to God's presence (see vv. 10, 23).

The justice of Jesus' mercy (Alma 42:13-15, 18-26). While God's justice requires that there be "punishment" for sin (Alma 42:16-18), if individuals paid for their own sins they would be "consigned . . . forever to be cut off from [God's] presence" (v. 14). Consequently, Alma explains that "an atonement should be made; therefore God himself atoneth for the sins of the world, to bring about the plan of mercy, to appease the demands of justice" (v. 15). Robert L. Millet has written about the "perfect balance" that could only be achieved "in and through a God." The sinless Jesus is one "upon whom justice has no claim" and personally "has no need of pardoning mercy."[19] Just as justice is violated by not punishing one who is guilty (see v. 22), so justice is also breached when one is punished who is innocent. Abinadi and Amulek powerfully explained the Savior's self-substitution earlier in the Book of Mormon (see Mosiah 13-15; especially 13:28-35; 15:7-9; see also Alma 34:8-17). This is how the "plan of mercy" (Alma 42:15) works. The eternal scales of violation and punishment must be in balance in the end (see v. 23). Corianton wanted mercy, but unless he complied with the terms of the atonement of Christ (who can and does offer to cover the punishment for him) there would be no justice (see v. 13). Hence, "justice exerciseth all his demands" according to eternal law, and "also mercy claimeth all which is her own" according to the individual's repentance (v. 24).

The necessity of repentance (Alma 42:13, 16-17, 22, 24). The Atonement provides for justice to be met in Jesus' acceptance of the punishment for sins, and mercy is extended through the removal of the natural consequences of sinful acts in the Resurrection for those who repent. Elder Dallin H. Oaks attests: "I cannot achieve my eternal goals on the basis of what I deserve. Though I try with all my might, I am still . . . an 'unprofitable servant' (see Mosiah 2:21). To achieve my eternal goals, I need more than I deserve. I need more

Alma to Corianton: A Pattern for Modern Parents

than justice. . . . [I need mercy through] the atonement of Jesus Christ." The apostle defines mercy as "an advantage greater than is deserved" and explains it "could come by the withholding of a deserved punishment or by the granting of an undeserved benefit." He continues, "If justice is exactly [the punishment] one deserves, then mercy is *more* benefit than one deserves. . . . *The Atonement* is the means by which justice is served and mercy is extended."[20]

"Therefore, O my son," Alma reasons, "whosoever will come may come and partake of the waters of life freely . . . but in the last day it shall be restored unto him according to his deeds.

"If he has desired to do evil, and has not repented in his days, behold, evil shall be done unto him, according to the restoration of God" (Alma 42:27–28; see also 41:15).

In the concluding chapters of the Book of Mormon, Moroni alludes to this remarkable possibility in Christ—that through his power we "may become the sons of God; that when he shall appear we shall be like him, for we shall see him as he his; that we may have this hope; that we may be purified even as he is pure" (Moroni 7:48).

Corianton is now doctrinally equipped to understand how Christ opens the way for all who will repent to be free from the natural effects of their sins. He can now see that he must repent in order to take advantage of Christ's merciful offer. Corianton's more complete understanding of individual accountability and the merciful effects of the Atonement can now catalyze his change to a more Christlike life. Alma encourages his son to begin this process by denying "the justice of God no more" and not trying "to excuse [himself] in the least point because of [his] sins, by denying the justice of God." Rather Corianton should "let the justice of God, and his mercy, and his long-suffering have full sway in [his] heart" which will bring him "down to the dust in humility" (Alma 42:30).

SHOW GREATER LOVE AND TRUST

Alma's entire approach with Corianton remarkably exemplifies the Lord's method of reproof. Compare his counsel with the revelation recorded in Doctrine and Covenants 121:41–44: Alma had reproved "with sharpness" as "moved upon by the Holy Ghost"; he had taught him "pure knowledge" that would "enlarge [his] soul"; and then, he showed Corianton the "increase of love" that let his son know that he was not "his enemy." In this way, the last words recorded between Alma and Corianton illustrate the appropriate love of a parent for his struggling child, along with the kind of persistent faith one should have in Christ's love and mercy toward the returning prodigal. Alma shows this greater love and trust by concluding his counsel with these words: "And now, O my son, ye are called of God to preach the word unto this people. . . . Go thy way, declare the word with truth and soberness, that thou mayest bring souls unto repentance, that the great plan of mercy may have claim upon them" (Alma 42:31; see also D&C 24:1–3).[21]

Conclusion

"Where there is no vision, the people perish" (Proverbs 29:18). The example set by Alma outlines a way for modern families to help their wayward loved ones obtain the gospel vision they need to find their way in this world.[22] Perhaps "our test of faith seems to be in believing our children of today are as able to understand spiritual truths as were the Nephite and Lamanite children of yore and in putting this belief into practice."[23] The key to applying Alma's exceptional pattern—whereby leaders, families, and friends effectively teach the doctrines of the gospel of Jesus Christ to succor those they love—is fundamentally a matter of believing in the power of true doctrine and to trusting in and trying "the virtue of the word of God" (Alma 31:5).

Notes

1. For a detailed treatment of father-to-son talks in the Book of Mormon, see Douglas Clark and Robert S. Clark, *Fathers and Sons in the Book of Mormon* (Salt Lake City: Deseret Book, 1991); for specifics on Alma to Corianton, see 140–46.

2. Alma's discourse to his sons comprises roughly 20 percent of his total recorded words (see Clark and Clark, *Fathers and Sons,* 133)—over half of which is devoted just to Corianton.

3. The Book of Mormon's account of Alma's discussion with Corianton can be contrasted with the biblical account of Eli and his sons (see 1 Samuel 2–4; especially 2:29; 3:13).

4. President Ezra Taft Benson has urged, "Are we using the *messages and the method* of teaching found in the Book of Mormon and other scriptures of the Restoration to teach this great plan of the Eternal

God?" (*A Witness and a Warning* [Salt Lake City: Deseret Book, 1988], 32; italics added).

5. On this point of forgiveness, President Boyd K. Packer has declared, "I repeat, save for the exception of the very few who defect to perdition, there is no habit, no addiction, no rebellion, no transgression, no apostasy, no crime exempted from the promise of complete forgiveness. That is the promise of the atonement of Christ" (in Conference Report, Sept.–Oct. 1995, 23; or *Ensign,* Nov. 1995, 20).

6. Boyd K. Packer, in Conference Report, Oct. 1986, 20; or *Ensign,* Nov. 1986, 17).

7. Moroni warns against discouragement: "If ye have no hope ye must needs be in despair; and despair cometh because of iniquity." Instead, this last prophet invites: "Come unto Christ, and be perfected in him." He explains that it is through the grace, or enabling power, of God, that we may be "perfect in Christ" and "sanctified in Christ." This sanctification yields the "remission of [our] sins, that [we] may become holy, without spot" (Moroni 10:22, 32–33). Alma's ultimate message is the same, but his approach is different to fit Corianton's needs.

8. Alma's wording in Alma 39:17 also indicates his discernment. It is a specific characteristic of Alma's record to have such details about the dialogues (see Clark and Clark, *Fathers and Sons,* 144; especially note 6).

9. Packer, in Conference Report, Oct. 1986, 20; or *Ensign,* Nov. 1986, 17).

10. Jacob's treatment of resurrection (see Jacob 4:11–12; 6:9), restoration (see Jacob 3:10–12; 6:3, 7, 10–11), and the Atonement (see Jacob 4:5, 11–12; 6:5, 8–9) is relatively brief. Jacob also taught about accountability (see Jacob 2:35; 3:3–9), but in a different context than Alma did.

11. Joseph Smith, *Teachings of the Prophet Joseph Smith,* sel. Joseph Fielding Smith (Salt Lake City: Deseret Book, 1938), 256.

12. John Taylor, in *Journal of Discourses,* 26 vols. (London: Latter-day Saints' Book Depot, 1854–86), 26:31.

13. Bruce R. McConkie, *Mormon Doctrine,* 2d ed. (Salt Lake City: Bookcraft, 1966), 97.

14. William James, *Psychology* (New York: Henry Holt and Co., 1892); cited in *Gospel Ideals* (Salt Lake City: Improvement Era, 1953), 350. These quotes bring added weight and significance to Alma 12:14, where Alma had earlier taught that "our words will condemn us, yea, all our works will condemn us; we shall not be found spotless; and our thoughts will also condemn us; and in this awful state we shall not dare to look up to our God."

15. Jeffrey R. Holland, *Christ and the New Covenant* (Salt Lake City: Deseret Book, 1997), 242; see also Dallin H. Oaks, *Sins, Crimes, and Atonement* (address to CES religious educators, 7 Feb. 1992).

16. Paul taught that there are three general types of bodies in the Resurrection, corresponding with the degrees of glory (see 1 Corinthians 15:40–42). Doctrine and Covenants 88:21–35 reveals four classes of resurrected bodies, each determined by the kind of law the individual was willing to obey. Celestial law provides celestial sanctification; terrestrial law produces terrestrial sanctification; telestial for telestial; and finally, inheritors of perdition, who "breaketh a law, and abideth not by law, but seeketh to become a law unto itself, . . . cannot be sanctified by law. . . . Therefore, they must remain filthy still" (v. 35).

17. Holland, *Christ and the New Covenant*, 242.

18. Ezra Taft Benson, *A Witness and a Warning* (Salt Lake City: Deseret Book, 1988), 33.

19. Robert L. Millet, "Justice, Mercy, and the Life Beyond," in Kent P. Jackson, ed., *Studies in Scripture: Volume Eight, Alma 30 to Moroni* (Salt Lake City: Deseret Book, 1988), 62.

20. Oaks, *Sins, Crimes, and Atonement*, 2.

21. Corianton's immediate recall to the work of preaching may be problematic to some, but as Alma indicated, the call came from God. Perhaps, as with the woman taken in adultery, Alma is actually only extending Corianton the opportunity to change his life without pardoning his sins. President Spencer W. Kimball commented on John 8:11 this way, "The woman had neither time nor opportunity to repent totally. . . . He was directing the sinful woman to *go her way, abandon her evil life, commit no more sin, transform her life.* He was saying, Go, woman, and start your repentance; and he was indicating to her the beginning step—*to abandon her transgressions*" (*The Miracle of Forgiveness* [Salt Lake City: Bookcraft, 1969], 68, 165; italics in original).

22. Alma's approach was evidently effective, as later passages indicate that Corianton became a righteous and responsible man (see Alma 43:1–2; 49:30; 63:1–2). For an extended explanation, see Clark and Clark, *Fathers and Sons*, 145–46.

23. H. Verlan Andersen, in Conference Report, Oct. 1991, 111; or *Ensign*, Nov. 1991, 80–81.

CHAPTER FOUR

The Book of Mosiah: A Primer for the Restoration

RICHARD E. BENNETT

> Such was the Boy—but for the growing Youth
> What soul was his, when from the naked top
> Of some bold heartland, he beheld the sun
> Rise up, and bathe the world in light!
> . . . .
> O then how beautiful, how bright, appeared
> The written promise! Early had he learned
> To reverence the volume that displays
> The mystery, the life which cannot die;
> But in the mountains did he feel his faith.
> All things, responsive to the writing, there
> Breathed immortality, revolving life,
> And greatness still revolving; infinite:
> There littleness was not.[1]

Few topics in early Church history are as critical to our understanding of the restoration of the gospel of Jesus Christ as is the inspired tutoring of the Prophet Joseph Smith. From out of that crucible of divine instruction, stretching from the theophany of the Sacred Grove to the translation of the Book of Mormon nine years later, came the "restoration of all things" (D&C 27:6). Yet, few

---

Richard E. Bennett is a professor of Church history and doctrine at Brigham Young University.

chapters in our history are less documented. Nevertheless, as we continue to study Joseph's own records and ponder more deeply the translation process of the Book of Mormon, our understanding and appreciation of the training of the boy prophet increase.

BLUEPRINT FOR THE RESTORATION

We continue to marvel at Moroni's careful mentoring of the young prophet. Long considered the guardian of the Book of Mormon, the Angel Moroni also knew well the Holy Bible. During his introductory commission to his seventeen-year-old student, Moroni cited key passages not only from Malachi, Isaiah, Acts, and Joel, but he also "quoted many other passages of scriptures, and offered many explanations" (JS–H 1:41). It was instruction enough for his tender pupil to realize that the Holy Bible was in part incomplete and sometimes incorrect, that prophecy was about to be fulfilled, and that he himself would play a central role in the unfolding drama of the Restoration. Subsequently, each year thereafter for four years, the master and his apprentice continued their lessons. In Joseph's own carefully selected words, "I . . . received instruction and intelligence from him at each of our interviews, respecting what the Lord was going to do, and how and in what manner his kingdom was to be conducted in the last days" (JS–H 1:54). Even before the work of translation began, the blueprint for the Restoration was well unfolding.

With Moroni's delivery of the gold plates in September 1827 to a more mature and experienced twenty-one-year-old young man, the apprenticeship only intensified. What Joseph learned from his early attempts at translation—the opposition, the hard work, the loss of the 116-page manuscript—all these constituted a school of hard knocks, a bittersweet experience that humbled and matured an imperfect human instrument. By the time he and his new scribe, Oliver Cowdery, embarked upon their intensive translation of the small plates of Nephi in the spring of 1829, Joseph had honed his skills and humbled his spirit and was prepared to be taught by a new teacher—this time the plates themselves—in ways we perhaps have underestimated.

This much, however, is clear and undeniable: the work of translating the plates was as much a divine schooling as the preparation required to receive them. In Joseph Smith's official *History of the Church*, little is said about the translation process itself. "During the month of April," he wrote, "I continued to translate and he [Oliver Cowdery] to write, with little cessation, during which time we received several revelations."[2] Little wonder Oliver later recorded: "These were days never to be forgotten—to sit under the sound of a voice dictated by the inspiration of heaven, awakened the utmost gratitude of this bosom. Day after day I continued, uninterrupted, to write from his mouth, as he translated, with the Urim and Thummim . . . the history, or record, called 'The book of Mormon.'"[3]

Though no one part of Moroni's record takes scriptural precedence over another, it appears increasingly likely that the book of Mosiah marked the first time the Book of Mormon spoke to its translators.[4] They undoubtedly were surprised by the relevancy and immediate application of what they were discovering to what they were embarking upon in early April 1829.

Over a century ago, George Reynolds, an early and avid student of the Book of Mormon, was one of the first to ponder the matter of sequence in translation. "Was the translation," he asked, "commenced at the beginning of the book and continued in regular order to the end?" His tentative conclusion was that they, the translators, probably started either with the Words of Mormon or the book of Mosiah and that "they worked more slowly at the commencement of their labors and with greater rapidity towards the end."[5]

Modern research corroborates Reynold's tentative conclusion. Dean Jessee, a student of the handwritings found in the original Book of Mormon manuscript, indicates that whereas Mosiah was written entirely in Oliver Cowdery's hand, most of 2 Nephi is in the hand of John Whitmer, a fact only made possible after the removal of Joseph Smith and Oliver from Harmony, Pennsylvania, to Fayette, New York, near the first of June 1829.[6] Milton Bachman and Richard Bushman have accepted Jessee's interpretations without argument. Bushman contends that Doctrine and Covenants 10, which speaks of the translation process, may have actually been dated "May 1829," rather than the "summer of 1828," a point that supports the argument of Mosiah being among writings to be translated.[7]

More recently, Jack Welch and Tim Rathbone have likewise argued the "Mosiah first" theory for several other reasons, including the fact that the title page to the Book of Mormon was translated before 11 June 1829; that there is no evidence of Emma Smith's handwriting in 1 Nephi, as might be expected since she assisted Joseph before Oliver's arrival; and that a Mosiah beginning is most consistent with the Doctrine and Covenants. In section 10, Joseph is commanded not to retranslate the lost pages but to "translate the engravings which are on the [small] plates of Nephi, down even till you come to the reign of King Benjamin, or until you come to that which you have translated, which you have retained" (D&C 10:41).[8]

More than mere translation from one language to another—as inscrutable as that effort was—the process was enormously instructional. It was as though the "message of Cumorah" came with its own manual of instructions for those commissioned to bring it forth—a primer for the Restoration. Within the first day or two, perhaps during the first few hours of translation, Joseph was reminded of the priceless value of the plates before him, as Moroni had taught several times before. "My sons, I would that ye should remember that were it not for these plates, which contain these records and these commandments, we must have suffered in ignorance . . . not knowing the mysteries of God" (Mosiah 1:3). Furthermore, the "engravings" on the plates and the "mysteries" of God thereon were to be read and taught to one generation after another, "even down to this present time" (v. 4). "These sayings are true, and also . . . these records are true . . . and we can know of their surety because we have them before our eyes" (v. 6). As a living witness of the tangible reality of the plates, Joseph's soul must have resonated with these poignant instructions regarding the truth and seriousness of the work he was embarking upon.

Essential Principles of the Gospel

A few chapters and a day or two of translating later, Joseph came upon special directives on the use of the Urim and Thummim—warnings and instructions that could only be applicable to one possessing them. "It is a gift from God," Ammon had once told King Limhi, as recorded in Mosiah 8:13. "And the things are called interpreters, and no man can look in them except he be commanded, lest he should look for that he ought not and he should perish." Little wonder that in the revelation given through Joseph to Oliver

Cowdery that same month of April 1829, they were counseled not to "trifle" with sacred things and to "not ask for that which you ought not" (D&C 8:10). From that same passage in Mosiah, Joseph was reminded of what Moroni had earlier told him, that "whosoever is commanded to look in them [the Urim and Thummim] the same is called seer . . . a revelator and a prophet" (Mosiah 8:13, 16).

Such reverence for the plates and instructions on the interpreters were, however, but the beginning. What they learned from the book of Mosiah alone about essential principles of the gospel prepared them well for the restoration of the Church of Jesus Christ. Within a matter of seven or eight days of translation, Joseph translated the sermons of King Benjamin (four chapters), Abinadi (seven chapters), Alma (four chapters), and his son, Alma the younger (two chapters) by mid-April 1829. Each one the cumulative experience of a lifetime, a measure of wisdom and of unfailing courage, these four masterful sermons taught the translators, as well as millions of later readers, the first principles and ordinances of the gospel.

At the risk of oversimplification, we see a pattern of instruction unfolding throughout the sermons. While the common denominator to all four is the mission and redemption of Christ, the Lord Omnipotent, who has been "prepared from the foundation of the world," King Benjamin's central message is surely that of service to one another and of faith in Christ who would come.

"Believe in God," he concludes, "believe that he is, and that he created all things, both in heaven and in earth; believe that he has all wisdom, and all power, both in heaven and in earth; believe that man doth not comprehend all the things which the Lord can comprehend.

"And again, believe that ye must repent of your sins and forsake them, and humble yourselves before God; and ask in sincerity of heart that he would forgive you; and now, if you believe all these things see that ye do them" (Mosiah 4:9–10).

If the principle of faith predominates within the teachings of King Benjamin, that of repentance is the central focus of Abinadi's message in Mosiah 11–17, as he warns King Noah and his wicked priests. A stern messenger of warning and rebuke, brave Abinadi makes clear his call: "Except they repent, I will visit them in mine anger" (Mosiah 11:20), "except they repent . . . I will deliver them into the hands of their enemies" (vv. 20–21), "except this people repent . . . they shall be brought into bondage" (v. 23), and "except they repent . . . I will not hear their prayers" (v. 25). Rehearsing unto his unbelieving audience the Ten Commandments and the Christ-centered prophecies of Isaiah, Abinadi concludes his warnings: "And now, ought ye not to tremble and repent of your sins, and remember that only in and through Christ ye can be saved?" (Mosiah 16:13).

Abinadi's sole convert, and one of King Noah's fugitive priests, Alma, flees for his life into the wilderness, preaching to his few followers "repentance, and redemption, and faith on the Lord" (Mosiah 18:7). Unique to Alma's teachings was his emphasis on the ordinance of baptism as a covenant and sequel to faith and repentance, a progression of the unfolding doctrine of Christ. "Now I say unto you," he said to his people near the waters of Mormon, "if this be the desire of your hearts, what have you against being baptized in the name of the Lord, as a witness before him that ye have entered into a covenant with him, that ye will serve him and keep his commandments, that he may pour out his Spirit more abundantly upon you?" (Mosiah 18:10).

Though the book of Mosiah is not the first place baptism is mentioned in the Book of Mormon as an essential ordinance of salvation (see 2 Nephi 31:12–13), it is the first place in which clear, practical instructions are given as to the manner of baptism. Not only does Alma teach the principle, but he likewise demonstrates the performance. After being "buried in the water" (Mosiah 18:14), he and Helam come out of the water rejoicing. Alma then baptized over two hundred others in the same manner he had baptized Helam, "only he did not bury himself again in the water" (Mosiah 18:15). If Joseph and Oliver did not know before translating this passage that baptism was by immersion, they certainly knew afterward. Approximately one month later, while translating Christ's further teachings in 3 Nephi regarding baptism for the remission of sins, the visitation of John the Baptist took place. From the very beginning of the translation, they were taught of the simple beauty and necessity of this ordinance, a truth which likely weighed upon their minds.

The fourth great sermon, not surprisingly, while alluding to all of the above principles, speaks perhaps most directly of the rebirth of the soul through the Spirit of God. The account of Alma the Younger's miraculous conversion near the end of Mosiah speaks less of baptism (in fact the term is not used at all) and much more of being "born of the Spirit":

"And the Lord said unto me: Marvel not that all mankind, yea, men and women, all nations, kindreds, tongues and people, must be born again; yea, born of God, changed from their carnal and fallen state, to a state of righteousness, being redeemed of God, becoming his sons and daughters;

"And thus they become new creatures; and unless they do this, they can in nowise inherit the kingdom of God" (Mosiah 27:25–26).

The incomparable spiritual instructions of these sermons of the book of Mosiah defy simple categorization and analysis. They are alive with the Spirit of the Lord—stunning testimonies to the fact that no unschooled farmboy could ever have composed such supremely simple yet profound verse. Nevertheless, we respectfully conclude that running through them all, like a doctrinal cord of everlasting truth, and taught in logical sequence, are the first principles and ordinances of the gospel—faith in the Lord Jesus Christ, repentance, baptism by immersion, and the Gift of the Holy Ghost—truths that impressed themselves upon these first readers in narrative form, as no mere creedal list could have ever done.

ORGANIZING AND OPERATING THE CHURCH

The teachings of the book of Mosiah, however, do not end with these foundation principles. More of what Joseph and Oliver would later be called upon to do, in organizing and operating the Church of Jesus Christ, finds specific parallels in Mosiah. Alma, in teaching of the necessity of baptism, spoke much of two complimentary doctrines in ways not found in 1 or 2 Nephi, nor covered so fully again until 3 Nephi. The first is the need for divine authority; the second is the need for the establishment of a Church of Christ.

The question of where Alma received his authority has long been a matter of discussion. Whatever the answer to that question, the important point is that the young Prophet Joseph recognized the need for authority to baptize and to perform other ordinances of the gospel. Alma is quoted as saying in Mosiah 18:13: "Helam, I baptize thee, *having authority from the Almighty God*" (italics added). This doctrine of authority is made even more clear later in the account of Ammon, a friend of Alma's, who deferred baptizing King Limhi until one could be found "that had authority from God" (Mosiah 21:33).

Further insight is given as to the governing authority over the priesthood, or "keys" of priesthood authority, when Alma, "their high priest" (Mosiah 23:16) "having authority from God, ordained priests; even one priest to every fifty of their number and . . . he commanded them that they should preach nothing save it were repentance and faith on the Lord, who had redeemed his people" (Mosiah 18:18, 20). Further on we read "that none received authority to preach or to teach except it were by him from God. Therefore he [Alma] consecrated all their priests and all their teachers; and none were consecrated except they were just men" (Mosiah 23:17). In other words, no man can assume such authority without consent of the prophet leader.

Likewise, such priesthood leaders must be men of personal integrity and righteousness, "walking in his ways and keeping his commandments" (Mosiah 23:14). No less important, they serve as a lay ministry, not reliant upon or supported by the people. "And the priests were not to depend upon the people for their support; but for their labor they were to receive the grace of God, that they might wax strong in the Spirit" (Mosiah 18:26).

Linked to the governing power of priesthood was the need for the establishment of the Church of Christ.[9] Alma clearly taught that it was not enough to be simply baptized; rather, "whosoever was baptized by the power and authority of God was added to his church" which was "called the church of God, or the church of Christ, from that time forward" (Mosiah 18:17). Such a church, Joseph understood, formed "through the strength and power of God" (Mosiah 21:30), would be as essential in A.D. 1830 as it had been back in 121 B.C.

One important reason for such an ecclesiastical organization was for guidance and instruction of the people, a shield from outside influences. "And there was one day in every week that was set apart that they should gather themselves together to teach the people, and to worship the Lord their God, and also, as often as it was in their power, to assemble themselves together" (Mosiah 18:25).

Joseph learned that there must not only be a church and that it should be named after the Son of God, but, in addition, he gained important insights into the code of member conduct: "And he [Alma] commanded them that there should be no contention one with another, but that they should look forward with one eye, having one faith and one baptism, having their hearts knit together in unity and in love one towards another" (Mosiah 18:21).

Alma even gave instruction in how to administer to both Saint and sinner and how to solve other difficult problems within the Church.

"For behold, this is my church; whosoever is baptized shall be baptized unto repentance. . . .

" . . . [Those] that will not hear my voice, the same shall ye not receive into my church. . . .

"And those that would not confess their sins and repent of their iniquity, the same were not numbered among the people of the church, and their names were blotted out" (Mosiah 26:22, 28, 36).

In this early priesthood handbook of instructions, Mosiah foreshadowed much of the articles and covenants of the Church, as given a year later in section 20 of the Doctrine and Covenants, hinting to Joseph that even in the Church of Christ in these latter days, defection and apostasy would be realities, requiring urgent attention and even disciplinary action.

Even the rudiments of the law of consecration, which Joseph revealed to the Church after the removal to Kirtland, Ohio, in 1831, were taught in Mosiah. Alma taught this law as an essential part of the Church he organized and the expectation of membership therein.

"And again Alma commanded that the people of the church should impart of their substance, every one according to that which he had; if he have more abundantly he should impart more abundantly; . . .

"And thus they should impart of their substance of their own free will . . .

" . . . imparting to one another both temporally and spiritually according to their needs and their wants" (Mosiah 18:27–29).

With the Church established and the first principles of the gospel in place, the book of Mosiah ends by establishing missionary work as a distinctive characteristic of the Church of Christ. The conversion of Alma the Younger and the sons of Mosiah clearly brought more than forgiveness; it brought commission—in this instance the commission to venture forth into the lands of the Lamanites to spread the gospel in difficult circumstances. Forsaking the opportunity to succeed their father in the kingship over the land, the sons of Mosiah "were desirous that salvation should be declared to every creature, for they could not bear that any human soul should perish" (Mosiah 28:3). In doing so, they laid the groundwork for much of the narrative in later Book of Mormon accounts, as well as for missionary efforts in modern times. One sign of the restoration of the Church must be a similar kind of missionary devotion, both to the Lamanite and to the Gentile.[10] As Abinadi repeated to his unbelieving audience: "How beautiful upon the mountains are the feet of him that bringeth good tidings; that publisheth peace; that bringeth good tidings of good; that publisheth salvation; that saith unto Zion, Thy God reigneth" (Mosiah 12:21).

There are many other points of doctrine and practice hinted at in the book of Mosiah that may have impressed its translators. When the people gathered throughout all the land to hear King Benjamin, was it coincidental that they went "up to the temple" to hear his words? (Mosiah 2:1). The doctrine of Christ's infinite grace and atonement, the universal resurrection of mankind, the innocence and redemption of children who die before the age of accountability (see Mosiah 15:25), the salvation of those who die without law (see Mosiah 15:24), the concept of Zion (see Mosiah 12:21), and so much more find repeated expression throughout.

It has not been the purpose of this chapter to argue the importance of Mosiah over any other part of Book of Mormon sacred writ. The books of Alma, Helaman, Nephi, Moroni—they all share a divine origin and purpose. One cannot artificially divide one from another as to their importance. What this study has attempted to show, however, is that Moroni's schooling of Joseph Smith did not end with the delivery of the plates in September 1827. The process continued thereafter, and perhaps intensified as Joseph began translating the engravings found on the plates Moroni gave him. If indeed the book of Mosiah served as the introduction to this very personal study of the Book of Mormon, no better blueprint of doctrine and instruction could be found for what he himself would soon have to organize and declare to all the world.

NOTES

1. William Wordsworth, "The Excursion," 1814, cited in Ernest Bernbaum, ed., *Anthology of Romanticism,* 3d ed. rev. and enl. (New York: Ronald Press Co., 1948), 278–79.

2. Joseph Smith, *History of The Church of Jesus Christ of Latter-day Saints,* ed. B. H. Roberts, 2d ed. rev., 7 vols. (Salt Lake City: Deseret Book, 1973), 1:35.

3. Oliver Cowdery, *Messenger and Advocate,* Oct. 1834, 14.

4. It is interesting to note that little has been written about the place of the Words of Mormon in the translation sequence. Whether this tiny portion of the Book of Mormon was translated first or last, its first eight verses speak to Mormon's searching "among the records which had been delivered into [his] hands" (Words of Mormon 1:3) and of his selecting the plates of Nephi from which to write his abridged account. "And I do this," he writes, "for a wise purpose; for thus it whispereth me, according to the workings of the Spirit" (v. 7). One would be hard pressed to find a clearer introduction to the plates of Nephi than these explanatory remarks.

5. George Reynolds, "History of the Book of Mormon," *The Contributor,* June 1894, 365.

6. Dean C. Jessee, "The Original Book of Mormon Manuscript," *Brigham Young University Studies,* spring 1970, 278.

7. Richard L. Bushman, *Joseph Smith and the Beginnings of Mormonism* (Urbana: University of Illinois Press, 1984), 99, 223–24; Milton V. Backman Jr., *Eyewitness Accounts of the Restoration* (Orem, Utah: Grandin Book Co., 1983), 173. See also Stanley R. Larson, "A Study of Some Textual Variations in the Book of Mormon Comparing the Original and the Printer's Manuscripts and the 1830, the 1837, and the 1840 Editions" (master's thesis, Brigham Young University, 1974), 9, 19–21.

8. John W. Welch and Tim Rathbone, "The Translation of the Book of Mormon: Preliminary Report on the Basic Historical Information" (Provo, Utah: Foundation for Ancient Research and Mormon Studies, n.d.), 37. The authors conclude: "The '1 Nephi first' theory does not appear to have been adopted by any writer who has considered the issue explicitly."

9. For more on the relationship of the Book of Mormon to the establishment of the Church, see Scott H. Faulring, "The Book of Mormon—A Blueprint for Organizing the Church," *Journal of Book of Mormon Studies,* 7, no. 1 (1998), 60–71.

10. It may not be coincidental that among the very first missions of the Church, Oliver Cowdery and others taught the gospel to the Delaware Indians "into the wilderness among the Lamanites" west of the Missouri River in the winter of 1830–31 (D&C 32:2).

CHAPTER FIVE

A Perfect Formula for Knowing Right from Wrong

RANDY L. BOTT

No one likes to look back on a past act and discover, to his embarrassment, that he made a poor judgment call. Telling the difference, however, between right and wrong, good and evil, or the sincere and the deceptive is not always easy. Two years before the Book of Mormon was published, the Lord told the Prophet Joseph Smith, "But as you cannot always judge the righteous, or as you cannot always tell the wicked from the righteous, therefore I say unto you, hold your peace until I shall see fit to make all things known unto the world concerning the matter" (D&C 10:37).

When the Book of Mormon was published in 1830, the Lord revealed with scripturally unparalleled clarity how to judge between good and evil:

"Wherefore, take heed, my beloved brethren, that ye do not judge that which is evil to be of God, or that which is good and of God to be of the devil.

"For behold, my brethren, it is given unto you to judge, that ye may know good from evil; and the way to judge is as plain, that ye may know with a perfect knowledge, as the daylight is from the dark night.

"For behold, the Spirit of Christ is given to every man, that he may know good from evil; wherefore, I show unto you the way to

---

Randy L. Bott is an associate professor of Church history and doctrine at Brigham Young University.

judge; for every thing which inviteth to do good, and to persuade to believe in Christ, is sent forth by the power and gift of Christ; wherefore ye may know with a perfect knowledge it is of God" (Moroni 7:14–16).

This chapter investigates the formula the Lord and his prophets have outlined concerning judging between good and evil and right and wrong. The formula consists of understanding how to use the "Spirit of Christ" to clarify eternal principles as revealed from the Lord through the scriptures, the modern prophets, and personal revelation.

THE SCRIPTURES

The doctrines, principles, and keys illuminated in the scriptures have been revealed and written for the purpose of giving us broad guidelines that delineate the extremities of acceptable behavior. Alma explains, "And now, it has hitherto been wisdom in God that these things [the scriptures] should be preserved; for behold, they have enlarged the memory of this people, yea, and convinced many of the error of their ways, and brought them to the knowledge of their God unto the salvation of their souls" (Alma 37:8).

President Harold B. Lee summarized the nature of the scriptures as a standard against which we can judge all things when he said:

"We have the standard Church works. Why do we call them standard? If there is any teacher who teaches a doctrine that can't be substantiated from the standard church works—and I make one qualification, and that is unless that one be the President of the Church, who alone has the right to declare new doctrine—then you may know by that same token that such a teacher is but expressing his own opinion. If, on the other hand, you have someone teaching a doctrine that cannot be substantiated by the scriptures, and more than that, if it contradicts what is in the standard Church works, you may know that that person is teaching false doctrine, no matter what his position in this church may be. The President of the Church alone may declare the mind and will of God to His people. No officer nor any other church in the world has this high and lofty prerogative. When the President proclaims any such new doctrine, he will declare it to be a revelation from the Lord."[1]

Having established that the Lord reveals his standard guidelines through authorized channels and forbids unauthorized man from adding to or taking from the canon of scripture (see Revelation 22:18–19), let us examine how the Book of Mormon establishes the formula for determining the mind and will of the Lord within those guidelines.

Too many people desire the Lord to make every decision for them. Every God-fearing person trembles at the thought of offending God by making a wrong decision. We should, however, be able to determine with confidence the acceptability of any proposition. Although the Bible gives some veiled directions, the Book of Mormon speaks with clarity and exactness, leaving the sincere inquirer in possession of succinct keys on how to make correct decisions. Mormon writes: "Wherefore, all things which are good cometh of God; and that which is evil cometh of the devil; for the devil is an enemy unto God, and fighteth against him continually, and inviteth and enticeth to sin, and to do that which is evil continually.

"But behold, that which is of God inviteth and enticeth to do good continually; wherefore, every thing which inviteth and enticeth to do good, and to love God, and to serve him, is inspired of God" (Moroni 7:12–13).

According to Mormon, individuals need only to consider the long-range impact of any proposal or course of action to determine whether it will take them closer to their eternal objectives of becoming like God and returning to live with him, or move them further away. In this same vein, the Lord revealed to the Prophet Joseph Smith, "But ye are commanded in all things to ask of God, who giveth liberally; and that which the Spirit testifies unto you even so I would that ye should do in all holiness of heart, walking uprightly before me, considering the end of your salvation, doing all things with prayer and thanksgiving, that ye may not be seduced by evil spirits, or doctrines of devils, or the commandments of men; for some are of men, and others of devils" (D&C 46:7).

Remembering God's stated objective—"For behold, this is my work and my glory—to bring to pass the immortality and eternal life of man" (Moses 1:39)—it would seem that everything revealed from God will facilitate man's quest to return to his heavenly home. Through Nephi, the Savior invited us to use him as our exemplar: "And he said unto the children of men: Follow thou me. Wherefore, my beloved brethren, can we follow Jesus save we shall be willing to keep the commandments of the Father?" (2 Nephi 31:10). Although numerous biblical references invite us to follow Christ, none specifies with such unmistakable clarity how we are to do it. Later, as a resurrected being, Jesus said: "Verily, verily, I say unto you, this is my gospel; and ye know the things that ye must do in my church; for the works which ye have seen me do that shall ye also do; for that which ye have seen me do even that shall ye do" (3 Nephi 27:21). Again, that unmistakable clearness is unique to the Book of Mormon.

Almost without exception, if a person will seriously and conscientiously consider the eternal impact of a decision, the right and wrong choice will be evident. In those rare cases in which the weakness of human reasoning would result in an erroneous decision, the Lord promises to intervene. Elder John H. Groberg of the Seventy said:

"In the past I have tried to figure out whether I should go into business or into teaching or into the arts or whatever. As I have begun to proceed along one path, having more or less gathered what facts I could, I have found that if that decision was wrong or was taking me down the wrong path—not necessarily an evil one, but one that was not right for me—without fail, the Lord has always let me know just this emphatically: 'That is wrong; do not go that way. That is not for you!'

"On the other hand, there may have been two or three ways that I could have gone, any one of which would have been right and would have been in the general area providing the experience and means whereby I could fulfill the mission that the Lord had in mind for me. Because he knows we need the growth, he generally does not point and say, 'Open that door and go twelve yards in that direction; then turn right and go two miles. . . .' But if it is wrong, he will let us know—we will feel it for sure. I am positive of that. So rather than saying, 'I will not move until I have this burning in my heart,' let us turn it around and say, 'I will move, unless I feel it is wrong; and if it is wrong, then I will not do it.' By eliminating all of these wrong courses, very quickly you will find yourself going in the direction that you ought to be going, and then you can receive the assurance: 'Yes, I am going in the right direction. I am doing what my Father in Heaven wants me to do because I am not doing the things he does not want me to do.' And you can know that for sure. That is part of the growth process and part of accomplishing what our Father in Heaven has in mind for us."²

A definition of the perfect pattern begins to emerge. God reveals the broad guidelines necessary for all mankind to avoid the deceptive tactics of the adversary. These guidelines are revealed through the example of his Son and the teachings of the prophets. They are given at different periods of time, but the principles underlying them have universal application in each dispensation. Only God can abridge these commandments, and he countermands his decisions so infrequently that such accounts are written in scripture. God sets his commandments in stone and expects them to be obeyed without debate or argument.

MODERN PROPHETS

Living prophets enlighten our understanding on how scriptural teachings apply in our time.

With stunning, unrivaled clarity, the Book of Mormon teaches us the indispensable value of living prophets and seers:

"And Ammon said that a seer is a revelator and a prophet also; and a gift which is greater can no man have, except he should possess the power of God, which no man can; yet a man may have great power given him from God.

"But a seer can know of things which are past, and also of things which are to come, and by them shall all things be revealed, or, rather, shall secret things be made manifest, and hidden things shall come to light, and things which are not known shall be made known by them, and also things shall be made known by them which otherwise could not be known.

"Thus God has provided a means that man, through faith, might work mighty miracles; therefore he becometh a great benefit to his fellow beings" (Mosiah 8:16–18).

Within the broad guidelines defined by the commandments and scriptures are ample opportunities to "choose for thyself, for it is given unto thee" (see Moses 3:17). Without living prophets and seers, however, one might still make serious judgmental errors in interpreting scripture. One might question why the Lord requires individuals to choose for themselves when something as important as eternal life hangs in the balance. An understanding of the scope of the plan of salvation provides the answer as well as an imperative to make correct decisions. From our birth into premortal existence, we desired to become like our heavenly parents (see Acts 17:29; Romans 8:16; Hebrews 12:9). Not only do they have perfected, resurrected bodies, in contrast to our spirit bodies, but they have also been perfected in their knowledge of good and evil. The Prophet Joseph Smith taught: "God himself, finding he was in the midst of spirits and glory, because he was more intelligent, saw proper to institute laws whereby the rest could have a privilege to advance like himself. The relationship we have with God places us in a situation to advance in knowledge. He has power to institute laws to instruct the weaker intelligences, that they may be exalted with himself, so that they might have one glory upon another, and all that knowledge, power, glory, and intelligence, which is requisite in order to save them in the world of spirits."[3]

Law, however, would be meaningless unless we have the freedom to choose to obey or disobey (see 2 Nephi 2:26–29).

Elder Bruce R. McConkie taught: "We know, of course, that we are the spirit offspring of God our Eternal Father, that he is a glorified, exalted, and perfected being, in whose image we have been created. Living as his spirit children in a pre-existent sphere before this life, we were endowed with agency, and we were subjected to eternal laws ordained by him. We were commanded to obey these laws in order to progress and advance. I suppose that we looked upon the exalted and glorified state of our Father and that we desired to progress and to become like him."[4]

The ancient patriarch Abraham was shown in a vision that among all of God's spirit offspring there were "many of the noble and great ones" (Abraham 3:22), the implication being that there were also those who were not as noble and great. Through the Prophet Joseph Smith, the Lord revealed the reason Satan and a third part of the spirit children of God were thrust down to become the devil and his angels:

"And it came to pass that Adam, being tempted of the devil—for, behold, the devil was before Adam, for he rebelled against me, saying, Give me thine honor, which is my power; and also a third part of the hosts of heaven turned he away from me because of their agency;

"And they were thrust down, and thus came the devil and his angels" (D&C 29:36–37).

Exercising their agency in open opposition to laws established by God caused them to be thrust out from his presence.

Understanding the essential nature of agency, the Holy Father confirmed man's agency while Adam was yet in the Garden of Eden: "The Lord said unto Enoch: Behold these thy brethren; they are the workmanship of mine own hands, and I gave unto them their knowledge, in the day I created them; and in the Garden of Eden, gave I unto man his agency" (Moses 7:32).

With the veil of forgetfulness securely in place, we are ready to try our hand at the final test called mortality. President Joseph F. Smith taught the essential nature of the veil when he said, "But in coming here, we forgot all, that our agency might be free indeed, to choose good or evil, that we might merit the reward of our own choice and conduct. But by the power of the Spirit, in the redemption of Christ, through obedience, we often catch a spark from the awakened memories of the immortal soul, which lights up our whole being as with the glory of our former home."[5]

The scriptures and the declarations of living prophets provide the easily recognizable guidelines that protect us (if we heed them) from wandering into forbidden paths and becoming lost, as Lehi saw in his expansive vision (see 1 Nephi 8:28). In order to progress to become like our eternal parents, it is necessary for us to learn to make wise and correct decisions. Therefore, it is unreasonable to expect the Omniscient One to condescend to make every decision for us. No one needs to ask, "Who makes God's decisions for him?" Since we essay to become like God, we too should make our own decisions. How could we learn to be master problem-solvers like God if he intervened and solved all our problems?

Perhaps an analogy would be beneficial. As children learn to walk, they cling tightly to the fingers of their parents. As they gain more experience and balance, their grip loosens. Eventually, the children are expected to release their grip and venture out on relatively untried legs to walk alone. Parents expect their children to fall multiple times before they successfully negotiate the complex task of walking. With constant encouragement, however, the child eventually learns not only to walk but also to run. It would be a sorry day if college freshmen still required the steadying hands of their parents to walk to their college classes.

The analogy holds true in the process of learning to make correct decisions. In our youth, parents decide for us. Wise parents, however, soon learn to encourage their children to make as many of their own decisions as possible. These parents provide a safe environment where mistakes can be made without fatal results. The same is true of our Heavenly Father. He knows that mistakes will be made as we learn to walk the spiritual path back to his divine presence.

As their children learn skills and develop expertise, mortal parents make fewer important decisions for them. It is hoped that by the time children leave home, they are prepared to make virtually all of their own decisions. Experience should have taught them to stay well within the guidelines outlined by their parents. They should also know that they alone are accountable for the consequences of their decisions.

Even when children have left home, parents are still available for counsel and advice. They should, however, not be expected (nor give in to the urge) to make the decisions for their children. So it is with our divine parents. They provide counsel and direction but should not be expected to make our decisions for us. We are commanded, "Look unto me in every thought; doubt not, fear not" (D&C 6:36). Alma taught his faithful son, "Counsel with the Lord in all thy doings, and he will direct thee for good" (Alma 37:37). Note that he did not teach him that the Lord would make the decision for him, but rather that he would direct him for good. Oliver Cowdery learned this principle when he attempted to translate a portion of the Book of Mormon. After he failed to continue as he commenced, the Lord revealed the reason for Oliver's failure:

"Behold, you have not understood; you have supposed that I would give it unto you, when you took no thought save it was to ask me.

"But, behold, I say unto you, that you must study it out in your mind; then you must ask me if it be right, and if it is right I will cause that your bosom shall burn within you; therefore, you shall feel that it is right" (D&C 9:7–8).

Mormon further emphasized: "And now, my brethren, seeing that ye know the light by which ye may judge, which light is the light of Christ, see that ye do not judge wrongfully; for with that same judgment which ye judge ye shall also be judged.

"Wherefore, I beseech of you, brethren, that ye should search diligently in the light of Christ that ye may know good from evil; and if ye will lay hold upon every good thing, and condemn it not, ye certainly will be a child of Christ" (Moroni 7:18–19).

As we make choices, narrowing our options within the guidelines of right and wrong established by the Lord, we are not left to wander without direction. The Lord revealed, "This is the light of Christ. . . .

"And the light which shineth, which giveth you light, is through him who enlighteneth your eyes, which is the same light that quickeneth your understandings;

"Which light proceedeth forth from the presence of God to fill the immensity of space—

"The light which is in all things, which giveth life to all things, which is the law by which all things are governed, even the power of God who sitteth upon his throne, who is in the bosom of eternity, who is in the midst of all things" (D&C 88:7, 11–13).

Individuals born into mortality receive the light of Christ (see John 1:9). By virtue of this gift, each is given the ability to know good from evil, and right from wrong. Through the Prophet Joseph Smith, the Lord revealed:

"And I now give unto you a commandment to beware concerning yourselves, to give diligent heed to the words of eternal life.

"For you shall live by every word that proceedeth forth from the mouth of God.

"For the word of the Lord is truth, and whatsoever is truth is light, and whatsoever is light is Spirit, even the Spirit of Jesus Christ.

"And the Spirit giveth light to every man that cometh into the world; and the Spirit enlighteneth every man through the world, that hearkeneth to the voice of the Spirit.

"And every one that hearkeneth to the voice of the Spirit cometh unto God, even the Father" (D&C 84:43–47).

Those who give heed to the enlightening influence of the light of Christ, and seek to enter into a covenant relationship with the Lord are promised an even greater opportunity to gain spiritual insight into scriptures and the words of living prophets. When faced with doctrines they did not fully understand as they translated the Book of Mormon, Joseph Smith and Oliver Cowdery retired to a secluded place where they inquired for further light and knowledge. In response, John the Baptist appeared and conferred upon them the Aaronic Priesthood and instructed them in the proper mode of baptism. After conforming to John's directions, both Joseph and Oliver were filled with the Holy Ghost. Joseph then records, "Our minds being now enlightened, we began to have the scriptures laid open to our understandings, and the true meaning and intention of their more mysterious passages revealed unto us in a manner which we never could attain to previously, nor ever before had thought of" (JS–H 1:74).

We have come almost full circle. God gives us the broad guidelines of right and wrong through scriptures. These principles are enlarged upon and fine-tuned for our particular day by living prophets who are guided by him. Guidelines do us little good if we do not study them and seek to apply them in our lives. At the conclusion of his long prophetic ministry, Nephi, son of Lehi, said:

"Angels speak by the power of the Holy Ghost; wherefore, they speak the words of Christ. Wherefore, I said unto you, feast upon the words of Christ; for behold, the words of Christ will tell you all things what ye should do.

"Wherefore, now after I have spoken these words, if ye cannot understand them it will be because ye ask not, neither do ye knock; wherefore, ye are not brought into the light, but must perish in the dark.

"For behold, again I say unto you that if ye will enter in by the way, and receive the Holy Ghost, it will show unto you all things what ye should do" (2 Nephi 32:3–5).

The light which emanates from the presence of God and fills the immensity of space is designed to bring us back to the Father (see D&C 84:43–47) through the covenants of salvation and exaltation. When we understand the Plan of Salvation, the purpose for mortality, the place of agency in that plan, and the fact that the Lord "doeth not anything save it be for the benefit of the world" (2 Nephi 26:24), we see that what Mormon has taught really is the key to

A Perfect Formula for Knowing Right from Wrong

discerning right from wrong: Anything that moves us closer to the light (Christ) and urges us to do good and to love God is inspired of God, while anything that focuses our attention on ourselves, leads us to disobey God, or to deny him in any way is of the devil.

If we view "search[ing] diligently in the light of Christ" like looking through a magnifying glass, then it becomes apparent that as we search the scriptures or the words of the prophets, we can see things in them we could not otherwise see. Mormon asks a simple question, "How is it possible that ye can lay hold upon every good thing?" (Moroni 7:20). He then explains that God knows all things, and that if we would exercise faith in his omniscience, and listen to his counsel through the ministering of angels, the words of living prophets, and other "divers ways" (Moroni 7:24), he would reveal Christ to us, and through Christ we could lay hold upon everything that is good.

Personal Revelation

One more vital key to knowing right from wrong is given by the scriptures and the living prophets: the need to establish an open line of communication with the Almighty through constant prayer. In every volume of scripture, and in none more so than the Book of Mormon, examples of prayer punctuate the essential nature of this dialogue; however, no volume of scripture is more explicit nor more powerfully illustrated than the Book of Mormon. The Prophet Joseph Smith taught:

"The Lord cannot always be known by the thunder of His voice, by the display of His glory or by the manifestation of His power, and those that are the most anxious to see these things, are the least prepared to meet them, and were the Lord to manifest His powers as He did to the children of Israel, such characters would be the first to say, 'Let not the Lord speak any more, lest we His people die.'

"We would say to the brethren, seek to know God in your closets, call upon him in the fields. Follow the directions of the Book of Mormon, and pray over, and for your families, your cattle, your flocks, your herds, your corn, and all things that you possess; ask the blessing of God upon all your labors, and everything that you engage in. Be virtuous and pure; be men of integrity and truth; keep the commandments of God; and then you will be able more perfectly to understand the difference between right and wrong—between the things of God and the things of men; and your path will be like that of the just, which shineth brighter and brighter unto the perfect day."[6]

At times, Latter-day Saints get the impression that this revelatory conduit between man and God is somehow limited to the very selected righteous or those of the true religion. President Brigham Young had a vastly different view:

"I do not believe for one moment that there has been a man or woman upon the face of the earth, from the days of Adam to this day, who has not been enlightened, instructed, and taught by the revelations of Jesus Christ. 'What! the ignorant heathen?' Yes, every human being who has possessed a sane mind. I am far from believing that the children of men have been deprived of the privilege of receiving the Spirit of the Lord to teach them right from wrong. No matter what the traditions of their fathers were, those who were honest before the Lord, and acted uprightly, according to the best knowledge they had, will have an opportunity to go into the Kingdom of God. I believe this privilege belonged to the sons and daughters of Adam, and descended from him, and his children who were contemporary with him, throughout all generations."[7]

How can people know the difference between right and wrong, and good and evil? The proof comes in the doing. Jesus taught: "If any man will do [God's] will, he shall know of the doctrine, whether it be of God, or whether I speak of myself" (John 7:17). Confirming that summary teaching and challenge, President Brigham Young taught: "You may know whether you are led right or wrong, as well as you know the way home; for every principle God has revealed carries its own convictions of its truth to the human mind, and there is no calling of God to man on earth but what brings with it the evidence of its authenticity."[8]

The Grand Father has not placed us here on earth to be victimized by the adversary, although many are through ignorance or open rebellion. He has graciously given us the keys to negotiate the maze of mortality successfully and find our way safely back to his celestial presence. Although they were revealed in clarity to Adam and other biblical prophets, many saving principles are obscure when only the Bible is relied upon. Nephi explains: "And after these plain and precious things were taken away [the Bible] goeth forth unto all the nations of the Gentiles; . . . thou seest—because of the many plain and precious things which have been taken out of the book, which were plain unto the understanding of the children of men, according to the plainness which is in the Lamb of God—because of these things which are taken away out of the gospel of the Lamb, an exceedingly great many do stumble, yea, insomuch that Satan hath great power over them" (1 Nephi 13:29).

If we choose to use them, the keys for making correct decisions are within easy reach, readily understandable by the learned as well as the unschooled. They are the scriptures, prophets, and prayer—sure ways of knowing good from evil, right from wrong, and that which exalts from that which destroys. Using these keys, searching within the light of Christ, no one need err. Nowhere are these principles more clearly taught than in the Book of Mormon.

Notes

1. Harold B. Lee, *Stand Ye in Holy Places* (Salt Lake City: Deseret Book, 1974), 109–10.

2. John H. Groberg, "What Is Your Mission?" in *1979 Devotional Speeches of the Year* (1980), 97–98.

3. Joseph Smith, *Teachings of the Prophet Joseph Smith,* sel. Joseph Fielding Smith (Salt Lake City: Deseret Book, 1976), 354.

4. Bruce R. McConkie, *The New and Everlasting Covenant of Marriage,* Brigham Young University Speeches of the Year (20 Apr. 1960), 2.

5. Joseph F. Smith, *Gospel Doctrine,* 5th ed. (Salt Lake City: Deseret Book, 1939), 13–14.

6. Smith, *Teachings of the Prophet Joseph Smith,* 247.

7. Brigham Young, *Discourses of Brigham Young,* sel. John A. Widtsoe (Salt Lake City: Deseret Book, 1941), 32.

8. Young, *Discourses of Brigham Young,* 65.

CHAPTER SIX

The Salvation of Children: A Case for Restoration and Revelation by Translation

GUY L. DORIUS

Early in his role as prophet, Joseph Smith Jr. was given the singular assignment to translate the sacred text known as the Book of Mormon. At one point the Lord states, "And you have a gift to translate the plates; and this is the first gift that I bestowed upon you; and I have commanded that you should pretend to no other gift until my purpose is fulfilled in this; for I will grant unto you no other gift until it is finished" (D&C 5:4). The process of translation was crucial in the restoration of doctrine that had either been lost or perverted to a point that it was unrecognizable. The translation of the Book of Mormon was especially crucial, for as the Lord stated, "For in [it] are all things written concerning the foundation of my church, my gospel, and my rock" (D&C 18:4).

The nature of children and their salvation through the atonement of Christ is one doctrine that had been lost and needed restoration through this process of translation. The chronology of the translation of the Book of Mormon and the Bible demonstrates the Lord's use of scripture in restoring this important doctrine line upon line. Understanding this process can increase our ability to be taught by study and revelation.

Guy L. Dorius is an assistant professor of Church history and doctrine at Brigham Young University.

The Sin of Infant Baptism

The question of infant baptism and salvation is attached to the larger issue of original sin. Prior to the translation process, the world had long lost the crucial doctrine necessary for them to understand the lack of necessity for infant baptism. The Book of Mormon warned that the world would lose many parts of the gospel that were "plain and most precious" (1 Nephi 13:26). Robert L. Millet observed: "Some of the most critical verities of salvation to be lifted or twisted from their pristine purity are the truths dealing with the Creation, the Fall, and the Atonement."[1] The practice of infant baptism sprang out of the notion that the original sin of Adam necessitated baptism for children immediately after birth because they had been born in sin.[2] This practice was evident throughout the Christian era, and scriptural evidence suggests even earlier involvement (see JST Genesis 17:3–7). Book of Mormon peoples seemed to have been plagued by this perversion as well (see Mormon 8:8–25). In the modern Christian world the practice is still prevalent.

This certainly would have been part of the religious atmosphere surrounding the Prophet Joseph Smith in his early years. Being connected to the larger issue of the fate of the unbaptized at any age, early in Joseph's life he would have encountered the doctrine. In November 1823 his brother Alvin died. Joseph's younger brother William reported the following: "Reverend Stockton had preached my brother's funeral sermon and intimated very strongly that he had gone to hell, for Alvin was not a church member, but he was a good boy, and my father did not like it."[3] Father Smith recognized that there was a lack of doctrinal understanding in this sermon and he turned against the Calvinist doctrine of the period.

Later in the summer of 1828, Joseph's wife, Emma, gave birth to their first baby boy, named Alvin, who died just hours after his birth. Both of these events must have had an effect on the Prophet Joseph in stirring questions about the fate of the unbaptized.

By the time of his son's death, Joseph had already translated the book of Lehi in the Book of Mormon.[4] There is no evidence that there was any doctrinal contribution to the question of the salvation of children found in these pages, which were subsequently lost at the hands of Martin Harris. The small plate replacements for the pages, 1 Nephi through Omni, are also silent on this doctrinal question. As a result of the lost manuscript, translation came to a stop for many months.

In the spring of 1829, the translation began again in earnest. Early in April, Oliver Cowdery arrived and the translation appears to begin somewhere in the beginning of Mosiah. There are different theories about the order of translation. Before going on with the translation of the remainder of the Book of Mormon, Joseph and Oliver may have stopped to translate the replacement for the lost manuscript.[5] Regardless of the theory adhered to, it is safe to assume that as early as April 1829, Joseph was involved with the doctrine found in the book of Mosiah. This is important because King Benjamin taught his people key concepts concerning the Atonement when he stated: "For behold he judgeth, and his judgment is just; and the infant perisheth not that dieth in his infancy; but men drink damnation to their own souls except they humble themselves and become as little children, and believe that salvation was, and is, and is to come, in and through the atoning blood of Christ, the Lord Omnipotent" (Mosiah 3:18). This verse may have been Joseph's earliest exposure to the doctrine of the innocence of children. It may well have caught his eye because of the death of his own son less than a year earlier.

Not much later in the translation process, Joseph found further clarification of this doctrine. Abinadi's teachings on the Atonement and the First Resurrection make reference to the salvation of little children. He stated: "And little children also have eternal life" (Mosiah 15:25). Though a more subtle reference, Joseph would have seen the eternal view of little children in this short verse. The translation process of the Book of Mormon would still have been in its early stages in April 1829.

By May 10–15, Joseph and Oliver were in 3 Nephi and the account of the Savior's visit to the Americas.[6] These passages inspired Joseph and Oliver to seek baptism, but they also contained more insight about the state of little children in the kingdom. The account records the observations of the multitude as they were with the Savior. It states:

"And when he had said these words, he wept, and the multitude bare record of it, and he took their little children, one by one, and blessed them, and prayed unto the Father for them.

"And when he had done this he wept again;

"And he spake unto the multitude, and said unto them: Behold your little ones.

"And as they looked to behold they cast their eyes towards heaven, and they saw the heavens open, and they saw angels descending out of heaven as it were in the midst of fire; and they came down and encircled those little ones about, and they were encircled about with fire; and the angels did minister unto them" (3 Nephi 17:21–24).

These scriptures alone do not directly address the doctrinal issues, but they certainly allude to the saved state of children. Joseph must have sensed the Savior's love for them. In reflecting on these verses, Elder Bruce R. McConkie stated: "Jesus loves and blesses children. They are the companions of angels. They shall be saved. Of such is the kingdom of heaven."[7]

The strongest Book of Mormon passages about the salvation of children occur in the book of Moroni. Mormon taught his son Moroni this doctrine when he stated:

"Listen to the words of Christ, your Redeemer, your Lord and your God. Behold, I came into the world not to call the righteous but sinners to repentance; the whole need no physician, but they that are sick; wherefore, little children are whole, for they are not capable of committing sin; wherefore the curse of Adam is taken from them in me, that it hath no power over them; and the law of circumcision is done away in me.

"And after this manner did the Holy Ghost manifest the word of God unto me; wherefore, my beloved son, I know that it is solemn mockery before God, that ye should baptize little children.

"Behold I say unto you that this thing shall ye teach—repentance and baptism unto those who are accountable and capable of committing sin; yea, teach parents that they must repent and be baptized, and humble themselves as their little children, and they shall all be saved with their little children.

"And their little children need no repentance, neither baptism. Behold, baptism is unto repentance to the fulfilling the commandments unto the remission of sins.

"But little children are alive in Christ, even from the foundation of the world; if not so, God is a partial God, and also a changeable

God, and a respecter to persons; for how many little children have died without baptism!

"Wherefore, if little children could not be saved without baptism, these must have gone to an endless hell.

"Behold I say unto you, that he that supposeth that little children need baptism is in the gall of bitterness and in the bonds of iniquity; for he hath neither faith, hope, nor charity; wherefore, should he be cut off while in the thought, he must go down to hell.

"For awful is the wickedness to suppose that God saveth one child because of baptism, and the other must perish because he hath no baptism" (Moroni 8:8–15).

It was at this point in the translation of the Book of Mormon that Joseph was taught by the strong words of Mormon about the sin of infant baptism. Whatever had been alluded to was now a matter of knowledge. Mormon continued in his epistle:

"Little children cannot repent; wherefore, it is awful wickedness to deny the pure mercies of God unto them, for they are all alive in him because of his mercy.

"And he that saith that little children need baptism denieth the mercies of Christ, and setteth at naught the atonement of him and the power of his redemption.

"Wo unto such, for they are in danger of death, hell, and an endless torment. I speak it boldly; God hath commanded me. Listen unto them and give heed, or they stand against you at the judgment-seat of Christ.

"For behold that all little children are alive in Christ, and also all they that are without the law. For the power of redemption cometh on all them that have no law; wherefore, he that is not condemned, or he that is under no condemnation, cannot repent; and unto such baptism availeth nothing" (Moroni 8:19–22).

The doctrine of the innocence of little children was powerfully presented to the Prophet and his scribe. They now understood the sin involved in the baptism of such. More importantly, the Book of Mormon had provided them with a greater understanding of the expansive reach of the Atonement. These verses even expounded the related doctrine of the salvation of those who die without law. Although the full restoration of work for the dead would be a future concern, it was tied to the salvation of children.

The Salvation of Children

The exact date the translation of the book of Moroni was completed is not known. Some evidence of its completion, however, may be provided in a letter from Oliver Cowdery to Hyrum Smith, dated 14 June 1829. Oliver taught some of the doctrine found in Doctrine and Covenants 18 and instructed Hyrum that the Savior "commandeth all men everywhere to repent and not only be baptized and not only men but women [and] children which have arrived to the years of accountability."[8] This indicates that as early as June 1829 Oliver had a clear understanding that children had to be accountable in order to be eligible for baptism. The wording he used is interesting in that he does not mention an age of accountability but years of accountability.

THE CONCEPT OF ACCOUNTABILITY

The concept of accountability began to appear in the revelations found in the Doctrine and Covenants. In section 20 the Lord instructed the brethren:

"Every member of the church of Christ having children is to bring them unto the elders before the church, who are to lay their hands upon them in the name of Jesus Christ, and bless them in his name.

"No one can be received into the church of Christ unless he has arrived unto the years of accountability before God, and is capable of repentance" (D&C 20:70–71).

These verses are followed by instructions on the manner of baptism in Christ's church. This revelation is dated April 1830 and appears in both the 1833 Book of Commandments and the 1835 edition of the Doctrine and Covenants. In September 1830, the Lord reiterated:

"But behold, I say unto you, that little children are redeemed from the foundation of the world through mine Only Begotten;

"Wherefore, they cannot sin, for power is not given unto Satan to tempt little children, until they begin to become accountable before me" (D&C 29:46–47).

It is clear that within a year of the organization of the Church, the brethren understood from the Book of Mormon that they should not baptize little children until they had arrived at the years of accountability. This verifies again the claim that the Book of Mormon contained "the fulness of the gospel of Jesus Christ to the Gentiles and to the Jews also" (D&C 20:9). The message that the atonement of the Savior would save little children was a fundamentally important, restorative step. President John Taylor stated: "These [little children] would embrace, according to the opinion of statisticians, more than one-half of the human family, who can attribute their salvation only to the mediation and atonement of the Savior."[9] The Book of Mormon illuminated the corruption of doctrine and restored this fundamental truth.

Without further revelation and instruction, it would be difficult to determine when a child is accountable. Although the foundation of doctrine and principal had been laid by the Book of Mormon's translation, the actual practice and age of youth baptisms had not been resolved. Elder Bruce R. McConkie stated: "Accountability does not burst full-bloom upon a child at any given moment in his life. Children become accountable gradually, over a number of years. Becoming accountable is a process, not a goal to be attained when a specified number of years, days, and hours have elapsed." Elder McConkie then clarified: "There comes a time, however, when accountability is real and actual and sin is attributed in the lives of those who develop normally. It is eight years of age, the age of baptism."[10] The revelation that instructed Joseph on the age of baptism may well have come as a result of translation.

The Book of Mormon was finished by the summer of 1829 and set the doctrinal foundation for the salvation of children, yet it lacked in the specificity necessary for an actual age of accountability. Soon after finishing the translation of the plates, the Lord gave Joseph another translation assignment. He was instructed to translate the Bible and recover some of the "plain and precious" parts that had been lost. The exact date he began is not known, but it appears to be as early as the summer of 1830.[11] Robert J. Matthews observed: "As the facts are assembled, it becomes clear that one of the benefits of the Bible translation is that it provided the Prophet with the spiritual involvement necessary for the revelation of many important doctrines."[12] It was important for the Prophet to continue in a translation process so that further revelation necessary for the complete Restoration might be given. More specifically, continued translation would provide Joseph with the knowledge necessary to restore the

The Salvation of Children

doctrine of baptism at the age of accountability, which had been introduced to him through the Book of Mormon.

The Prophet began his translation of the Bible in the Old Testament. Early in his work he came across more information concerning the salvation of children and the age of accountability. When Joseph came to the instructions the Lord gave to Abraham, he encountered the following:

"My people have gone astray from my precepts, and have not kept mine ordinances, which I gave unto their fathers;

"And they have not observed mine anointing, and the burial, or baptism wherewith I commanded them;

"But have turned from the commandment, and taken unto themselves the washing of children, and the blood of sprinkling;

"And have said that the blood of the righteous Abel was shed for sins; and have not known wherein they are accountable before me" (JST Genesis 17:4–7).

Infant baptisms were occurring in the early days of Abraham. Joseph was again taught of the misunderstanding concerning the Atonement that led to the practice. He was then given the most specific doctrine concerning the accountability of children. The Lord taught Abraham: "And I will establish a covenant of circumcision with thee, and it shall be my covenant between me and thee, and thy seed after thee, in their generations; that thou mayest know for ever that children are not accountable before me until they are eight years old" (JST Genesis 17:11).

This verse clearly informed the Prophet Joseph Smith that children were not accountable before they were eight years old. This appears to be the first record in which Joseph encountered the age of accountability for children.[13] The latest date this translation might have occurred would have been 7 March 1831 because after that date Joseph was instructed to move in his translation to the New Testament. Chronologically, this predates the statement in the Doctrine and Covenants wherein the Lord states:

"And again, inasmuch as parents have children in Zion, or in any of her stakes which are organized, that teach them not to understand the doctrine of repentance, faith in Christ the Son of the living God, and of baptism and the gift of the Holy Ghost by the laying on of the hands, *when eight years old,* the sin be upon the heads of the parents.

"For this shall be a law unto the inhabitants of Zion, or in any of her stakes which are organized.

"And their children shall be baptized for the remission of their sins when eight years old, and receive the laying on of the hands" (D&C 68:25–27; italics added).

The date of this revelation was November 1831, many months after Joseph had received the inspired version of Genesis. It is now evident that not only had the doctrine of accountability of little children been restored to the Prophet, but also the more specific understanding of when the Lord views that children are accountable before him.

Joseph encountered this doctrine again while translating the New Testament. Matthew recorded:

"Then were there brought unto him little children, that he should put his hands on them and pray. And the disciples rebuked them, saying, There is no need, for Jesus hath said, Such shall be saved.

"But Jesus said, Suffer little children to come unto me, and forbid them not, for of such is the kingdom of heaven.

"And he laid [his] hands on them, and departed thence" (JST Matthew 19:13–15). Again the Prophet was reminded of the important doctrine of the salvation of little children.

Celestial Inhabitants

These early lessons, learned through the process of translation, restored the knowledge of the age of accountability and thus the age at which we baptize our children in The Church of Jesus Christ of Latter-day Saints. But this was not all. Through the revelations and Restoration we gained greater understanding of not only the salvation of little children, but of all who die in ignorance. On 21 January 1836, Joseph received further insight when, in the upper floor of the unfinished Kirtland Temple, he saw the celestial kingdom and some of its inhabitants. He stated:

"I saw Father Adam and Abraham; and my father and my mother; my brother Alvin, that has long since slept;

"And marveled how it was that he had obtained an inheritance in that kingdom, seeing that he had departed this life before the Lord had set his hand to gather Israel the second time, and had not been baptized for the remission of sins.

The Salvation of Children

"Thus came the voice of the Lord unto me, saying: All who have died without a knowledge of this gospel, who would have received it if they had been permitted to tarry, shall be heirs of the celestial kingdom of God;

"Also all that shall die henceforth without a knowledge of it, who would have received it with all their hearts, shall be heirs of that kingdom;

"For I, the Lord, will judge all men according to their works, according to the desire of their hearts.

"And I also beheld that all children who die before they arrive at the years of accountability are saved in the celestial kingdom of heaven" (D&C 137:5–10).

Summary

As previously stated, these two doctrines are related by the common thread of the Atonement. A proper understanding of Christ's mission clarified for the Prophet Joseph the administration of ordinances. It is significant that this understanding began with the translation of the Book of Mormon. It is there that Joseph had the foundational doctrines of the gospel revealed to him. The Lord provided a step-by-step process through which he restored doctrine to the Prophet. His early work in the Book of Mormon, subsequent work in translation, and other revelatory experiences gave him the knowledge necessary to be the instrument of the Restoration.

This process is important for Latter-day Saints to understand. Robert J. Matthews, in referring to the Joseph Smith Translation of the Bible, stated: "That these revelations came as a result of intense study of the holy scriptures is a lesson in itself. Answers are found while searching the scriptures because inspiration comes from studying the Lord's own words. They are an unfailing source of light and inspiration."[14] Readers of scripture must have the expectation that their study will yield personal revelation. Elder Dallin H. Oaks stated: "For us, the scriptures are not the ultimate source of knowledge, but what precedes the ultimate source. The ultimate knowledge comes by revelation."[15]

For Joseph, his translation and study of the Book of Mormon provided a springboard for receiving the revelations necessary for the Restoration. For Latter-day Saints, a study of the Book of Mormon will restore in their hearts the doctrines of the gospel and Atonement so crucial for their exaltation. Then, added study of all the canon of scripture will provide an understanding of the specific ordinances and covenants necessary to return to God's presence.

NOTES

1. Robert L. Millet, "Alive in Christ: The Salvation of Little Children," in Monte S. Nyman and Charles D. Tate Jr., ed., *The Book of Mormon: Fourth Nephi through Moroni, from Zion to Destruction* (Salt Lake City: Bookcraft, 1995), 2.

2. For a thorough treatment of this issue, see Millet, "Alive in Christ."

3. J. W. Peterson, "The Testimony of William Smith," *Millennial Star,* 26 Feb. 1894, 133.

4. See John W. Welch and Tim Rathbone, "The Translation of the Book of Mormon: Preliminary Report on the Basic Historical Information" (Provo, Utah: Foundation for Ancient Research and Mormon Studies, n.d.), 11.

5. Ibid., 33–39.

6. See Oliver Cowdery, *LDS Messenger and Advocate,* 7 Sept. 1834, 14–15.

7. Bruce R. McConkie, "The Salvation of Little Children," *Ensign,* Apr. 1977, 3.

8. Letter cited in Larry C. Porter, "The Restoration of the Aaronic and Melchizedek Priesthoods," *Ensign,* Dec. 1996, 38.

9. John Taylor, *Mediation and Atonement* (Salt Lake City: Deseret News Co., 1882), 148.

10. McConkie, "The Salvation of Little Children," 6.

11. See Robert J. Matthews, *"A Plainer Translation," Joseph Smith's Translation of the Bible: A History and Commentary* (Provo, Utah: Brigham Young University Press, 1975), 26.

12. Robert J. Matthews, *A Bible! A Bible!* (Salt Lake City: Bookcraft, 1990), 134.

13. See Matthews,*"A Plainer Translation,"* 317.

14. Matthews, *A Bible! A Bible!* 134.

15. Dallin H. Oaks, "Scripture Reading and Revelation," *Ensign,* Jan. 1995, 7.

CHAPTER SEVEN

THE FIRST COMING OF THE LORD TO THE JEWS: A BOOK OF MORMON PERSPECTIVE

RICHARD D. DRAPER

Speaking prophetically, Alma told the Saints at Gideon that "there be many things to come; and behold, there is one thing which is of more importance than they all—for behold, the time is not far distant that the Redeemer liveth and cometh among his people" (Alma 7:7). Alma knew, as he reminded his hearers, that there was one future event more important than any other. That event was the coming of the Savior to the earth.

Alma was not the only Book of Mormon prophet who knew of things to come. In fact, others' prophecies included some very specific items; some are more clearly stated than most found in the Bible. For instance, the Nephite prophets knew from the time God called Lehi to his work that the Savior would come six hundred years in the future; they knew that his mother would be named Mary and that she would dwell in Nazareth; and they also knew that he would not appear unto them as a mortal man. There were additional details that God revealed to them concerning the Lord's first coming—details that he wanted them to understand. Their understanding of the mortal Messiah and his mission came solely from God. As a result, the Book of Mormon emphasizes what the Father felt was

---

Richard D. Draper is an associate professor of ancient scripture at Brigham Young University.

important about Jesus' first coming. By bringing all these prophetic elements together, we can get a clear picture of the essentials. The purpose of this chapter is to bring together those items so that we might better understand what the Father wants to emphasize concerning the Lord's first coming. For the sake of space, this chapter will be limited to revealed information about the Savior's ministry among the Jews.

Though this study is about the Lord's first coming, it also has something to say about the foreknowledge of God and how God uses that foreknowledge to further his work. The Book of Mormon shows us that God knows the future down to the smallest details, such as the names by which his mortal children shall be known and where they shall reside. It also shows us that God willingly reveals details of the future to his prophets and through them to his other children. He does this so that all might be prepared to take full advantage of that which is to come.

The Book of Mormon also shows us that not all respond to prophecy with faith. Many, especially among the Nephite intellectuals, found the doctrine impossible to believe. Sherem took Jacob to task for perverting the way of truth by promoting the "worship of a being which ye say shall come many hundred years hence." He assured Jacob that "this is blasphemy; for no man knoweth of such things; for he cannot tell of things to come" (Jacob 7:7). Korihor preached "unto the people against the prophecies which had been spoken by the prophets, concerning the coming of Christ" (Alma 30:6). He boldly asked, "Why do ye look for a Christ? For no man can know of anything which is to come" (Alma 30:13). The prophetic witness of the first coming of the Lord proves both of these men wrong. In the book's witness of the first coming of the Savior, we see just how much righteous men and women knew about the future.

"God Should Come Down among the Children of Men"

One of the strongest messages that comes through the pages of the Book of Mormon is that the Messiah would be the Son of God. Alma testified that "he shall be born of Mary, . . . who shall be overshadowed and conceive by the power of the Holy Ghost, and bring forth a son, yea, even the Son of God" (Alma 7:10). An angel assured Nephi that Mary was "the mother of the Son of God, after the manner of the flesh" (1 Nephi 11:18). That is a striking statement. The great Jehovah, the Creator of heaven and earth, would enter the world just as any other baby. Though his conception might be miraculous, his birth would not be. Like us, he would in the natural way take upon himself flesh and blood and go forth among the children of men (see Mosiah 7:26–27). How apropos, if homey, is King Benjamin's statement that the Redeemer would "dwell in a tabernacle of clay" (Mosiah 3:5).

We must be careful, however, not to make the mortal Savior too much like ourselves. The Book of Mormon testifies that he was something special, something unique. Though he might dwell in a tabernacle of clay, he would come "with power" and "go forth amongst men, working mighty miracles" (Mosiah 3:5). He would have the power to do his mighty works as a direct result of being the "Only Begotten of the Father" (2 Nephi 25:12). Never in the history of this telestial world would there be another born as Son of Elohim. His conception and birth allowed him to retain his station as God. Abinadi avowed that "God himself [shall] come down among the children of men, and take upon him the form of man, and go forth in mighty power" (Mosiah 13:33–34). It is of note that Abinadi does not say that Jesus will be a man, but rather he would have man's form, through which he would be able to manifest his "mighty power."

Alma elaborated on this point, saying that the Redeemer would "take upon him the image of man, and it should be the image after which man was created in the beginning; or in other words, he said that man was created after the image of God, and that God should come down among the children of men" (Mosiah 7:27). The point is that Jesus stood apart from all others born of mortal woman, even though we look like him and he lived like us. It was because he was different that he could fulfill his mission, for "he shall suffer temptations, and pain of body, hunger, thirst, and fatigue, even more than man can suffer, except it be unto death; for behold, blood cometh from every pore, so great shall be his anguish for the wickedness and the abominations of his people" (Mosiah 3:7). Two important points come out of this scripture. First, the Savior is separate from the class of beings called "man"—he endured what no "man" could in terms of spiritual and physical suffering. Second, his godly abilities allowed his body to withstand the physical anguish the Atonement required.

Amulek also stressed that Jesus was something other than man when he taught the Zoramites. Explaining the need for a great and last sacrifice, he said that it would "not [be] a sacrifice of man, neither of beast, neither of any manner of fowl; for it shall not be a human sacrifice; but it must be an infinite and eternal sacrifice" (Alma 34:10). His testimony, like that of Abinadi and Benjamin, seems startling. How could the Savior, born after the manner of the flesh, be considered anything other than human? Amulek is herein making an important point. He expands upon Abinadi's division—that mortals fall into two categories, by distinguishing whether or not they are infinite and eternal. If one is not infinite and eternal then one is man; if one is infinite and eternal, then one is not man. Jesus was the Son of God and, consequently, even as a mortal was infinite and eternal. Therefore, he carried with him attributes no other mortal ever carried. Amulek could therefore affirm that the "great and last sacrifice will be the Son of God, yea, infinite and eternal" (Alma 34:14).

He Became the Father and the Son

The Savior was unique in two other ways: First, he was the Only Begotten of God. No other would ever be born in the flesh as God's child. Second, as a mortal he was the Eternal Father. Therefore, he was at the same time, the Son of God and the Eternal Father. Benjamin testified that he would "be called Jesus Christ, the Son of God, the Father of heaven and earth" (Mosiah 3:8). Nephi quoted Isaiah saying that "Unto us a child is born, . . . and his name shall be called, . . . The Mighty God, The Everlasting Father" (2 Nephi 19:6).

Abinadi, in an extremely difficult passage, explained this dual characteristic. He noted that "God himself shall come down among the children of men" (Mosiah 15:1), and that he would come as "the Father and the Son" (Mosiah 15:2). What gave him the power to be the Father? Abinadi said it was because "he was conceived by the power of God" (v. 3). Just what Abinadi meant by that phrase is puzzling, but it seems clear that the Savior's power as Father came as a direct result of something he inherited from God. What made him the Son? The act by which God gave him "the flesh" (vv. 2–3). Thus,

Abinadi observed, he became "the Father and the Son" (v. 3). The prophet went on to testify that "they are one God, yea, the very Eternal Father of heaven and earth" (v. 4), and that Jesus, even though he came in the dual role of Son and Father, would be that "one God, [who] suffereth temptation, and yieldeth not to the temptation, but suffereth himself to be mocked, and scourged, and cast out, and disowned by his people" (v. 5). All this stresses the point that the Savior, even as a mortal, was unlike anyone else.

We should not get the idea from all this, however, that the Savior could not relate to us. The testimony of the Book of Mormon is that nothing could be further from the truth. Just because he was God and the Son of God, he was not, as Abinadi testified, shielded from temptation or pain or sorrow. Alma knew that the Savior would "go forth, suffering pains and afflictions and temptations of every kind; and this that the word might be fulfilled which saith he will take upon him the pains and the sicknesses of his people" (Alma 7:11). Indeed, he would "take upon him their infirmities" (v. 12). There was a divine reason for this: "That his bowels may be filled with mercy, according to the flesh, that he [might] know according to the flesh how to succor his people" (v. 12). Therefore, as "the Spirit knoweth all things," the flesh also needed to know. Consequently, the mortal Christ would suffer "according to the flesh" (v. 13)—and, remember, he would suffer even more than man can suffer without dying.

Someone once pointed out a myth that many believe. According to the myth, good people know little of temptation because only bad people are ever really touched by it. Nothing could be further from the truth. What does a person know about the seductive force or unrelenting pressure of temptation if he never resists? Only those who hold out against temptation ever really feel its depth and power. Christ never yielded. Therefore, he not only sympathizes with those who must struggle against it, he also empathizes. Thus, he could ascend "into heaven, having the bowels of mercy; being filled with compassion towards the children of men" (Mosiah 15:9).

Before that Ascension, he had first to come to earth and fulfill his mission. The Nephite prophets were well aware that the Lord would come six hundred years after Lehi left Jerusalem, but they did not keep their dating system based on this prophecy. Instead, they followed a more traditional method of keeping track of years according to the reign of kings and judges. As a result, we don't know if the general population knew that the exact year of the Lord's first coming had been revealed. That uncertainty changed with the preaching of Samuel the Lamanite. He told them the Lord would come in five years, and gave the people a very specific sign by which they would know that the Lord had indeed come. There would be "one day and a night and a day, as if it were one day and there were no night" (Helaman 14:4). In addition, "There shall a new star arise, such an one as ye never have beheld" (v. 5). By this they would know that the Son of God had come "to redeem all those who shall believe on his name" (v. 2).

"Baptized the Lamb of God"

In addition to knowing when he would be born, they also knew it would be some time before he would start his actual ministry. During that period "the Spirit of the Lord shall rest upon him, the spirit of wisdom and understanding, the spirit of counsel and might, the spirit of knowledge and of the fear of the Lord;

"And shall make him of quick understanding in the fear of the Lord" (2 Nephi 21:2–3). Then, after he had matured, he would go forth.

Before the ministry, he would have to take care of a very important matter: his baptism. The Father, through the amount of detail he revealed about this event, underscored its importance. Nephi taught that John the Baptist would play the principal role in the ordinance. Though John is never mentioned by name, his status is. Lehi called him "a prophet who should come before the Messiah, to prepare the way of the Lord" (1 Nephi 10:7), and knew that he would "baptize in Bethabara, beyond Jordan" (v. 9). Nephi also saw "the prophet who should prepare the way before" the Lord (1 Nephi 11:27). They knew that he would come out of the wilderness and tell the people to make straight the path of the Lord. He would testify that one stands "among you whom ye know not; and he is mightier than I, whose shoe's latchet I am not worthy to unloose" (1 Nephi 10:8). The mission of John would also include an additional witness. "And after he had baptized the Messiah with water," Lehi taught, "he should behold and bear record that he had baptized the Lamb of God" (1 Nephi 10:10).

Concerning Jesus himself, Nephi predicted that "after he was baptized, . . . the Holy Ghost [would] come down . . . and abide upon him in the form of a dove" (1 Nephi 11:27). The dove came as a sign that the Savior had been "obedient unto him [the Father] in keeping his commandments" (2 Nephi 31:7; see also v. 8). It also showed that the power of the Holy Ghost comes only after one has entered into the water (see 2 Nephi 31:12).

Nephi helps us understand why the Father revealed so much detail about the Savior's baptism. He shows us two points in particular. The first has to do with the condescension of God. The term denotes the act of voluntarily laying aside privilege, rank, or dignity. In vision, Nephi saw the Savior do this. "The angel said to me again: Look and behold the condescension of God!

"And I looked and beheld the Redeemer of the world, of whom my father had spoken; . . . and the Lamb of God went forth and was baptized" by a man (1 Nephi 11:26–27). He who was holy, and the Redeemer of humankind, condescended to be baptized by a man who, though one of the greatest born of woman, was not worthy to untie his sandal straps.

The second point deals with the Savior's need to fulfill all righteousness. The Lord had done all that had been required of him up to the point when he was about to start his ministry. That includes living for thirty years in a state of holiness. But he could not stop now. He had to continue until he had done all that the Father required. At this point, the Father required that Jesus show "unto the children of men that, according to the flesh he humbleth himself before the Father, and witnesseth unto the Father that he would be obedient unto him in keeping his commandments" (2 Nephi 31:7). Further, he had to show "the children of men the straitness of the path, and the narrowness of the gate, by which they should enter, he having set the example before them" (v. 9). Indeed, he did show the way, for if the Savior was holy and still had to fulfill the Father's will by being baptized, "how much more need have we, being unholy, to be baptized" (v. 5).

"MINISTERING UNTO THE PEOPLE"

Once the Savior had met that requirement, he was ready to move on to the next phase of his mission. That phase was to go "forth ministering unto the people, in power and great glory" (1 Nephi 11:28). Abinadi testified he would "go forth in mighty power upon the face of the earth" (Mosiah 13:34). The power would be manifest, among other ways, through miracles. The prophets were well aware of the breadth of those miracles, which would include "healing the sick, rasing the dead, causing the lame to walk, the blind to receive their sight, and the deaf to hear, and curing all manner of diseases.

"And he shall cast out devils, or the evil spirits which dwell in the hearts of the children of men" (Mosiah 3:5–6). As Nephi saw, these miracles were not few and far between. "I beheld multitudes of people who were sick, and who were afflicted with all manner of diseases, and with devils and unclean spirits; . . . And they were healed by the power of the Lamb of God; and the devils and the unclean spirits were cast out" (1 Nephi 11:31).

As a result of these deeds, "multitudes were gathered together to hear him" (1 Nephi 11:28). Among these Nephi saw "many fall down at his feet and worship him" (v. 24). Of these, there would be twelve called to his service. Nephi knew, by angelic testimony, that their title would be "apostles" (v. 34) and that, someday, they would "judge the twelve tribes of Israel" (1 Nephi 12:9). Before that day, they would assist the Lord in his ministry. One of their main functions would be to "bear record" of the Lamb of God (1 Nephi 13:24).

The Book of Mormon prophets knew that the Savior would devote most of his time to teaching the people. His message would carry the pure "word of God" (1 Nephi 11:25). Through it, those who would hear would be brought to "the love of God" (v. 25). Such love, as Nephi understood, "sheddeth itself abroad in the hearts of the children of men; wherefore, it is the most desirable above all things" (v. 22). Indeed, it is "the most joyous to the soul" (v. 23).

THE ATONEMENT: POWER TO REDEEM

Both his teachings and miracles were the foundations to the Lord's central work. "A prophet would the Lord God raise up among the Jews," Lehi testified, "even a Messiah, or, in other words, a Savior of the world" (1 Nephi 10:4). This Messiah, he went on to say, would also be the "Redeemer of the world" (v. 5). The two tasks—redemption and salvation—though closely related, are not identical. Redemption carries the idea of paying the price necessary to bring a person or people out of bondage. Salvation, on the other hand, goes beyond merely freeing them; it carries with it the assurance of further existence in which they can enjoy security and happiness.

The Savior's power to redeem grew out of the Atonement. It was through the Atonement that he paid the necessary price to save humankind. Jacob assured his people that "redemption cometh in and through the Holy Messiah; for he is full of grace and truth."

"Behold he offereth himself a sacrifice for sin, to answer the ends of the law, unto all those who have a broken heart and a contrite spirit" (2 Nephi 2:6–7). He paid the price of himself. "His blood atoneth for the sins of those who have fallen by the transgression of Adam," King Benjamin taught. It covered those "who have died not knowing the will of God concerning them, or who have ignorantly sinned" (Mosiah 3:11). This sentence gives us a feel for the breadth of the Savior's redeeming power. Its full force, however, would not come upon all people, only those who met the proper criteria. "He shall come into the world to redeem his people," Amulek taught, "and he shall take upon him the transgressions of those who believe on his name" (Alma 11:40). It is true that there is a universal aspect of the redemption: "Because of the intercession for all, all men come unto God; wherefore, they stand . . . to be judged of him according to the truth and holiness which is in him" (2 Nephi 2:10). Thus, some aspects of the Savior's atonement benefit everyone.

That is not the whole story, however. As Nephi, the son of Helaman, testified, Jesus "hath power given unto him . . . to redeem them from their sins because of repentance" (Helaman 5:11). The Nephites understood that the Savior payed the price to redeem us from the Fall; however, it would be up to each individual to accept the redemption and the freedom it brought. The means God has provided, by which we may show our acceptance, is repentance. Seeing repentance in this way allows us to focus on its positive aspects. So often we see it as the burden we pay to have our sins remitted. The truth of the matter is that Christ has given us a gift. That gift is redemption. It is freely given, but we must accept it. We do that by repenting. When we accept the Lord's gift, he forgives our sins. Samuel the Lamanite said, "Repent of all your sins, that thereby ye may have a remission of them through his merits" (Helaman 14:13).

That redemption opens the way for full salvation, through which the individual can secure eternal life and joy. Benjamin testified that the Lord "cometh unto his own, that salvation might come unto the children of men even through faith on his name" (Mosiah 3:9). It is of note that God designed the Savior's mission to the Jews as the means of taking salvation to all his children. The Father sent Jesus specifically to the Jews, but the objective was not Jewish salvation alone. What happened to the Savior while he was with the Jews would open the way for the salvation of all people. In Benjamin's seemingly simple statement, we see that God made the wicked among the Jews, like he made Assyria or Babylon, instruments in bringing about his will.

The Book of Mormon shows that the Savior designed the teachings, acts, signs, and miracles of his ministry to promote faith in him so he could save the people. The Book of Mormon prophets knew that "there is no other way nor means whereby man can be saved, only through the atoning blood of Jesus Christ" (Helaman 5:9). But people had to have faith in that blood, or they would not do what was required of them to be saved. Amulek explained why it was a necessity for sinners to accept the Lord, forsake their sins, and become clean. It was because the Lord "cannot save them in their sins; for I cannot deny his word, and he hath said that no unclean thing can inherit the kingdom of heaven; therefore, how can ye be saved, except ye inherit the kingdom of heaven? Therefore, ye cannot be saved in your sins" (Alma 11:37). The Lord's power operated only to save people from their sins. That meant that they had to forsake their sins through faith and repentance.

"SLAIN FOR THE SINS OF THE WORLD"

Through his teachings, signs, miracles, and loving kindness, the Lord sought to create that faith by which he could save the people. But "even after all this," taught King Benjamin, "they shall consider him a man, and say that he hath a devil" (Mosiah 3:9). Among the multitudes that came to hear him, there were many who would turn away and "cast him out from among them" (1 Nephi 11:28). Eventually, the prophets saw, the Jews' fear and hatred would turn murderous. Nephi saw in vision that "the Son of the everlasting God was judged of the world" (1 Nephi 11:32). The irony is amazing. The righteous God and judge of all would be judged by the world. Their

The First Coming of the Lord to the Jews

judgment, however, would not be righteous. "And the world, because of their iniquity, shall judge him to be a thing of naught; wherefore they scourge him, and he suffereth it; and they smite him, and he suffereth it. Yea, they spit upon him, and he suffereth it, because of his loving kindness and his long-suffering towards the children of men" (1 Nephi 19:9). Benjamin said these people, unyielding to his loving kindness, "shall scourge him, and shall crucify him" (Mosiah 3:9). In this way, "he was lifted up upon the cross and slain for the sins of the world" (1 Nephi 11:33).

He was slain not only for the sins of the world, but also because of them. People do not seem to realize that sin is blinding; however, sin cannot blind in and of itself. Rather, it is the instrument whereby people blind themselves. Having done so, a Jewish mob moved against their God, and he "yieldeth himself, according to the words of the angel, as a man, into the hands of wicked men, to be lifted up" (1 Nephi 19:10).

The use of the word *wicked* is arresting. It points to much more than simply not measuring up to a spiritual standard. The word describes a conscious and deliberate opposition to and violation of moral law. Though many of the Lord's initial followers may have inadvertently blinded themselves with sin, the Book of Mormon makes it clear that the Jewish leadership knew what they were doing. Therefore, its prophets could say that the Messiah will "come among the Jews, among those who are the more wicked part of the world; and they shall crucify him—for thus it behooveth our God, and there is none other nation on earth that would crucify their God.

"For should the mighty miracles be wrought among other nations they would repent, and know that he be their God.

"But because of priestcrafts and iniquities, they at Jerusalem will stiffen their necks against him, that he be crucified" (2 Nephi 10:3–5).

Due to their murderous hatred, they would do more than just crucify him. They would first put him through tremendous humiliation and torture. He saw it coming and said, "I gave my back to the smiter, and my cheeks to them that plucked off the hair. I hid not my face from shame and spitting" (2 Nephi 7:6). Further, he would not fight them. "He shall be led, yea, even as Isaiah said, as a sheep before the shearer is dumb, so he opened not his mouth" (Mosiah

15:6). So, wicked men judged the God of judgment, shamed him, humiliated him, and then crucified him.

The Book of Mormon shows, however, that the situation is not as black as it appears. At least two positive things came out of it. The first was for the Lord himself. At the time "when his soul has been made an offering for sin he shall see his seed" (Mosiah 15:10). Just when he would see his seed Abinadi does not make clear. Could it have been during the agony of Gethsemane or on the cross? Or was it after, as he ministered to the spirit world, or later, to people on two continents? The text is not clear; however, one thing that is clear is that Abinadi knew who it was the Lord would see. It was those who "looked forward to that day for a remission of their sins, . . . or they [who] are the heirs of the kingdom of God" (Mosiah 15:11). The Savior would see these, and his soul would rejoice.

The second item was that all the suffering and torture worked to God's end: "Christ shall come among the children of men, to take upon him the transgressions of his people, and that he shall atone for the sins of the world" (Alma 34:8). His mission was twofold. First, he would take upon him the transgressions of his people. In that way he would pay the debt of sin and redeem them from death and hell. In addition, he would save them by making an atonement on their behalf. The word *atonement* carries with it the idea of reconciliation. An atonement is needed when two estranged parties must come together for the benefit of either or both. Alma taught that, due to sin, people suffer both temporal and spiritual death. As a result of this, when they die physically, their souls are "miserable, being cut off from the presence of the Lord" (Alma 42:11). The only way to reclaim them from their fallen state is to reconcile them to God. But justice had claim on them, due to sin, and demanded their separation from God. The Savior gave his blood and thus redeemed them from sin and also freed them from justice, but on the condition that they accept his mercy. He would not, however, force anyone to live according to the *law* of mercy.

Justice and Mercy

Two points need to be understood. First, the Savior's death allowed the *law* of mercy to operate within the bounds of the *law* of justice. Second, Jesus did not die to move his people from law to lawlessness.

The First Coming of the Lord to the Jews

His death made it possible for them to live according to the law of mercy rather than the law of justice. Those who chose mercy still lived according to the law and, therefore, the Savior could reconcile them to the Father. The means by which they could choose to come under the law of mercy was repentance. So, Alma explains, "The plan of mercy could not be brought about except an atonement should be made; therefore God himself atoneth for the sins of the world, to bring about the plan of mercy, to appease the demands of justice" (Alma 42:15). In doing so, Jesus made it possible for us to return to the Father. Of all the prophecies dealing with the first coming, the Lord's mission as Savior and Redeemer are central.

The Book of Mormon prophets told their people that they would know when Jesus made that atonement. Nephi explained that there would be "three days of darkness, which should be a sign given of this death unto those who should inhabit the isles of the sea, more especially given unto those who are of the house of Israel" (1 Nephi 19:10). The event, however, would be signaled by far more severe conditions than mere darkness. Indeed, "the rocks of the earth must rend; and because of the groanings of the earth, many of the kings of the isles of the sea shall be wrought upon by the Spirit of God, to exclaim: The God of nature suffers" (1 Nephi 19:12).

RESURRECTION

His suffering and death would not be the last event that defined his first coming to the Jews. He still had to be resurrected and ascend in order to prepare for his second coming. Therefore, "after he is laid in a sepulchre for the space of three days he shall rise from the dead, with healing in his wings" (2 Nephi 25:13; see also 1 Nephi 19:10). It is of note that the Lord's healing ministry would continue even into the Resurrection. It would focus on healing the breach between man and God. Through the power of the Resurrection, the Father "breaketh the bands of death, having gained the victory over death; giving the Son power to make intercession for the children of men" (Mosiah 15:8).

"Behold, the resurrection of Christ redeemeth mankind, yea, even all mankind, and bringeth them back into the presence of the Lord.

"Yea, and it bringeth to pass the condition of repentance, that whosoever repenteth the same is not hewn down and cast into the fire; and there cometh upon them again a spiritual death, yea, a second death, for they are cut off again as to things pertaining to righteousness" (Helaman 14:17–18).

With the Resurrection and reconciliation made, the Savior's first coming to the Jews met all of its objectives, and he departed from these people, never to return until he would come to them again in the last days.

An observation in closing. Most of what the Book of Mormon teaches about the Lord's first coming is laid out in the books of Nephi. God had already revealed the essential elements of his Son's mission before Lehi ever left the old world. Therefore, the righteous Nephites had a clear picture of the Savior's mortal mission from the beginning. Later prophets generally did little more than confirm what was already known. The point is that God saw fit to reveal all the essentials about his Son's mortal ministry early, so that the Nephite people, far removed from the place of the first coming of the Lord, could still be prepared for and take advantage of what he offered.

CHAPTER EIGHT

A Banner Is Unfurled: The Doctrine of the Gathering in the Book of Mormon

Timothy W. Durkin

Seven centuries before Israel's watchmen first spotted Assyrian chariots descending upon their Northern Kingdom, the Lord revealed the doctrine of the scattering and gathering. In that early day, while Moses prepared the children of Israel to enter the promised land, he warned that if Israel forsook the covenant of the Lord, foreign nations would enslave them (see Deuteronomy 28:64; 29:24–28). Sadly, Moses' prophecies of conquering, subjugation, and slavery were fulfilled.[1] Even as the lengthening shadow of destruction loomed over the Lord's people, however, the Lord's prophets extended the light of hope. Of the sixteen prophets whose books are canonized in the Old Testament, ten recorded detailed descriptions, warnings, and prophecies about Israel's exile and future gathering.[2] With so much Old Testament prophecy implicating the gathering of Israel, it is not surprising to find a proportionate amount of interpretive commentary. A survey of non-LDS interpretations of the gathering prophecies reveals little more than confusion and disagreement.

It is against this opaque backdrop that the doctrine of the gathering in the Book of Mormon is revealed. By tracing the doctrine of the

---

Timothy W. Durkin is director of the institute of religion in Columbus, Ohio.

gathering from its Old Testament roots through its current non-LDS formulations, we are in a better position to appreciate three vital contributions the Book of Mormon makes to our understanding of this important doctrine: First, the Book of Mormon functions as a key that unlocks the door of the gathering. Second, the Book of Mormon restores many plain and precious truths relative to the gathering. Finally, and perhaps most significantly, the Book of Mormon is the key that unlocks the individual door of the heart, inviting the reader to find personal significance in the doctrine of the gathering.

The Gathering of Israel's Remnant as Old Testament Prophecy

The restoration of the house of Israel to their covenants and covenant lands is a central theme of Old Testament prophets. The first prophet to speak to Israel about the gathering was Moses. He reminded them that the Lord would remember his covenant with Abraham, and "turn thy captivity, and have compassion upon thee, and will return and gather thee from all the nations, whither the Lord thy God hath scattered thee" (Deuteronomy 30:3). Subsequent prophets picked up the theme of Israel's scattering and gathering. Isaiah, whose prophetic mission so thoroughly embraced the doctrine of the gathering that he named his son Shear-jashub (a remnant shall return), prophesied that the Lord would "assemble the outcasts of Israel, and gather together the dispersed of Judah from the four corners of the earth" (Isaiah 11:12). Likewise, Jeremiah reminded Israel that the Lord would send hunters and fishers to "bring them again into their land that I gave unto their fathers" (Jeremiah 16:15–16; see also 30:1–3).

Ezekiel promised that the Lord would gather Israel with a "mighty hand, and with a stretched out arm" (Ezekiel 20:33), and that he would "gather [Israel] out of all countries" (Ezekiel 36:24). Ezekiel symbolically illustrated his point by bringing together in his hand two sticks, representing the regathering of Judah and Joseph (see Ezekiel 37:15–22).[3] Hosea declared that "the children of Judah and the children of Israel [would] be gathered together" (Hosea 1:11), while Micah expressed his assurance that the Lord "will surely gather the remnant of Israel" (Micah 2:12). Zechariah prophesied of the future gathering, declaring that the Lord would "gather them; for I have redeemed them" (Zechariah 10:8). The theme of Israel's gathering is so prevalent in the pages of the Old Testament that scholars and theologians are obliged to offer interpretation.

Contemporary Interpretations of the Prophesied Gathering

There is disagreement among Jews and Christians about the nature and scope of the predicted gathering. At one end of the spectrum are those who argue that Old Testament preexilic references to the gathering are not prophecies at all but rather reformulations of history by national and religious loyalists seeking to shore up Israel's status as a nation. On Isaiah's prophecy of the Babylonian exile (which occurred more than a century after Isaiah's death), J. R. Dummelow commented:

"However far an O[ld] T[estament] prophet may project his vision into the future, the standpoint from which he does so is always that of his own time, and his words are for the warning or encouragement of those of his own age. But on the supposition that Isaiah is the author of these [scattering and gathering prophecies], not only does he project his vision into the future, but first projects himself to a standpoint in the future, and though living while the kingdom of Judah was still in existence and Jerusalem outwardly flourishing, addresses himself to the encouragement of the Jews of a future age, when they should be in exile, and their city and Temple a heap of ruins. But this would be a case without parallel in O[ld] T[estament] prophecy, and it is therefore much more likely that these [gathering prophecies] are the work of one who actually lived towards the close of the exile."[4]

Unfortunately, this view reduces prophecy to interpretation, and prophets to mere historical commentators. The Book of Mormon, however, stands as a powerful witness of a prophet's unique role. Ammon explained to King Limhi that "a seer is a revelator and a prophet also; and a gift which is greater can no man have, except he should possess the power of God, which no man can; yet a man may have great power given him from God.

"But a seer can know of things which are past, and also of things which are to come. . . .

" . . . therefore he becometh a great benefit to his fellow beings" (Mosiah 8:16–18).

Not only does the Book of Mormon stand as a second witness that Jesus is the Christ, it stands as a witness that Isaiah (and others) were the authors of the prophecies attributed to them. Moreover, the Book of Mormon affirms that prophets may indeed project themselves into the future and speak to the hope and comfort of future generations. Moroni declared: "I speak unto you as if ye were present, and yet ye are not. But behold, Jesus Christ hath shown you unto me, and I know your doing" (Mormon 8:35). The Book of Mormon authenticates Old Testament gathering prophecies, "proving to the world that the holy scriptures are true, and that God does inspire men and call them to his holy work in this age and generation, as well as in generations of old" (D&C 20:11).

Those who accept the authenticity of the gathering prophecies often debate over their fulfillment and theological significance. Although some rabbis argue that the ten tribes of Israel would never return,[5] the prevailing view among Jews is that the ten tribes would be gathered to their homeland.[6] So significant to the Jews is the concept of the "ingathering," that the rabbis rival its importance with the creation of heaven and earth.[7] While it is generally conceded by modern theologians that Israel's remnant would be gathered, there is disagreement about how the gathering would be accomplished.

Arthur W. Kac argues that the "restoration of which the Bible speaks is the reconstitution of a fully independent sovereign State."[8] Likewise, Mendell Lewittes sees the creation of the modern state of Israel in 1948 as a "sure sign of Israel's redemption."[9] These two views express a basic concept of religious Zionism, which attributes the mass immigration to the state of Israel of Jews from the Diaspora to fulfillment of God's gathering prophecies. Many Orthodox Jews reject this view, claiming that Israel's restoration will only be effected by divine means.[10] This view is also refuted by the Book of Mormon, as we shall see.

Christian-Hebraist J. F. Walvoord argues that the creation of the state of Israel was a "first stage" of the gathering, but ultimate fulfillment of the gathering would not be realized until "Israel's Messiah returns to the earth in power and glory to reign."[11] Other theologians find fulfillment of the prophesied gathering in Israel's return from

Babylon to Palestine under Zerubbabel in 536 B.C.[12] Old Testament scholar J. Barton Payne offers a millennial interpretation of the gathering, arguing that the prophecies would be fulfilled by the "regathering of converted Jews, after Christ has set up His future kingdom."[13] Other Christian interpretations hold that the gathering prophecies were fulfilled in the meridian of time, when Christ revealed himself to Israel.[14] What is arguably the most pervasive Christian interpretation is the view that the gathering is purely a spiritual event, as converted Christians gather to Christ.[15]

With so much interpretive disparity, it is not surprising that some commentators either choose to ignore or eviscerate theological significance from the gathering.[16] Elder Russell M. Nelson, commenting on the significance of the gathering, decried the current state of ignorance. He observed: "This big picture [of the gathering] is obscure to the eye of many who focus upon bargains at supermarkets and rankings of favorite football teams."[17] The Book of Mormon not only focuses on the "big picture" of the gathering, it plays a vital role in accomplishing the gathering.

THE ROLE OF THE BOOK OF MORMON IN THE GATHERING PROCESS

The Book of Mormon is the key that unlocks the door of the gathering of Israel in the last days. Elder Bruce R. McConkie wrote: "The Book of Mormon will be the means of gathering in the remnants of scattered Israel."[18] Elsewhere he recorded: "As far as the gathering of Israel is concerned, the Book of Mormon is the most important book that ever has been or ever will be written. It is the book that gathers Israel." He continued: "If there were no Book of Mormon . . . the gathering of the Lord's people in the last days would come to a standstill."[19]

Evoking the ancient practice of the tribes of Israel rallying around their tribal banner, Isaiah symbolically described a latter-day gathering around what he variously termed an "ensign," "standard," or "banner" (see Isaiah 5:26; 11:10–12; 13:2; 18:3; 49:22). Isaiah envisioned this standard (or flag) being lifted high in the air so it would be visible to all nations. The lifting of the banner would be accompanied by an audible "hiss" (or whistle),[20] and the clarion call of a trumpet (see Isaiah 5:26; 18:3). The prophet Nephi identified Isaiah's ensign. He declared it to be "the words of [his] seed; . . . [which]

words shall hiss forth unto the ends of the earth, for a standard unto my people which are the house of Israel" (2 Nephi 29:2).[21] The resurrected Lord explained to the Nephites that the coming forth of the Book of Mormon was indeed a sign that his latter-day work of gathering had commenced (see 3 Nephi 21:1–2). The Book of Mormon is a visible sign to all nations of the Lord's great latter-day restoration. It is accompanied by a voice, which speaks from the dust and has a familiar spirit (see 2 Nephi 26:16). When the Book of Mormon is read with real intent, the clarion call of the Holy Ghost sounds in the heart of each reader, signaling the call to gather to Zion and unite with Christ and his church. The message of the Book of Mormon, coupled with the testifying voice of the Holy Ghost, functions as the rallying point around which Israel gathers. Readers of the Book of Mormon are invited to come unto Christ, embrace the true points of his gospel, and unite with his authorized Church. The Book of Mormon literally gathers Israel to Christ, and Christ gathers Israel to covenants and covenant lands.

BOOK OF MORMON CONTRIBUTIONS TO THE DOCTRINE OF THE GATHERING

When Nephi declared that the writings of his people would restore many plain and precious truths, he undoubtedly had in mind precious truths relative to the gathering of Israel. The title page of the Book of Mormon affirms as much. In it, the prophet Mormon wrote that one of the purposes of the Nephite record was "to show unto the remnant of the House of Israel what great things the Lord hath done for their fathers; and that they may know the covenants of the Lord" (Book of Mormon title page).[22] In the pages of his abridged record, Mormon "shows" us the Lord's gathering covenant. The Book of Mormon enhances our view of the gathering by providing us with an important scriptural definition.

Nephi explained that "after the house of Israel should be scattered they should be gathered together again; or, in fine, after the Gentiles had received the fulness of the Gospel, the natural branches of the olive-tree, or the remnants of the house of Israel, should be grafted in, or come to the knowledge of the true Messiah, their Lord and their Redeemer" (1 Nephi 10:14). Elsewhere Nephi recorded that the remnant of his seed would be grafted in when they "come to the knowledge of their forefathers, and also to the knowledge of the gospel of their Redeemer, which was ministered unto their fathers by him; wherefore, they shall come to the knowledge of their Redeemer and the very points of his doctrine, that they may know how to come unto him and be saved" (1 Nephi 15:14).

Jacob also spoke of the Lord's covenant to gather Israel. He taught that the Jews would be gathered when they were "restored to the true church and fold of God" (2 Nephi 9:2). Thus, the Book of Mormon defines the gathering as primarily a spiritual event, and secondarily a temporal one. Moreover, the Book of Mormon makes it clear that the spiritual gathering requires far more than simply uniting with the great ecumenical church of modern Christendom. Israel's gathering is accomplished when members of the house of Israel gain an awareness of the Lord's ancient covenants, come to a knowledge of the gospel of their Redeemer, embrace the true points of his doctrine, and unite with the Lord's true church.

While the emphasis in the Book of Mormon is on a spiritual gathering to Christ and his church, the promises of a literal gathering "are as real as the dirt and dust upon which [Abraham] set his feet of flesh and blood."[23] The Book of Mormon both affirms and enhances our understanding of Israel's physical gathering to lands of inheritance. It does so by identifying two primary gathering places: one in Jerusalem and one in the Western Hemisphere. The writings of Ether in the Book of Mormon record that the Jews will be restored to their lands of inheritance in Palestine and that Jerusalem shall be "built up again, a holy city unto the Lord" (Ether 13:5). The Book of Mormon also teaches that a "New Jerusalem should be built up upon this land, unto the remnant of the seed of Joseph" (Ether 13:6).[24]

Similarly, while instructing the Nephites in the Americas, the Savior said he would establish a remnant of Jacob "in this land," and that "it shall be a New Jerusalem" (3 Nephi 20:22; see also 21:1–7). From the Book of Mormon, we learn that the physical gathering to specified lands of inheritance is an important part of the Lord's covenant with members of the house of Israel. The Book of Mormon represents only a portion, however, of the Lord's revealed word on the subject of the physical gathering. Latter-day prophets have taught that the physical gathering in the last days is to consist of individuals gathering to "multiple Zions" throughout the world.[25]

While affirming that the physical gathering to covenant lands is a concomitant of the spiritual gathering to Christ and his church, the Book of Mormon specifies the proper sequence.[26] Referring to the Jews, the Savior taught:

"And it shall come to pass that the time cometh, when the fulness of my gospel shall be preached unto them;

"And they shall believe in me, that I am Jesus Christ, the Son of God, and shall pray unto the Father in my name. . . .

"Then will the Father gather them together again, and give unto them Jerusalem for the land of their inheritance" (3 Nephi 20:30–31, 33).

Jacob also taught that "after they [those from whence we came] are driven to and fro, . . . they shall be scattered, and smitten, and hated; nevertheless, the Lord will be merciful unto them, that when they shall come to the knowledge of their Redeemer, they shall be gathered together again to the lands of their inheritance" (2 Nephi 6:11).[27] The Book of Mormon makes it abundantly clear that the spiritual gathering to Christ and his church is to precede the physical gathering to lands of promise. Moreover, the Book of Mormon declares that much of the work of the gathering is to occur during the Millennium. While instructing the people of Nephi, the resurrected Lord revealed a covenant chronology. First, he declared he would establish his church among the Gentiles and invite them to be numbered among the remnant of Jacob. Then, the Lord would invite the remnant of Jacob and others to participate in the establishment of New Jerusalem. These events would be followed by the "power of heaven [coming] down among them," and the Lord being in their midst. *Then,* instructed the resurrected Lord, "shall the work of the Father commence . . . among all the dispersed of my people, yea, even the tribes which have been lost, which the Father hath led away out of Jerusalem" (3 Nephi 21:25–26; see also vv. 22–24).

Elder McConkie provided additional commentary on this chronology. He wrote: "We do not say that occasional blood descendants of Reuben or Naphtali or others of the other tribal heads shall not return to their Palestinian Zion, or assemble in an American Zion, or find their way into the stakes of Zion of all nations, all before the Second Coming of Christ. Some shall no doubt return to Canaan as true believers and members of the true Church, with the intent and purpose of fulfilling the scriptures and building up the ancient cities of Israel. This may well happen in some small measure, and to it there can be no objection. Great movements have small beginnings, and floods that sweep forth from bursting dams are first forecast when small rivulets trickle from pent-up reservoirs. But we do say that the great day of the return of the Ten Tribes, the day when the assembling hosts shall fulfill the prophetic promises, shall come after our Lord's return."[28]

The sequence of the gathering revealed in the Book of Mormon challenges the view equating fulfillment of the gathering prophecies with the creation of the modern state of Israel. Elder McConkie explained: "The present gathering of the Jews to Palestine is political, not spiritual and it is not the gathering of Israel of which the prophecies speak."[29]

Personal Significance of the Gathering

In an 1835 letter to the elders of the Church in Kirtland, Ohio, Joseph Smith wrote: "[The] subject of the gathering . . . is a principle I esteem to be of the greatest importance to those who are looking for salvation in this generation."[30] Many individuals fail to see the "importance" the Prophet Joseph attached to the doctrine of the gathering. This was illustrated to me in a dramatic way. Several years ago, I was invited to participate on a panel of religionists. The host of the event wanted to expose members of his congregation to the doctrinal beliefs of other faiths. Each panelist was allotted ten minutes to make a formal presentation. I drew my remarks from our Articles of Faith. At the conclusion of the presentations, the audience asked panel members questions, inviting us to clarify our doctrinal positions. As might be expected, LDS doctrine generated a considerable amount of interest. The tenth article of faith, expressing our belief in "the literal gathering of Israel and in the restoration of the Ten Tribes" generated the most questions. Recognizing that this doctrine was primarily biblical, I invited my fellow panelists to share their perspectives. The debate and confusion that followed caused me to reflect upon the doctrine of the gathering. I wondered how a doctrine so significant, and so thoroughly established in the biblical record, could also be so misunderstood. What I realized at that time, and have come to appreciate more fully since, is that the Book of

Mormon removes the doctrine of the gathering from the historic and academic arena and lodges it squarely in a personal one. In no other volume of scripture do we see as clearly the personal, individual relevance of the gathering of Israel.

Nephi recorded early in his record that it was his intent to show his readers "the tender mercies of the Lord [that] are over all those whom he hath chosen, because of their faith, to make them mighty even unto the power of deliverance" (1 Nephi 1:20). We see the tender mercies of the Lord in Zenos' allegory of the tame and wild olive trees (see Jacob 5). In this parable, which dramatizes the Lord's intimate involvement in the scattering and gathering of the house of Israel, Zenos paints a portrait of a loving, caring, watchful, and diligent Lord. The Lord's every move relative to the scattering and gathering of Israel is motivated by love and concern. We are informed that the Lord grieves at the prospect of losing even one of his children (see Jacob 5:13). Zenos' allegory reveals a Lord who is diligently at work nourishing his vineyard. When the vineyard becomes corrupted, the Lord weeps, asking "What could I have done more?" (Jacob 5:47).

The Book of Mormon reveals the powerful motivating forces behind the Lord's work of scattering and gathering. Nephi declared that the Lord "doeth not anything save it be for the benefit of the world; for he loveth the world" (2 Nephi 26:24). Without the added light of the Book of Mormon, readers of the biblical record might conclude that the scattering was conducted primarily as punishment for sin, or that it was the natural result of failing to follow the Lord's prophets. The Book of Mormon, however, reveals a unique view of the Lord's protective and redemptive purposes in the scattering and gathering of Israel. Lehi, a righteous member of the house of Israel, declared that his people would be led "into the land of promise, unto the fulfilling of the word of the Lord, that we should be scattered upon all the face of the earth" (1 Nephi 10:13). Later, Nephi recorded that the Lord "leadeth away the righteous into precious lands" (1 Nephi 17:38). From these verses, we learn that the purposes of the scattering are much broader than the biblical record suggests. When the Lord led the Nephites to lands of promise, he was fulfilling scattering prophecies. How many other righteous branches of the house of Israel may have been led away by the Lord to fulfill his protective, covenantal purposes we can only guess. What is certain is that the scattering was an act of love. Although the scattering of Israel and Judah was precipitated by national apostasy, it was conducted by a loving Father who knows exactly what is necessary for the redemption of each individual and individual nation. The scattering of Israel was part of the Lord's great plan of redemption.

The Book of Mormon provides additional evidence of the Lord's redemptive purposes in the scattering and gathering of Israel. Nephi indicated that he included in his record the words of Isaiah to "more fully persuade [his people] to believe in the Lord their Redeemer" (1 Nephi 19:23). Some wonder at Nephi's selection of Isaiah passages. If his intent was to persuade his people to believe in Christ, why did he include the passages he did and ignore others? Eleven of the thirteen Isaiah chapters quoted by Nephi teach the doctrine of the scattering and gathering of Israel. It is not unreasonable to conclude that Nephi viewed the promises of the Lord to gather Israel as prima facie evidence of the Lord's redemptive love for Israel. By including Isaiah's prophecies in his record, Nephi takes the diffuse Old Testament doctrine of the gathering and inextricably links it to the mission and atonement of Jesus Christ.

The Book of Mormon reveals the Lord's redemptive purposes behind the gathering in yet another way. The Savior explained to the Nephites:

"I shall speak unto the Jews and they shall write it; and I shall also speak unto the Nephites and they shall write it; and I shall also speak unto the other tribes of the house of Israel, which I have led away, and they shall write it; and I shall also speak unto all nations of the earth and they shall write it.

"And it shall come to pass that the Jews shall have the words of the Nephites, and the Nephites shall have the words of the Jews; and the Nephites and the Jews shall have the words of the lost tribes of Israel; and the lost tribes of Israel shall have the words of the Nephites and the Jews" (2 Nephi 29:12–13).

Six hundred years after the Lord uttered these words, he told the Nephites that he had other sheep, "not of this land, neither of the land of Jerusalem, neither in any parts of the land round about whither I have been to minister. . . .

"But I have received a commandment of the Father that I shall go unto them, and that they shall hear my voice, and shall be numbered among my sheep, that there may be one fold and one shepherd" (3 Nephi 16:1, 3). The Savior's love and concern for his lost sheep is evidenced by his commitment to visit them in their lost and fallen state. While we know little of these visits, we may suppose that his work among his lost sheep of Israel paralleled his postmortal ministry among the Nephites. We may also suppose that his ministry among the lost tribes of Israel had tremendous redemptive value for those he visited. What we may overlook, however, is how redemptive the Savior's visits to the lost tribes of Israel will be to Latter-day Saints already safely gathered in Zion.

When the lost tribes return, they will bring additional convincing and testifying records with them.[31] Who can estimate the spiritual impact of additional witnessing records of the Lord's great plan of redemption? Individuals will have not two, but multiple records bearing witness of the Lord's love for his people, and the infinite Atonement he worked on their behalf. Saints will thrill as they read these records, which, like the Bible and the Book of Mormon, testify of the Lord's infinite love for all mankind. Like a powerful testimony meeting, where witness after witness is borne, and faith, testimony, and resolve are strengthened, so will be the spiritual impact of multiple records brought together.

What motivates the Lord to work so diligently to recover lost Israel? At least nine times in the pages of the Book of Mormon, the Lord forcefully declares "I will remember my covenant which I have made unto my people, O house of Israel" (3 Nephi 16:11; see also 1 Nephi 19:15; 2 Nephi 29:1–2; 3 Nephi 16:12; 20:29; 29:3; Mormon 5:20; 8:23; 9:37). While the world speculates and debates over the doctrine of the gathering, careful readers of the Book of Mormon may come to a clear and convincing understanding of this fundamental truth: The Lord's covenants are precious to him, and they will be fulfilled. He makes and keeps covenants with Israel because he loves Israel. In the end, the Book of Mormon unfurls a view of the gathering ripe with personal significance. A loving Father and a Redeeming Son tenaciously cleave unto their covenants. What remains unanswered is whether we will cleave unto ours.

Notes

1. The scattering of Israel occurred in three primary phases. First, the Assyrians conquered the Northern Kingdom of Israel in 722 B.C., carrying members of the ten tribes into the north countries. In 587 B.C., the kingdom of Judah fell to Babylonian conquerors, resulting in the deportation of large portions of the Judean population. Finally, in A.D. 66–70, the Judean state and the Jerusalem temple were destroyed by Romans.

2. See Stephen D. Ricks, "A Watchman to the House of Israel," in Kent P. Jackson, ed., *Studies in Scripture: Volume Four, 1 Kings to Malachi* (Salt Lake City: Deseret Book, 1989), 267. Ricks identifies scattering and gathering prophecies in the books of Amos, Hosea, Micah, Isaiah, Zephaniah, Jeremiah, Obadiah, Ezekiel, Zechariah, and Joel.

3. Latter-day Saints find fulfillment of this prophecy in the joining together of the Bible and the Book of Mormon. This is an appropriate interpretation. The prophecy was given, however, in the context of reuniting the nations of Israel and Judah (see Ezekiel 37).

4. J. R. Dummelow, *A Commentary on the Holy Bible* (New York: Macmillan Publishing, 1908), 412.

5. See Rabbi Akiba, in Herbert Danby, trans., *The Mishna* (London: Oxford University Press, 1933), 398; Sanhedrin 10:3.

6. See R. J. Zwi Werblowsky, ed., *The Oxford Dictionary of the Jewish Religion* (New York: Oxford University Press, 1997), 244.

7. Ibid., 244.

8. Arthur W. Kac, *The Rebirth of the State of Israel: Is It of God or of Men?* (Grand Rapids, Mich.: Moody Press, 1958), 39.

9. Mendell Lewittes, *Religious Foundations of the Jewish State* (New York: Ktav Publishing House, 1977), 193–94.

10. See Werblowsky, *Oxford Dictionary of the Jewish Religion,* 704.

11. J. F. Walvoord, cited in Hans K. LaRondelle, *The Israel of God in Prophecy: Principles of Prophetic Interpretation* (Berrin Springs, Mich.: Andrews University Press, 1983), 156.

12. This interpretation is untenable because it fails to account for the gathering prophecies that were extended to include the ten tribes, who never did return. Those who press this interpretation argue that before the Assyrian captivity, substantial numbers from the ten tribes in the Northern Kingdom of Israel had migrated to the Southern Kingdom of Judah (see 2 Chronicles 11:16–17). Thus, when Judah was exiled and then returned from Babylon, representatives from all the tribes were among them.

13. J. Barton Payne, *Encyclopedia of Biblical Prophecy: The Complete Guide to Scriptural Predictions and Their Fulfillment* (Grand Rapids, Mich.: Harper and Row, 1973), 300.

14. See LaRondelle, *Israel of God in Prophecy,* 99.

15. Ibid., 153. This interpretation ignores any allusion to a physical gathering.

16. In preparation for this chapter, I searched the dictionaries, encyclopedias, and canons of faith of dozens of religions. Entries distinguishing the doctrine of the gathering were limited to Jewish and Latter-day Saint commentaries.

17. Russell M. Nelson, "Remnants Gathered, Covenants Fulfilled," in *Voices of Old Testament Prophets: The 26th Annual Sidney B. Sperry Symposium* (Salt Lake City: Deseret Book, 1997), 2.

18. Bruce R. McConkie, *The Mortal Messiah: From Bethlehem to Calvary*, 4 vols. (Salt Lake City: Deseret Book, 1979–81), 4:313.

19. Bruce R. McConkie, *A New Witness for the Articles of Faith* (Salt Lake City: Deseret Book, 1985), 554.

20. The King James Version uses the word *hiss*. The Hebrew word may be translated "whistle"; see also Donald W. Parry, *Understanding Isaiah* (Salt Lake City: Deseret Book, 1998), 59.

21. Elsewhere *ensign* is identified with Zion, the Lord, and his gospel (see D&C 64:42; 45:9).

22. The promise to regather Israel is one of the most pervasive covenants detailed in the Book of Mormon.

23. Joseph F. McConkie, "The Final Gathering to Christ," in Kent P. Jackson, ed., *Studies in Scripture: Volume Eight, Alma 30 to Moroni* (Salt Lake City: Deseret Book, 1988), 193–94.

24. From Latter-day revelation we learn that the New Jerusalem spoken of is to be in Jackson County, Missouri (see D&C 57:1–3).

25. See Spencer W. Kimball, *The Teachings of Spencer W. Kimball*, ed. Edward L. Kimball (Salt Lake City: Bookcraft, 1982), 439–40.

26. For an excellent and thorough discussion of the process of the gathering, see Robert L. Millet and Joseph Fielding McConkie, *Our Destiny: The Calling and Election of the House of Israel* (Salt Lake City: Bookcraft, 1993).

27. See also 2 Nephi 9:2; 25:15–17, which make clear that conversion to Christ precedes gathering to lands of inheritance.

28. Bruce R. McConkie, *The Millennial Messiah: The Second Coming of the Son of Man* (Salt Lake City: Deseret Book, 1982), 323.

29. McConkie, *New Witness for the Articles of Faith*, 564–65.

30. Joseph Smith, *The Teachings of Joseph Smith*, eds. Larry E. Dahl and Donald Q. Cannon (Salt Lake City: Bookcraft, 1997), 278.

31. See Neal A. Maxwell, *Plain and Precious Things* (Salt Lake City: Deseret Book, 1983), 11–12.

CHAPTER NINE

THY WALLS ARE CONTINUALLY BEFORE ME: THE INDISPENSABLE ROLE OF ZION IN THE PLAN OF SALVATION

STEVE FOTHERINGHAM

If Nephi stood before a class, with marker in hand, would he depict the plan of salvation as we traditionally do? Would he draw circles for kingdoms and lines for veils? The vision of section 76 shines so brightly that the goal and conditions for salvation are often considered the plan. The Book of Mormon focuses on the plan. Its prophets constantly prophesied of the formation of the New Jerusalem, the gathering of Israel, the Second Coming, and the Millennium. These are indispensable features of the plan of redemption. They tell us how God intends to help us return to him. Surprisingly, these elements are often omitted in our traditional models. Nephi would not omit such crucial events in an overview of the plan and neither should we.

AN APOSTOLIC CHALLENGE

In a 1993 address, Elder Boyd K. Packer assigned seminary and institute teachers to "prepare a brief synopsis or overview of the plan of happiness—the plan of salvation." He said this would provide "a

---

Steve Fotheringham is an instructor at the Las Vegas Institute of Religion.

framework on which your students can organize the truths you will share with them." He continued:

"At first you may think that a simple assignment. I assure you, it is not. Brevity and simplicity are remarkably difficult to achieve. At first you will be tempted to include too much. The plan in its fulness encompasses every gospel truth. . . .

"I will give you the barest outline of the plan as a beginning, but you must assemble your framework yourself.

"The essential components of the *great plan of happiness, of redemption, of salvation,* are these:

"Premortal existence

"Spiritual creation

"Agency

"War in heaven

"Physical creation

"The Fall and mortality

"Principles and ordinances of the gospel of Jesus Christ (first principles: faith in the Lord Jesus Christ, repentance, baptism, . . .)

"The Atonement

"Life beyond the grave

"Spirit world

"Judgment

"Resurrection"[1]

It is not hard to imagine that many teachers, on hearing this assignment, thought something like, "Oh, I have that plan already on a transparency in my file drawer under *P.*" Yet when Elder Packer said, "This may be the most difficult, and surely the most rewarding, assignment of your teaching career,"[2] no doubt he had something more profound than an old transparency in mind. If an overview of the plan was what he requested, it would take the effort he predicted. If the model is to be worthy of repetition and continual use in the classroom, and if it is to be a framework for organizing truths, it will need to be something different from what has been generally used in the past.

Although the prophets repeatedly wrote of the latter-day Zion, the gathering of Israel, the Second Coming, and the Millennium, it is fascinating that these concepts are seldom found in our depictions of the plan. In many ways, these doctrines *are* the plan. They are how several of the elements enumerated by Elder Packer will be employed for our salvation. Incorporate the establishment and destiny of Zion into a model and it will make all the difference. There will hardly be a verse in scripture that will not have a home on such a framework.

THE PLAN

A plan must show how. That is what a plan is! Whether we want to bake a cake or build a house, it is the how that makes it a plan. The question needs to be asked, "How does God intend to save his children?" Before the how of salvation can be discussed, however, the why needs to be established. Knowing why is crucial to understanding how. Elder Packer addressed this point in his discussion on portraying the plan:

"Young people wonder 'why?'—Why are we commanded *to do* some things, and why are we commanded *not* to do other things? A knowledge of the plan of happiness, even in outline form, can give young minds a 'why.' . . .

"Providing your students with a collection of unrelated truths will hurt as much as it helps. Provide a basic feeling for the whole plan, even with just a few details, and it will help them ever so much more. Let them know what it's all about, then they will have the 'why.'"[3]

The ultimate answer to why is found in the promises made to the fathers, which are to be with God and to be like God. Abraham was promised that he would be like God in that his seed would "continue; both in the world and out of the world should they continue" (D&C 132:30). Abraham was also promised land on this earth for an eternal inheritance (see 3 Nephi 20:29; Abraham 2; D&C 88:17–20). This will allow him to enjoy the presence of God because the earth will become a celestial orb. The terms *land* and *seed* are used repeatedly throughout the scriptures. They describe the promises that were made to the fathers and to all those who enter into the covenant. The promised blessings are the reason for our existence. Therefore, they do much to answer the question why.

When we realize that our destiny is to inherit this earth with resurrected celestial bodies that can have a continuation of seed, the question of how becomes easier to approach. How does the Lord intend to renovate this earth and give it to his people? The answer centers on a city. The city is called Zion.

The idea of Zion predates mortality and is centered on the Atonement, but it begins to take shape in the Restoration. It is in the latter-days when "the work of the Father shall commence, in preparing the way for the fulfilling of his covenants, which he hath made to his people who are of the house of Israel" (1 Nephi 14:17). Zion has much to do with "the way" the covenants will be fulfilled. It is a city we will make and inherit on this earth. The Savior taught the Nephites that Zion would be built by "the remnant of Jacob" (3 Nephi 21:23). Brigham Young put it this way:

"Where is Zion? Where the organization of the Church of God is. And may it dwell spiritually in every heart; and may we so live as to enjoy the spirit of Zion always!

"Do we realize that if we enjoy a Zion in time or in eternity we must make it for ourselves? That all, who have a Zion in the eternities of the Gods, organized, framed, consolidated, and perfected it themselves, and consequently are entitled to enjoy it?

"This is the Gospel; this is the plan of salvation; this is the Kingdom of God; this is the Zion that has been spoken and written of by all the Prophets since the world began. This is the work of Zion which the Lord has promised to bring forth."[4]

A Proposed Model

If a teacher can illustrate the following, it will do much to help students visualize the Lord's plan to save his children. Begin by drawing the earth with a few continents. Dot the continents to represent the scattering of Israel. Draw a cross in the Middle East to represent the Atonement. Depict a wall on part of the American continent representing Zion. Within the wall draw a temple. Outside the wall, portray two elders carrying a Book of Mormon, representing the gathering of Israel.

Above the earth draw a figure representing the Savior's second coming. Next to him draw a circle representing the millennial earth. Draw a final circle with a couple in it representing our ultimate destination, the celestial earth.

This diagram does not portray the entire plan, but it does display much of the "how" of the plan. It contains only nine items, and yet a surprising number of scriptural truths can be organized on this framework.

THE SCATTERING OF ISRAEL

Salting the earth with the seed of Abraham is part of the Lord's plan to bless the world in the latter days. President Joseph Fielding Smith explained: "Moreover we have learned that the Lord said that he would scatter Israel among the Gentile nations, and by doing so he would bless the Gentile nations with the blood of Abraham."[5] Abraham was promised that through his seed "shall all the kindreds of the earth be blessed" (1 Nephi 15:18). The scattering is connected with the fulfillment of that promise.

THE ATONEMENT

The Atonement must be portrayed in any discussion of the plan. It is the heart of the plan. Without the Atonement, there is no salvation, nor the possibility of obtaining the promises of the covenant. Christ's sacrifice is also central to Zion. It makes Zion possible. To have a community that is of one heart and who are pure in heart requires the Atonement. Referring to the portion of Zion that will be in Jerusalem, the Savior explained: "And they shall believe in me, that I am Jesus Christ, the Son of God, and shall pray unto the Father in my name" (3 Nephi 20:31). As a result, those in Zion would be of one heart, for it was prophesied that "With the voice together shall they sing; for they shall see eye to eye" (3 Nephi 20:32). Zion would eventually be asked to "put on thy beautiful garments, O Jerusalem, the holy city, for henceforth there shall no more come unto thee the uncircumcised and the unclean" (3 Nephi 20:36). None of this could be done without the Atonement.

Christ is the stone upon which Zion will be built. Peter wrote, "Wherefore also it is contained in the scripture, Behold, I lay in Sion a chief corner stone, elect, precious: and he that believeth on him shall not be confounded" (1 Peter 2:6).

THE TEMPLE

The temple is the center of Zion. It is a major component of the plan of salvation. Christ foretold that the watchmen of Zion would sing: "The Father hath made bare his holy arm in the eyes of all the nations; and all the ends of the earth shall see the salvation of the Father. . . .

"And then shall be brought to pass that which is written: Awake, awake again, and put on thy strength, O Zion" (3 Nephi 20:35–36). Zion derives her strength from the Lord's arm being revealed. Nephi taught that the Father will make bare his arm by "bringing about his covenants and his gospel unto those who are of the house of Israel" (1 Nephi 22:11).

The temple aids us in becoming one with each other and God. The following is a simplistic illustration of how the temple can assist in establishing Zion. In the Lord's house we take upon us his name. One of his names is "The Prince of Peace" (Isaiah 9:6). Therefore, we covenant to be a people of peace—we covenant to be kind. The Lord spoke of the everlasting covenant as a "covenant of peace" (Ezekiel 37:26; see also 3 Nephi 22:10). As we keep that covenant, we form a peaceful community. The word *Jerusalem* is, by definition, the "city of peace." Zion is the New Jerusalem, and the temple is central to its formation.

The depiction of a temple in the drawing also implies the Restoration. There would obviously be no temple without a restoration. Hence, Joseph Smith is integral to the plan of salvation and the foundation of Zion (see 2 Nephi 3:15).

Zion

The wall in the model represents Zion. A wall implies a community that is different and set apart from the world. Eventually, "all they who fight against Zion shall be cut off" (1 Nephi 22:19; see also 3 Nephi 20:22–23).

The wall also represents refuge. Ether taught that the New Jerusalem would come down out of heaven and be "the holy sanctuary of the Lord" (Ether 13:3).

The wall implies location. The Savior prophesied: "And behold, this people will I establish in this land, unto the fulfilling of the covenant which I made with your father Jacob; and it shall be a New Jerusalem" (3 Nephi 20:22; see also Ether 13:6).

The amazing thing about this wall is that it can expand. Moroni, quoting Isaiah, finished his record exhorting Zion to "strengthen thy stakes and enlarge thy borders forever" (Moroni 10:31). Zion will be enlarged until it fills the entire earth.

THE GATHERING OF ISRAEL

Israel is gathered to the covenant (see 3 Nephi 5:23–26), to Zion (see 3 Nephi 21:1), to lands of inheritance (see 2 Nephi 9:2), and to the Savior (see 3 Nephi 20:29–31). The gathering is crucial to the plan. The ultimate fulfillment of the gathering is in obtaining a resurrected body in a land of inheritance. Jacob apparently connects the gathering with the Resurrection in the following: "But behold, thus saith the Lord God: When the day cometh that they shall believe in me, that I am Christ, then have I covenanted with their fathers that they shall be restored in the flesh, upon the earth, unto the lands of their inheritance" (2 Nephi 10:7). Similarly, the Lord prophesied to Ezekiel: "Thus saith the Lord God; Behold, O my people, I will open your graves, and cause you to come up out of your graves, and bring you into the land of Israel" (Ezekiel 37:12). The gathering is the process by which the covenant is entered into and eventually fulfilled.

THE BOOK OF MORMON

The Book of Mormon is the tool for gathering. It must be depicted because it is indispensable to the plan. The Lord prophesied that when he shall set his hand the second time to recover his people, which are of the house of Israel, the words of Nephi and his seed would proceed forth out of his mouth for a standard unto his people (see 2 Nephi 29:1–2). He also foretold that the coming forth of the Book of Mormon was the sign "that the work of the Father hath already commenced unto the fulfilling of the covenant which he hath made unto the people who are of the house of Israel" (3 Nephi 21:7).

THE SECOND COMING OF CHRIST

The Second Coming is the day when Christ will come to fulfill the promises of the covenant. In 3 Nephi the Savior quotes Isaiah's prophecy about the servant who shall be exalted and extolled very high, in whom many were astonished because his "visage was so marred" (3 Nephi 20:43–44). Elder Bruce R. McConkie saw in these words "a triumphant millennial Christ."[6]

After Jesus finished quoting Isaiah, he said, "Verily, verily, I say unto you, all these things shall surely come, even as the Father hath commanded me. Then shall this covenant which the Father hath covenanted with his people be fulfilled; and then shall Jerusalem be inhabited again with my people, and it shall be the land of their inheritance" (3 Nephi 20:46).

On this, Elder McConkie explained: "Then shall the children of the covenant inherit, receive, and possess—equally and fully—with their fathers of old! Then shall the Lamanites flourish in the Americas; then shall the Jews prosper in Jerusalem; then shall Ephraim—the Lord's firstborn!—confer on all the tribes their eternal blessings; and then shall all the promises relative to Israel and Zion be fulfilled."[7]

THE MILLENNIUM

The Millennium is the time when the author of our faith will finish our redemption. The Savior will dwell in righteousness with men on earth a thousand years (see 1 Nephi 22:24–26; 3 Nephi 20:22; D&C 29:11). The Zion of Enoch will come and join the Zion on earth (see Ether 13:3–11). In that day, Zion's borders will be enlarged in a wonderful way. Of that day, Nephi prophesied "that the righteous must be led up as calves of the stall, and the Holy One of Israel must reign in dominion, and might, and power, and great glory.

"And he gathereth his children from the four quarters of the earth; and he numbereth his sheep, and they know him; and there shall be one fold and one shepherd; and he shall feed his sheep, and in him they shall find pasture" (1 Nephi 22:24–25). As the sheep come to know the shepherd and are fed by him, they will be prepared to inherit the celestial world (see D&C 76:106–7).

THE CELESTIAL EARTH

The last realm in the suggested model represents the celestial earth. From the title page to the final phrase, obtaining the presence of God through the covenant is a continual theme throughout the Book of Mormon. In the oft-repeated phrase "Inasmuch as ye shall keep the commandments of God ye shall prosper in the land; and inasmuch as ye will not keep the commandments of God ye shall be cut off from his presence" (Alma 38:1), the words *land* and *presence* bear corresponding meanings.

At the end of his life, after recapping some of the trials of their journey, Lehi tells his children it was worth it because "the Lord hath covenanted this land unto me, and to my children forever" (2 Nephi 1:5). The Saints in the last days were promised the same through Joseph Smith: "And this shall be my covenant with you, ye shall have it for the land of your inheritance, and for the inheritance of your children forever, while the earth shall stand, and ye shall possess it again in eternity, no more to pass away" (D&C 38:20).

Zion, a Prophetic View

When Jarom concluded the small plates, he asked, "For have not they revealed the plan of salvation? I say unto you, Yea; and this sufficeth me" (Jarom 1:2). Nephi included in his record three witnesses who had seen the Savior and the plan—Jacob, Isaiah, and himself. They prophesied of Zion continually.

As part of the vision of the tree of life, "Nephi sees in vision . . . the restoration of the gospel, the coming forth of latter-day scripture, and the building up of Zion" (1 Nephi 13 chapter heading). In the last chapter of his first book, Nephi enumerates these latter-day events in wonderful detail. He repeatedly informs us that "all these things must come according to the flesh" (1 Nephi 22:27; see also vv. 2, 18). The promises can be obtained in no other way. For instance, Israel was, in reality, scattered throughout the world. The Savior suffered "according to the flesh" (Alma 7:13), and will come again as a resurrected being. The covenant was restored to men in the flesh (see 2 Nephi 10:15). Zion will be established in the last days on the earth (see 3 Nephi 20:16–22). Israel will be literally gathered "in time and in eternity" (D&C 39:22; see also 3 Nephi 21:24). And the righteous will inherit the land in the Resurrection (see 2 Nephi 10:7; Ezekiel 37).

Jesus clearly reinforced that the promises would be fulfilled in the flesh:

"A city reserved until a day of righteousness shall come—a day which was sought for by all holy men, and they found it not because of wickedness and abominations;

"And confessed they were strangers and pilgrims on the earth;

"But obtained a promise that they should find it and see it in their flesh. . . .

"And I will show it plainly as I showed it unto my disciples as I stood before them in the flesh, and spake unto them saying; As ye have asked of me concerning the signs of my coming, in the day when I shall come in my glory in the clouds of heaven, to fulfil the promises that I have made unto your fathers,

"For as ye have looked upon the long absence of your spirits from your bodies to be a bondage, I will show unto you how the day of redemption shall come, and also the restoration of the scattered Israel" (D&C 45:12–14, 16–17).

The day of redemption and the restoration of scattered Israel go together. Thus, Nephi couched these latter-day events in the context of the Resurrection.

Jacob taught the same thing—in the same way as his brother. Like Nephi, he also quoted Isaiah, who wrote about the latter-day gathering and Zion. Then in the context of covenants, gathering, and lands of inheritance, he taught: "For I know that ye have searched much, many of you, to know of things to come; wherefore I know that ye know that our flesh must waste away and die; nevertheless, in our bodies we shall see God" (2 Nephi 9:4). This is followed by a powerful explanation of the Resurrection: "All these things must come according to the flesh" (1 Nephi 22:27).

Nephi understood that the words he inscribed in gold would be instrumental to the holy city. He realized how foundational Joseph Smith and the restored covenant would be to "the city of the heritage of God" (D&C 58:13). He knew that the gathering would be "in time and in eternity" (D&C 39:22), and that Christ would be the center of it all. It is easy to understand why Nephi wrote of little else. A glance at the chapter headings of 1 and 2 Nephi leave no doubt as to his emphasis.

If Nephi stood before a class, he would invariably talk of Christ. He would surely enumerate the goal and requirements of salvation. If, however, he entered into the idea of the plan, if the question of "how" was brought up, he would discuss the promises, the Atonement, the gathering, the establishment of Zion, the Second

Coming, and the Millennium. The Book of Mormon authors did not vary significantly from these latter-day themes.

Mormon had the same wonderful assignment as Nephi. He was to compile a record about the plan that would play a major role in the plan. He did so "according to the manifestations of the Spirit which had testified of things to come" (Mormon 3:16). Therefore, he did much to portray events that reflected the Lord's latter-day work of salvation. Knowing how crucial the gathering would be to the plan, Mormon used considerable space to describe the missionary efforts of Alma and the sons of Mosiah. The establishment of a covenant people, before the coming of Christ, was also a major theme in his abridgment efforts. The central role of the Atonement was woven throughout his record. Christ's coming to the Nephites, followed by a Zion-like community and a millennium-like period of peace can clearly be seen as types.

Mormon's account of the Savior's ministry to the Nephites, established beyond controversy, the reality of the Atonement. In 3 Nephi, the recorded prophecies of Jesus center almost entirely on the details of how the Father plans to save Israel in the latter-days (see 3 Nephi 16, 20–22, 24–25). The Savior foretold that his people would be "gathered in, who are scattered upon all the face of the land, in unto the New Jerusalem.

"And then shall the power of heaven come down among them; and I also will be in the midst" (3 Nephi 21:24–25). He taught that this gathering to the New Jerusalem, with him in their midst, is how the Father will prepare "the way whereby his people may be gathered home to the land of their inheritance" (3 Nephi 21:28).

Being gathered home to a land of inheritance takes on significance when it is remembered that the land will become a new earth. Like the Savior, and the prophets before him, Moroni also taught that the establishment of Zion was part of the process for obtaining such an inheritance. In his synopsis of the writings of Ether, Moroni prophesied:

"A New Jerusalem should be built up upon this land, unto the remnant of the seed of Joseph, for which things there has been a type.

"For as Joseph brought his father down into the land of Egypt, even so he died there; wherefore, the Lord brought a remnant of the seed of Joseph out of the land of Jerusalem, that he might be merciful unto the seed of Joseph that they should perish not, even as he was merciful unto the father of Joseph that he should perish not.

"Wherefore, the remnant of the house of Joseph shall be built upon this land; and it shall be a land of their inheritance; and they shall build up a holy city unto the Lord, like unto the Jerusalem of old; and they shall no more be confounded, until the end come when the earth shall pass away.

"And there shall be a new heaven and a new earth; and they shall be like unto the old save the old have passed away, and all things have become new" (Ether 13:6–9).

When the New Jerusalem is viewed in the context of salvation, it is easy to see how Joseph could be considered a type. Like Joseph's store of food, his posterity stored up God's word for a time of famine. As Joseph saved his brethren anciently, his descendent (Joseph Smith) brought forth the word of God to save Israel. In the latter-days, that nourishing word is being offered to a needy world by a remnant of the seed of Joseph. Anciently, Israel found refuge in a foreign land. In the last days, Israel finds refuge in the holy city built "up upon this land" (Ether 13:6). As Joseph saved his father, Joseph's descendants are saving their fathers in the temples of Zion.

Referring to the seer that would lay the foundation of Zion, the Lord told Joseph anciently, "And he shall be like unto you; for the thing which the Lord shall bring forth by his hand shall bring my people unto salvation" (JST Genesis 50:33).

Throughout the Book of Mormon, this redemptive theme is consistent and repetitive. The Book of Mormon foreshadows, foretells, and facilitates the plan. It is indeed a marvelous instrument for a marvelous work and a wonder.

The proposed model is merely an attempt to depict what the Book of Mormon describes over and over again. But if, using a traditional depiction of the plan, you ask a class, "What is missing?" Zion will, most likely, not be brought up. Zion has not been our traditional emphasis when discussing the plan. And yet it was emphasized by all of the prophets. That is evident both by their choice of topics, and also by the fact that we are clearly told where God focused their attention.

Anciently, Israel felt forsaken and forgotten. In response the Lord said, "Behold, I have graven thee upon the palms of my hands; thy walls are continually before me" (Isaiah 49:16). What are the walls the Lord always has his eyes on? Wilford Woodruff suggests that they are the walls of the latter-day Zion:

"Any man who has ever read the book of Isaiah, which we frequently have quoted to us, can see that he, with other prophets, had his eye upon the latter-day Zion of God. He says in one place, 'Sing O heavens, rejoice O earth, break forth into singing, O ye mountains, for the Lord hath comforted his people, he will have mercy upon his afflicted. But Zion said: The Lord hath forsaken me, and my Lord hath forgotten me,' 'Ah,' says the Lord, 'Can a woman forget her sucking child, that she should not have compassion on the son of her womb? Yea, they may forget, yet will not I forget thee. Behold, I have graven thee upon the palms of my hands; thy walls are continually before me.'"[8]

Individuals who comment on this verse in Isaiah generally focus on the palms being graven as an allusion to the Atonement. But the walls are the reason for the palms being graven. The Atonement makes the walls possible and the Lord's eyes, as well as his hands, are committed to that latter-day objective. Elder Woodruff continues his commentary on the walls of Zion by declaring that all of this has to do with the redemption of the world: "The Lord never created this world at random; he has never done any of his work at random. The earth was created for certain purposes; and one of these purposes was its final redemption, and the establishment of his government and kingdom upon it in the latter days, to prepare it for the reign of the Lord Jesus Christ, whose right it is to reign."[9]

A verse from the Apocrypha, attributed to Baruch (a scribe for Jeremiah) is consistent with Elder Woodruff's interpretation of what walls the Lord has his eyes on. The Lord tells Baruch that the city, for which he carved his hands and on which he fixed his view, was not ancient Jerusalem. Speaking of the temple, and the Jerusalem of Jeremiah's day, the following was recorded:

"And the Lord said to me: this city will be delivered up for a time, and the people will be chastened for a time, and the world will not be forgotten.

"Or do you think that this is the city of which I said: On the palms of my hands I have carved you? It is not this building that is in your midst now; it is that which will be revealed, with me, that was already prepared from the moment that I decided to create Paradise. And I showed it to Adam before he sinned. . . . After these things I showed it to my servant Abraham in the night between the portions of the victims. And again I showed it also to Moses on Mount Sinai when I showed him the likeness of the tabernacle and all its vessels. Behold, now it is preserved with me—as also Paradise."[10]

Many scriptures support this idea that the Lord showed this glorious city to his prophets. The apostle Paul, referring to Abraham, wrote, "For he looked for a city which hath foundations, whose builder and maker is God" (Hebrews 11:10). Peter, James, and John were shown a pattern of how the earth would be transfigured on the mount of transfiguration (see D&C 63:20–21). The Lord himself revealed that this city was "sought for by all holy men" (D&C 45:12–14). Brigham Young said: "I have Zion in my view constantly."[11]

Joseph Smith wrote: "The building up of Zion is a cause that has interested the people of God in every age; it is a theme upon which prophets, priests and kings have dwelt with peculiar delight; they have looked forward with joyful anticipation to the day in which we live; and fired with heavenly and joyful anticipations they have sung and written and prophesied of this our day."[12] Referring to the privilege of laying the foundation of Zion, he continued: " . . . a work that God and angels have contemplated with delight for generations past; that fired the souls of the ancient patriarchs and prophets; a work that is destined to bring about the destruction of the powers of darkness, the renovation of the earth, the glory of God, and the salvation of the human family."[13]

ZION, A LATTER-DAY VIEW

Late in August 1831, the Lord commented to the members of the Church that they too should be looking toward Zion. The Prophet's introduction of Doctrine and Covenants 63 had Zion in view:

"In these infant days of the Church, there was a great anxiety to obtain the word of the Lord upon every subject that in any way concerned our salvation; and as the land of Zion was now the most important temporal object in view, I inquired of the Lord for further information upon the gathering of the Saints, and the purchase of the land, and other matters."

Although temporal matters are discussed in this section, the Lord will make it clear that there is nothing transitory about Zion. In this revelation on salvation, of which "Zion was now the most important temporal object in view," the Lord will leave no doubt as to where we should be looking.

"Yea, and blessed are the dead that die in the Lord, from henceforth, when the Lord shall come, and old things shall pass away, and all things become new, they shall rise from the dead and shall not die after, and shall receive an inheritance before the Lord, in his holy city. . . .

"Wherefore, for this cause preached the apostles unto the world the resurrection of the dead.

"These things are the things that ye must look for; and, speaking after the manner of the Lord, they are now nigh at hand, and in a time to come, even in the day of the coming of the Son of Man" (D&C 63:49, 52–53).

The apostles taught the Resurrection for the same reason the Book of Mormon authors taught it—to show the fulfillment of the promises. Both the promises and the Resurrection are connected to the coming of the Son of Man. These subjects deal much with the establishment and destiny of Zion and our salvation.

Zion is the "work that God and angels have contemplated with delight for generations past; that fired the souls of the ancient patriarchs and prophets."[14] Zion is the "cause that has interested the people of God in every age; it is a theme upon which prophets, priests and kings have dwelt with peculiar delight."[15] Zion "is the plan of salvation."[16] And now to us, whose fortune it is to be involved in this marvelous work, the Lord commends, "These things are the things that ye must look for" (D&C 63:53). As we look, we realize the promises and the opportunities. We catch a "basic feeling for the whole plan."[17] We begin to see "what it's all about" and we find we have the "why."[18]

Notes

1. Boyd K. Packer, *The Great Plan of Happiness* (address to religious educators at a symposium on the Doctrine and Covenants/Church history, Brigham Young University, 10 Aug. 1993), 2–3.

2. Ibid., 3.

3. Ibid., 3.

4. Brigham Young, *Discourses of Brigham Young,* sel. John A. Widtsoe (Salt Lake City: Deseret Book, 1941), 118.

5. Joseph Fielding Smith, *Answers to Gospel Questions,* 5 vols. (Salt Lake City: Deseret Book, 1960), 3:63.

6. Bruce R. McConkie, *The Mortal Messiah: From Bethlehem to Calvary,* 4 vols. (Salt Lake City: Deseret Book, 1979–81), 4:344.

7. Ibid., 345.

8. Wilford Woodruff, in *Journal of Discourses,* 26 vols. (London: Latter-day Saints' Book Depot, 1854–86), 15:7–8.

9. Ibid., 8.

10. Baruch, in *The Old Testament Pseudepigrapha,* ed. James H. Charlesworth, 2 vols. (New York: Doubleday, 1983), 1:622.

11. Brigham Young, in *Journal of Discourses,* 9:284.

12. Joseph Smith, *History of The Church of Jesus Christ of Latter-day Saints,* ed. B. H. Roberts, 2d ed. rev., 7 vols. (Salt Lake City: Deseret Book, 1973), 4:609–10.

13. Ibid., 4:610.

14. Ibid., 6:610.

15. Ibid., 6:609.

16. Young, *Discourses of Brigham Young,* 118.

17. Packer, *Great Plan of Happiness,* 3.

18. Ibid., 3.

CHAPTER TEN

FOREORDINATION IN THE BOOK OF MORMON

BRIAN M. HAUGLID

With the Restoration inaugurated by the First Vision, many plain and precious truths have been and continue to be revealed from the heavens. Among these important truths is the doctrine of foreordination. It is significant that the restoration of this doctrine began with the translation and publication of the Book of Mormon. In this sacred record are found several implicit references to foreordination. In addition, Alma 13:3–5 explicitly refers to this precious truth that, until the Restoration, had been lost for centuries.

To more fully appreciate the significance of the restoration of foreordination through the Book of Mormon, we must first briefly outline the loss of this plain and precious truth during the early periods of Christian history. Second, we will briefly review the emergence of foreordination in the early part of the Restoration after the translation of the Book of Mormon. Third, a few notable implicit references to foreordination in the Book of Mormon will be discussed. Fourth, Alma 13:3–5 will be examined in light of other prominent biblical references that refer to foreordination to demonstrate the unique contributions of the Book of Mormon. Finally, we will discuss some of the thoughts of General Authorities on foreordination, particularly Elder Neal A. Maxwell's statement that "this doctrine brings unarguable identity but also severe accountability to our lives."[1] It is

---

Brian M. Hauglid is an assistant professor of ancient scripture at Brigham Young University.

hoped that this discussion will enhance our appreciation of the Book of Mormon and its contribution to our understanding of the doctrine of foreordination.

Loss of a Belief in Foreordination in Early Christian History

To underscore the need for a restoration of the doctrine of foreordination and to better see the significant contributions of the Book of Mormon, we must first note that the loss of this doctrine likely occurred in the early stages of the Great Apostasy. If we accept the idea that foreordination is inherently connected to the concept of premortality, we see that when the early Christian church rejected the idea of a premortal life it implicitly rejected a belief in foreordination. This seems to be what occurred in the very early centuries after Christ. According to Stephen E. Robinson, the historical agent (Hellenism) that excised the doctrine of premortality, and many other truths, "would have had its origins in the second half of the first century and would have done much of its work by the middle of the second century."[2]

It appears that with the emergence and imposition of Greek culture and philosophy upon the early Christian community, belief in a premortal life quickly waned and eventually disappeared from general acceptance.[3] The most influential Greek beliefs that seem to have adversely affected the belief in premortality were the idea that God was a spiritual, not a physical, being, and the doctrine of *creation ex nihilo* (creation out of nothing). Eventually, within Judaism, Christianity, and Islam, Neoplatonism became generally accepted, and God emerged an incorporeal being who is both unknowable and mysterious. These major religions argue that one cannot determine what God is, but only what God cannot be. The culmination of this long process of philosophical speculation in early Christianity, at least in the Western Church, emerges in the writings of St. Augustine (A.D. 354–430), who adopted the Neoplatonic concept of God that was accepted by Catholicism and later by Protestantism.

"For Augustine it is impossible for any man to know God, or even any of his attributes, for man is entirely different from his Maker and exists on a completely different plane of reality. The only reliable information about God is negative—what he is not. God is, by philosophical definition, incomprehensible to the mind or senses of man, and it is impious to assert any direct knowledge of him."[4] In the Islamic philosophical tradition, Neoplatonism also made an indelible mark on the nature of God, especially in terms of what God is not. According to the Mu'tazila, a Muslim rationalist group of the ninth century, "God is one; there is no thing like him; he is hearing, seeing; he is not a body . . . , not a form, not flesh and blood, not an individual . . . , not substance nor attribute; he has no colour, taste, smell, feel, no heat, cold, moisture nor dryness, no length, breadth nor depth, no joining together nor separation, no movement, rest nor division; . . . no place comprehends him, no time passes over him; . . . not begetting nor begotten; . . . he is not comparable with men and does not resemble creatures in any respect."[5]

This way of thinking, of course, greatly inhibited man's understanding of his Creator. This thinking not only affected the understanding of the doctrine of foreordination but other important doctrines, such as the concept of the Godhead as three distinct personages and the physical resurrection of mankind. Significantly, when the Book of Mormon was unearthed and translated, it shed much-needed light on these precious truths.

Doctrine of Foreordination Restored

Concerning the restoration of truths in the latter days, Elder Neal A. Maxwell has noted that "as when dinner guests arrive nearly all at once, Joseph, as host, received, welcomed, and duly noted each truth. Only later was there time and matured perceptivity to see their relationships and the antiquity of their credentials.

"Among these plain and precious truths was the doctrine of the premortal existence of mankind. (See 1 Nephi 13:39–40.) Early on, Joseph received much concerning this truth, but just as the revelations concerning it came incrementally, so did Joseph's understanding." Elder Maxwell also observes that "so far as we know . . . the restoration of this responsive doctrine began with the translation by Joseph Smith of a few verses in the book of Alma, late 1829 or early 1830. (See Alma 13:3–5)."[6] It is interesting to note that Alma 13:3–5, which specifically mentions the doctrine of foreordination, initiated the restoration of its sister doctrine—the concept of premortality.[7] "Orson Pratt indicated that it was Joseph Smith's translation of the

Bible, which began soon after the publication of the Book of Mormon, that first drew his attention to the idea of a preexistence in latter-day revelation. The first seven chapters of the revised account of the creation (revealed in June 1830) as recorded in the Book of Moses make repeated reference to man's spiritual creation."[8]

Note a few examples of the incremental, "line upon line," restoration of the doctrine of foreordination (premortality) as given by revelation according to the year of reception:

1829–30 *Alma 13:3–5:* Priests were "called and prepared from the foundation of the world according to the foreknowledge of God." *Ether 3:13–16:* Jesus Christ shows himself to the brother of Jared and reveals his foreordained mission to atone for the sins of man.

June 1830 *Moses 4:2:* Jesus Christ was the Beloved and Chosen "from the beginning."

May 1833 *Doctrine and Covenants 93:29–33:* "Man was also in the beginning with God," for man is spirit. The elements are eternal.

1835–36 *Abraham 3:22–23:* Intelligences "were organized before the world was." Abraham was chosen before he was born. *Abraham 3:27:* "And the Lord said: I will send the first."

October 1918 *Doctrine and Covenants 138:55:* "Noble and great ones . . . were chosen in the beginning to be rulers in the Church of God."

Joseph Smith's first public discourse concerning the doctrine of premortality in general did not occur until August 1839. There, the Prophet taught that "the Spirit of Man is not a created being; it existed from Eternity & will exist to eternity."[9] Concerning foreordination specifically, the Prophet said in 1844 that "every man who has a calling to minister to the inhabitants of the world was ordained to that very purpose in the Grand Council of heaven before this world was. I suppose I was ordained to this very office in that Grand Council."[10]

With the translation of the Book of Mormon, the doctrine of foreordination was restored to the earth and, although incrementally added upon later in other scriptures and statements of general authorities, the Book of Mormon itself contains within its pages several implicit and explicit examples of foreordination that demonstrate the power of this sacred text. It also shows that foreordination intricately intertwines our roles here upon the earth with the divine purposes of God.

IMPLICIT REFERENCES TO FOREORDINATION IN THE BOOK OF MORMON

The doctrine of foreordination is implicitly referred to in the first chapter of 1 Nephi. In verses 9–11 we read: "And it came to pass that he saw One descending out of the midst of heaven, and he beheld that his luster was above that of the sun at noon-day. And he also saw twelve others following him, and their brightness did exceed that of the stars in the firmament. And they came down and went forth upon the face of the earth; and the first came and stood before my father, and gave unto him a book, and bade him that he should read."

This event in the first chapter sets the tone and central message for the entire Book of Mormon—that Jesus is the Christ, referred to in verse 9 as the One. It also demonstrates that Jesus Christ and his apostles existed premortally and were foreordained to their respective missions. Elder Bruce R. McConkie notes that the "twelve others" in Lehi's vision were "Apostles of the Lord Jesus Christ—mighty men of faith; pillars of personal righteousness; chosen spirits who were before ordained to walk with Christ, teach his doctrine, and testify of his divine Sonship! . . . There was no happenstance in their calls; they had been foreordained by Him who knows all things and who had prepared them from all eternity to be his ministers in the meridian day."[11]

We also find several examples of implicit references to foreordination in the vision given to Nephi in 1 Nephi 11–14. In fact, Nephi is so specific that we can identify some of the individuals he refers to by name. For example, in 1 Nephi 11:13, 18–20, we read:

"I looked and beheld the great city of Jerusalem, and also other cities. And I beheld the city of Nazareth; and in the city of Nazareth I beheld a virgin, and she was exceedingly fair and white. . . .

"And an angel . . . said unto me: Behold, the virgin whom thou seest is the mother of the Son of God, after the manner of the flesh.

"And it came to pass that I beheld that she was carried away in the Spirit; and after she had been carried away in the Spirit for the space of a time the angel spake unto me, saying: Look!

"And I looked and beheld the virgin again, bearing a child in her arms."

Concerning these verses, Elder Bruce R. McConkie said: "Nearly six hundred years before Mary was with child of God, by the power of the Holy Ghost, Nephi saw in vision what would transpire in time's meridian.... Clearly the vision was intended to show the high and holy place of Mary. She was foreordained. There is only one Mary, even as there is only one Christ."[12] In Alma 7:10, Alma names Mary, stating that Christ "shall be born of Mary, at Jerusalem," thus again underscoring the doctrine of foreordination in relation to Jesus Christ and Mary.

In 1 Nephi 12:6–10 of Nephi's vision, foreordination is again emphasized with the Savior's future visit to the Nephites in the land of Bountiful and his subsequent choosing of the twelve disciples of the new world. Nephi is, of course, again viewing events that were still over six hundred years into the future. Just as the Twelve in the old world were foreordained, however, so also were the Twelve chosen by Jesus in the new world.

In 1 Nephi 13:12, Nephi sees "a man among the Gentiles, who was separated from the seed of my brethren by the many waters; and I beheld the Spirit of God, that it came down and wrought upon the man; and he went forth upon the many waters, even unto the seed of my brethren, who were in the promised land." According to President Ezra Taft Benson, "God inspired 'a man among the Gentiles' (1 Nephi 13:12) who, by the Spirit of God was led to rediscover the land of America and bring this rich new land to the attention of the people in Europe. That man, of course, was Christopher Columbus, who testified that he was inspired in what he did."[13] Concerning the foreordination of Columbus, Elder Bruce R. McConkie stated, "The mission of Columbus to bring the American nations to the knowledge of the old world, and the Lord's dealings with the Gentile nations which should inhabit the areas thus re-discovered, was all foreknown and foreordained."[14]

Toward the end of Nephi's recorded vision, Nephi "beheld a man, and he was dressed in a white robe.

"And the angel said unto me: Behold one of the twelve apostles of the Lamb.

"Behold, he shall see and write the remainder of these things; yea, and also many things which have been.

"And he shall also write concerning the end of the world....

"And I, Nephi, heard and bear record, that the name of the apostle of the Lamb was John, according to the word of the angel" (1 Nephi 14:19–22, 27).

Again, it is not unreasonable to accept that long before, John the Revelator was chosen and foreordained to have the responsibility of recording the remainder of Nephi's vision as it is now found in the book of Revelation.

There are many other implicit references to foreordination in the Book of Mormon. Some of these references identify individuals by name; others give enough information that it is readily apparent to whom it is referring. A few examples of these references include (but are not limited to) the following:

2 Nephi 3:14–15. Joseph Smith and Joseph Smith Sr.
2 Nephi 27:12. Three Witnesses (see also Ether 5:4)
2 Nephi 27:13. Eight Witnesses
2 Nephi 27:15–19. Joseph Smith and Martin Harris
Alma 7:10. Mary

As the central purpose of the Book of Mormon is to bring us to Christ, numerous implicit references to his foreordained mission to work out the infinite and eternal Atonement are found throughout the Book of Mormon (see Topical Guide, "Jesus Christ," 240–58). The most explicit reference to the foreordained mission of Jesus Christ is found in Ether 3:14, wherein the Savior manifests himself to the brother of Jared: "Behold, I am he who was prepared from the foundation of the world to redeem my people. Behold, I am Jesus Christ. I am the Father and the Son. In me shall all mankind have life, and that eternally, even they who shall believe on my name; and they shall become my sons and my daughters."

Elder Bruce R. McConkie said that Jesus Christ was "chosen and foreordained to be the One who would work out the infinite and eternal atonement. . . . And so before mortal men were, before Adam fell that men might be, before there was mortality and procreation and death—before all this, provision was made for the redemption."[15]

These implicit references in the Book of Mormon help us see two important things. First, that Jesus Christ was foreordained to come to this earth to work out the infinite and eternal Atonement. Second, that many individuals would be foreordained to come to this earth to aid in bringing about the purposes of the Lord. It is in the Book of Mormon that we can clearly see that our roles upon this earth are not merely coincidental nor happenstance but are intertwined with the divine purposes of an all-loving God.

Alma 13:3–5 and Biblical Passages

As already noted, there are many implicit references to the doctrine of foreordination relating to individuals, and more particularly to the mission of Jesus Christ. The most explicit and expansive teaching on foreordination in the Book of Mormon, however, is found in Alma 13:3–5. It reads:

"And this is the manner after which they were ordained—being called and prepared from the foundation of the world according to the foreknowledge of God, on account of their exceeding faith and good works; in the first place being left to choose good or evil; therefore they having chosen good, and exercising exceedingly great faith, are called with a holy calling, yea, with that holy calling which was prepared with, and according to, a preparatory redemption for such.

"And thus they have been called to this holy calling on account of their faith, while others would reject the Spirit of God on account of the hardness of their hearts and blindness of their minds, while, if it had not been for this they might have had as great privilege as their brethren.

"Or in fine, in the first place they were on the same standing with their brethren; thus this holy calling being prepared from the foundation of the world."

Biblical verses related to foreordination are few, and none are so explicit as those found here in Alma. Though only three of this passage's verses specifically point to foreordination, these verses add much to the knowledge and understanding provided through the Bible. To see this more clearly, several biblical passages will be compared to Alma 13:3–5.

"Before I formed thee in the belly I knew thee; and before thou camest forth out of the womb I sanctified thee, and I ordained thee a prophet unto the nations" (Jeremiah 1:5).

From a general Christian commentary, this verse "follows upon a decree of God's, fixed before he [Jeremiah] was conceived or born. . . . He has accordingly so influenced our origin and our growth in the womb, as to prepare us for what we are to become, and for what we are to accomplish on behalf of His kingdom."[16] Note that there is no connecting man to a premortal existence, but that God's will is worked into us in the womb. Alma, however, specifically states that priests "were ordained—being called and prepared from the foundation of the world . . . on account of their exceeding faith and good works; in the first place being left to choose good or evil; therefore they having chosen good, and exercising exceedingly great faith, are called with a holy calling" (Alma 13:3). Here Alma makes it clear that there was a period prior to this life in which one could demonstrate one's faithfulness. Therefore, with Alma's teachings in mind, Jeremiah 1:5 takes on added meaning, showing that Jeremiah may have been one of these priests that Alma refers to as exercising great faith in a premortal existence.

"And hath made of one blood all nations of men for to dwell on all the face of the earth, and hath determined the times before appointed, and the bounds of their habitations" (Acts 17:26; see also Deuteronomy 32:8).

"For whom he did foreknow, he also did predestinate to be conformed to the image of his Son, that he might be the firstborn among many brethren.

"Moreover whom he did predestinate, them he also called" (Romans 8:29–30).

"Who verily was foreordained before the foundation of the world, but was manifest in these last times for you" (1 Peter 1:20).

One Christian author notes that there is a "complete absence in Paul's epistles of any suggestion of the Hellenistic notion of the soul's pre-existence before the existence of the body."[17] In one commentary, Acts 17:26 is viewed as "a standard statement of God's creative power, which has as one of its essential elements the 'separating' (*horizò*) of space and time in orderly fashion."[18] In still another commentary, "The idea of allotted periods and boundaries reflects apocalyptic motifs (cf. I Enoch 2:1) and shows that the Creator is also ruler of history."[19] Another commentator argues that Paul, in Romans 8:29, is not referring to the individual premortality of man but is "applying the biblical privilege of election communally to the Christian community made up of Jews and Gentiles."[20] Accordingly, God's foreknowledge or foreordination in the above verses does not refer to any individual premortal existence, but instead is viewed as his ultimate knowledge before individual existence. In Christian thought, only

Christ existed premortally, as evidenced by Peter's remark in 1 Peter 1:20.[21]

Alma 13:3–5 clarifies that these verses should be applied to the doctrine of individual premortality and foreordination. Just as Jesus Christ existed premortally, every spirit also existed in a premortal realm, exercised agency, received foreordination, and was assigned to a specific time, place, and mission. With the aid of Alma's comments on premortality and foreordination, the biblical verses that refer to the doctrine can be better understood and applied in a much more individual and personal way.[22]

Premortality and Our Earthly Identity

Alma 13:3–5 inaugurated a flood of additional light on the doctrines of premortality and foreordination. One of the most significant results attending the restoration of these doctrines is its dramatic expansion of our concept of eternal identities. Although our identities are certainly shaped by our genetics and environment in this life, our identity should not and cannot be limited to this existence. In fact, the Lord states that we were "also in the beginning with God" (D&C 93:29). In this same revelation, we are told that our premortal existence was in a state called intelligence. Abraham said he saw "the intelligences that were organized before the world was" (Abraham 3:22).

According to Elder Bruce R. McConkie: "Abraham used the name *intelligences* to apply to the spirit children of the Eternal Father. The intelligence or spirit element became intelligences after the spirits were born as individual entities. . . . Use of this name designates both the primal element from which the spirit offspring were created and also their inherited capacity to grow in grace, knowledge, power, and intelligence itself, until such intelligences, gaining the fulness of all things, become like their Father, the Supreme Intelligence."[23]

As mentioned, within just a few centuries after Christ, the early Christian communities came to believe and accept the Greek philosophical view that God is the first cause of all existence. That is to say that man's core essence or existence is entirely dependent on God. From the Prophet Joseph Smith, however, we learn that "the intelligence of spirits had no beginning, neither will it have an end. . . . There never was a time when there were not spirits; for they are co-equal [co-eternal] with our Father in heaven."[24] Therefore, man exists on the same eternal principles as God. Speaking of the creation of the earth, this principle was also clarified in 1916 by the First Presidency in "The Father and the Son: A Doctrinal Exposition," in which it is stated that "God created the earth as an organized sphere; but He certainly did not create, in the sense of bringing into primal existence, the ultimate elements of the materials of which the earth consists, for 'the elements are eternal' (D&C 93:33)."[25]

At some point in our primal existence, our intelligences (i.e., the self-existing part of us that was "not created or made" [D&C 93:29]) were clothed with spirit bodies. This process involved an eternal father and an eternal mother. President Marion G. Romney noted that "in origin, man is a son of God. The spirits of men 'are begotten sons and daughters unto God' (D&C 76:24). Through that birth process, self-existing intelligence was organized into individual spirit beings."[26] We also learn from revelation to prophets and apostles that our spirit bodies have the same form as our earthly bodies (see D&C 77:2; Ether 3:16–17) and, although made of a finer material, spirit bodies have "all the organs and parts exactly corresponding to the outward tabernacle."[27]

From Alma 13:5 we learn that spirits were "on the same standing" with each other in the "first place." It is not clear what the phrase "same standing" is referring to in the context of these verses. From Doctrine and Covenants 93:38 we learn that "every spirit of man was innocent in the beginning." This seems to imply that though there are varying grades of intelligences (i.e., spirit children of God; see Abraham 3:18–19; 22–23), all began their progress from a state of innocence and moral agency in the "first place," or in the premortal life. There is also no question that before we came to this existence we had already developed certain tendencies, capacities, and predilections that would affect our sojourn here on earth. We must not, however, confuse this idea with the concept of predestination. It would perhaps be better to use the term *predisposition*.[28] We are all, in a sense, predisposed to certain likes and dislikes, and to various types of behavior, some of which must be cultivated and some of which must be avoided or overcome. In other words, all of us developed to a large extent our identities before we came to the earth.

For example, Elder Bruce R. McConkie notes: "Being subject to law, and having their agency, all the spirits of men, while yet in the Eternal Presence, developed aptitudes, talents, capacities, and abilities of every sort, kind, and degree. During the long expanse of life which then was, an infinite variety of talents and abilities came into being. As the ages rolled, no two spirits remained alike. Mozart became a musician; Einstein centered his interest in mathematics; Michelangelo turned his attention to painting. Cain was a liar, a schemer, a rebel who maintained a close affinity to Lucifer. Abraham and Moses and all of the prophets sought and obtained the talent for spirituality."[29]

When we come to this life "we bring with us the traits and talents there developed. True, we forget what went before because we are here being tested, but the capacities and abilities that then were ours are yet resident within us. . . . And all men with their infinitely varied talents and personalities pick up the course of progression where they left it off when they left the heavenly realms."[30] Noting the connection between our former life and mortality, President Harold B. Lee said, "Rewards were seemingly promised, or foreordained, before the world was. Surely these matters must have been determined by the kind of lives we had lived in that premortal spirit world. Some may question these assumptions, but at the same time they will accept without any question the belief that each one of us will be judged when we leave this earth according to his or her deeds during our lives here in mortality. Isn't it just as reasonable to believe that what we have received here in this earth [life] was given to each of us according to the merits of our conduct before we came here?"[31]

As Elder Neal A. Maxwell said, "This doctrine [premortality explicitly but foreordination implicitly] brings unarguable identity but also severe accountability to our lives."[32] As shown, our identities began their development long before we came to this earth. "Unarguable" identity can best be seen only from an eternal perspective. "Severe accountability" can be better understood when we see that our tendencies here may have had their shaping in the premortal realms and must be either cultivated, controlled, or rejected through moral agency.[33]

According to President Joseph Fielding Smith, "Notwithstanding this fact that our recollection of former things was taken away, the character of our lives in the spirit world has much to do with our disposition, desires, and mentality here in mortal life. . . . We must not lose sight of the fact that the characteristics of the spirit, which were developed through many ages of a former existence, play a very important part in our progression through mortal life."[34]

Without the perspective of an eternal identity supplied by this doctrine, we can become one-dimensional, and "one-dimensional man with only a one-dimensional view of the world will surely focus upon the cares of the world, yielding to the things of the moment."[35] Finally, a few thoughts from Elder Neal A. Maxwell will summarize the idea of the connection between our premortal and earthly identities:

"Premortality is not a relaxing doctrine. For each of us, there are choices to be made, incessant and difficult chores to be done, ironies and adversities to be experienced, time to be well spent, talents and gifts to be well employed. Just because we were chosen 'there and then,' surely does not mean we can be indifferent 'here and now.' Whether foreordination for men, or foredesignation for women, those called and prepared must also prove 'chosen, and faithful.' (See Rev. 17:14; D&C 121:34–36.)

"In fact, adequacy in the first estate may merely have ensured a stern, second estate with more duties and no immunities! Additional tutoring and suffering appears to be the pattern for the Lord's most apt pupils. (See Mosiah 3:19; 1 Pet. 4:19.) Our existence, therefore, is a continuum matched by God's stretching curriculum.

"This doctrine brings unarguable identity but also severe accountability to our lives. It uniquely underscores the actuality of the Fatherhood of God and the brotherhood of man.

"It also reminds us that we do not have all of the data. There are many times when we must withhold judgment and trust God, even in the midst of 'all these things.' Only with the help of this doctrine can we begin to understand things as they really were, are, and will become. (See Jacob 4:13; D&C 93:24.)"[36]

Conclusion

Not many years after the death and resurrection of Christ, the precious doctrine of premortality, which ultimately affected a belief in foreordination, was lost to the world. This was due to the influx of Greek philosophical ideas into early Christianity that championed the concept of a God as an amorphous Spiritual Being as opposed to a physical being in the form of a man. In addition, Greek philosophy argued that God's creative powers were of such nature that all things, including mankind, could be brought into existence out of nothing. Any idea of premortality or foreordination did not survive this type of thinking.

By the time Joseph Smith began the restoration process, a disbelief in premortality had already been firmly embedded into Christianity and was an integral part of early nineteenth-century religious thought. Therefore, in translating the Book of Mormon, Joseph Smith unlocked a doctrine that had been lost for many centuries. Following this first introduction to a premortal life, many more revelations followed that served to add to the knowledge of our life before.

In the Book of Mormon we find many implicit references to Christ's foreordained mission and to individual foreordained roles of people, such as Joseph Smith, Mary, and Columbus. This helps us see that our lives are inextricably connected to events, callings, and rewards that occurred in the life before and that these premortal occurrences have a significant impact on our lives in mortality and in the working out of the purposes of God upon the earth.

Alma 13:3–5, the only expansive, explicit teaching on the doctrine of foreordination in the Book of Mormon, enhances the biblical teachings on premortality and foreordination. It is significant that without the Book of Mormon and later revelations, our knowledge would be at the same level as the world's understanding. We, too, would be groping to find meanings for obscure biblical references with little success had not the Lord provided further information.

Finally, an enlightened view of this precious doctrine, given by the Lord and his servants, informs us that we have come from an eternal home. Our identities were not created but have been developing for ages before this life. Each of us has come to this earth with many strengths and talents, in addition to some predisposed weaknesses that must be overcome in this life as we exercise our agency. We also know that since we have come from a prior existence, we will be held accountable for how we have used our predisposed strengths or weaknesses, which will ultimately affect our progress back to our eternal home.

In sum, the Book of Mormon teachings on the doctrine of foreordination, whether implicit or explicit, are truly a restoration of a "plain and precious truth." This precious truth helps us see more clearly with the eye of faith our eternal heritage in the premortal world and strengthens our resolve to carry out our foreordained missions upon the earth so that ultimately we can be led back home to a loving Father in Heaven to live in his presence forever.

NOTES

1. Neal A. Maxwell, in Conference Report, Oct. 1985, 21; or *Ensign*, Nov. 1985, 17. For a general discussion of the doctrines of foreordination and, more particularly, premortality, see Brent L. Top, *The Life Before* (Salt Lake City: Bookcraft, 1988).

2. Stephen E. Robinson, "Warring against the Saints of God," *Ensign*, Jan. 1988, 38–39. Robinson says, "This period might be called the blind spot in Christian history, for it is here that the fewest primary historical sources have been preserved. We have good sources for New Testament Christianity; then the lights go out, so to speak, and we hear the muffled sounds of a great struggle. When the lights come on again a hundred or so years later, we find that someone has rearranged all the furniture and Christianity has become something very different from what it was in the beginning. That different entity can accurately be described as hellenized Christianity."

3. Ironically, though Greek influence eventually diminishes belief in a premortal life in the Catholic and Protestant religions, "it is found in a well-developed form in Greek religion and philosophy, in Judaism, in the early Christian Church, in the religions of India, and to a very considerable extent associated with modern thought in the West. . . . In the Talmud and the Midrash the preexistence of souls is clearly taught. They are created by God and given a distinct existence as living beings. . . . Through the influence of Hellenistic philosophy and the Zoroastrian and Buddhist religions, it soon made its appearance among certain sects who derived part of their teaching from Christianity, notably the Mandeans, originating in Palestine in the 1st century; and the Gnostics, spreading from Antioch and Alexandria in the 2d century; and the Manichaeans from Persia in the 3d." James Hastings, ed., *Encyclopedia of Religion and Ethics*, 12 vols. (New York: Charles Scribner's Sons, 1961), 10:236, 238, s.v. "preexistence."

4. Keith Norman, "Ex Nihilo: The Development of the Doctrines of God and Creation in Early Christianity," in *Brigham Young University Studies*, spring 1977, 293.

5. Cited in W. Montgomery Watt, *The Formative Period of Islamic Thought* (Edinburgh: Edinburgh University Press, 1973), 246–47.

6. Maxwell, in Conference Report, Oct. 1985, 19; or *Ensign,* Nov. 1985, 15–16.

7. Orson Pratt spoke of this doctrine as found in the book of Alma in 1872: "I do not think that I should have ever discerned it in that book had it not been for the new translation of the Scriptures" (in *Journal of Discourses,* 26 vols. [London: Latter-day Saints' Book Depot, 1854–86], 15:249).

8. Charles R. Harrell, "The Development of the Doctrine of Preexistence, 1830–1844," in *Brigham Young University Studies,* spring 1988, 80.

9. Andrew F. Ehat and Lyndon W. Cook, ed., *The Words of Joseph Smith* (Provo, Utah: Brigham Young University, 1980), 9. For an excellent, albeit brief, review of the revelations and teachings of the Prophet on premortality, see Donald Q. Cannon, Larry E. Dahl, and John W. Welch, "The Restoration of Major Doctrines through Joseph Smith," *Ensign,* Jan. 1989, 30–31.

10. Joseph Smith, *Teachings of the Prophet Joseph Smith,* sel. Joseph Fielding Smith (Salt Lake City: Deseret Book, 1976), 365.

11. Bruce R. McConkie, *The Mortal Messiah: From Bethlehem to Calvary,* 4 vols. (Salt Lake City: Deseret Book, 1979–81), 2:100–101.

12. Bruce R. McConkie, *The Promised Messiah: The First Coming of Christ* (Salt Lake City: Deseret Book, 1981), 466.

13. Ezra Taft Benson, *The Teachings of Ezra Taft Benson* (Salt Lake City: Bookcraft, 1988), 577.

14. Bruce R. McConkie, *Mormon Doctrine,* 2d ed. (Salt Lake City: Bookcraft, 1966), 292.

15. Bruce R. McConkie, *A New Witness for the Articles of Faith* (Salt Lake City: Deseret Book, 1985), 110.

16. C. F. Keil and F. Delitzsch, *Commentary on the Old Testament,* 10 vols. (Peabody, Mass.: Hendrickson Publishers, 1989), 8:39.

17. Donald Guthrie, *New Testament Theology* (England: Inter-Varsity Press, 1981), 165.

18. Luke Timothy Johnson, "The Acts of the Apostles," in Daniel J. Harrington, ed., *Sacra Pagina Series,* 10 vols. (Collegeville, Minn.: Liturgical Press, 1992), 5:315.

19. Charles M. Laymon, ed., *The Interpreter's One-Volume Commentary on the Bible* (New York: Abingdon Press, 1971), 752.

20. Brendan Byrne, "Romans," in Harrington, *Sacra Pagina Series,* 6:272.

21. For a discussion on the premortal existence of Christ from a Christian perspective, see Guthrie, *New Testament Theology,* 345–48.

22. Restoration of the doctrines of premortality and foreordination

have also illuminated many other biblical references not generally viewed as such by Christianity (see Topical Guide, s.v. "man, antemortal existence of"; "man, a spirit child of Heavenly Father"; "foreordination").

23. McConkie, *Mormon Doctrine*, 387. Brigham Young noted, "The matter composing our bodies and spirits has been organized from the eternity of matter that fills immensity" (in *Journal of Discourses*, 7:285). Note also that the terms *intelligence* and *spirit element* are synonymous (see D&C 93:29–30; McConkie, *Mormon Doctrine*, 316, 442). See also Robert H. Craig, comp., "The Pre-Existence," LDS Study Briefs Series (Sonora, Calif.: Yankee Hill, 1988) for a compilation of many quotations from general authorities on the doctrine of premortal existence.

24. Smith, *Teachings of the Prophet Joseph Smith*, 353–54. "Intelligence is eternal and exists upon a self-existent principle. It is a spirit from age to age, and there is no creation about it."

25. In Daniel H. Ludlow, ed., "Doctrinal Expositions of the First Presidency," *Encyclopedia of Mormonism*, 5 vols. (New York: Macmillan Publishing, 1992), 4:1670.

26. Marion G. Romney, in Conference Report, Oct. 1978, 18; or *Ensign*, Nov. 1978, 14.

27. Parley P. Pratt, *Key to the Science of Theology* (Salt Lake City: Deseret Book, 1978), 79.

28. I am grateful to Larry E. Dahl for helping me see the distinction between the terms *predestination* and *predisposition*.

29. McConkie, *Mortal Messiah*, 1:23. For a discussion of foreordination in relation to the house of Israel, see Robert L. Millet, "The House of Israel: From Everlasting to Everlasting," in Richard D. Draper, ed., *A Witness of Jesus Christ: The 1989 Sperry Symposium on the Old Testament* (Salt Lake City: Deseret Book, 1990), 179–82.

30. McConkie, *Mortal Messiah*, 1:25.

31. Harold B. Lee, in Conference Report, Oct. 1973, 7–8; or *Ensign*, Jan. 1974, 5.

32. Maxwell, in Conference Report, Oct. 1985, 21; or *Ensign*, Nov. 1985, 17.

33. President Joseph Fielding Smith said: "No person was foreordained or appointed to sin or to perform a mission of evil. No person is ever predestined to salvation or damnation. Every person has free agency" (*Doctrines of Salvation*, comp. Bruce R. McConkie, 3 vols. [Salt Lake City: Bookcraft, 1954–56], 1:61).

34. Smith, *Doctrines of Salvation*, 1:60.

35. Maxwell, in Conference Report, Oct. 1985, 21; or *Ensign*, Nov. 1985, 17.

36. Ibid.

CHAPTER ELEVEN

SHOWING, KNOWING, AND CONVINCING: THREE WAYS THE BOOK OF MORMON RESTORES HOPE FOR THE LATTER-DAY SAINT FAMILY

RICHARD D. HAWKS

As early as 1 Nephi 2, Laman and Lemuel began their incessant complaining: "And thus Laman and Lemuel, being the eldest, did murmur against their father" (v. 12). What would it have been like to grow up in Lehi and Sariah's home? Was there bickering and contention, or was there peace and harmony in their home? What kinds of conversations did Lehi and Sariah have at the end of the day when it was quiet and they had time to reflect on the choices their children were making? This scenario, although taken from a context nearly twenty-six hundred years old, is reflective of the challenges that Latter-day Saint families face today.

The same questions can be asked of modern parents in Zion, who, like Lehi and Sariah, bear the noble responsibility of training up their children in the way they should go, so that when they are old, they will not depart from it (see Proverbs 22:6). Where can parents turn for the rejuvenation of their hope? The Book of Mormon teaches that

---

Richard D. Hawks is a doctoral candidate in the Department of Educational Policy and Administration at the University of Minnesota.

LDS families can find true hope in Jesus Christ. Moroni, referring to both the Jaredite and Nephite records, writes that these have been preserved "to show unto the remnant of the House of Israel what great things the Lord hath done for their fathers; and that they may know the covenants of the Lord, that they are not cast off forever— And also to the convincing of the Jew and Gentile that Jesus is the Christ, the Eternal God, manifesting himself unto all nations" (Book of Mormon title page).

This knowledge is important because it represents three "perverted" or "taken away" truths (see 1 Nephi 13:26, 29, 40) that the Book of Mormon restores or "establishes" (see 1 Nephi 13:40). These are (1) that Jehovah is a God of grace and mercy, and that he has done and will continue to do great things for his people and their families; (2) that salvation is a covenant affair—we are "not cast off forever"; and (3) that Jesus is the Christ, the literal Son of God, and that he will manifest himself to all people. The restoration of these three fundamental truths by the Book of Mormon provides families of the last days with greater faith in God and hope for enduring the challenges of this final dispensation. Our study of the Book of Mormon must include each if we are to "exercise faith in God unto life and salvation," for "a correct idea of his character, perfections, and attributes."[1]

SHOWING

What "great things" is the Lord showing me? Why is he showing me these great things? How can these great things benefit my family?[2]

The Book of Mormon, because of the truths it restores, is a message of hope for LDS families. It begins with a focus on one small family in Jerusalem and the efforts of the parents and a child to protect and preserve their family. As the record unfolds, however, it represents much, much more. It reveals the greater family of God and the painstaking efforts of a Heavenly Parent and his child to protect and preserve their family (see 1 Nephi 1:20; Moroni 10:3).

Inasmuch as the Book of Mormon was written "to show unto the remnant of the House of Israel what great things the Lord hath done for their fathers," Book of Mormon writers occasionally use identifying phrases to draw the reader's attention to the great things the Lord has done. Nephi pleads with his brothers, "Yea, and how is it that ye have forgotten what great things the Lord hath done for us, in delivering us out of the hands of Laban, and also that we should obtain the record?" (1 Nephi 7:11). In addition, Nephi "rehearsed unto [his brothers], how great things the Lord had done for them in bringing them out of the land of Jerusalem" (2 Nephi 1:1). In Alma 62, the people of Nephi remembered the "great things the Lord had done for them, that he had delivered them from death, and from bonds, and from prisons, and from all manner of afflictions, and he had delivered them out of the hands of their enemies" (v. 50).

Continuing, the righteous King Orihah reigns in prosperity because he "did walk humbly before the Lord, and did remember how great things the Lord had done for his father, and also taught his people how great things the Lord had done for their fathers" (Ether 6:30). Shule, a contemporary of Orihah, also "remembered the great things that the Lord had done for his fathers in bringing them across the great deep into the promised land; wherefore he did execute judgment in righteousness all his days" (Ether 7:27). Shule remembered the great things the Lord had done and it caused him to "execute judgment in righteousness."

These references show us the great things the Lord is willing to do for his children. In addition, we learn a few reasons why the Lord desires us to remember the great things he has done for us. What was the result of Shule recognizing the great things the Lord had done for his fathers? It was righteousness—more than just obedience, a righteousness consistent with any holder of the priesthood who desires to serve in a godly manner (see Abraham 1:1–3; D&C 121:36–37, 41–46). If parents in the Church could help themselves and their children see the great things the Lord has done for them, and continually remember those things, it would help keep them in the right way—both seeking and cleaving unto righteousness. Is it any surprise that we are taught in the Church to study the Book of Mormon daily, as individuals and as families? Following this teaching will cause us to continually reflect and remember the great things the Lord has done.

Another reason the Lord shows us great things is to give us hope. By showing us that he is full of grace (see 2 Nephi 2:6; Alma 5:48; 9:26; 13:9), we gain hope that we can qualify for a bestowal of that grace. We can also use that hope to inspire family members to change their lives in order to more fully qualify for the blessings of the Lord.

This concept is illustrated in 1 Nephi 17. Here Nephi has the overwhelming task of soliciting support from his rebellious brothers to build a ship. To win their support, he reminds them of the great things the Lord has done for their fathers (see vv. 23–43). Then he continues:

"And it came to pass that I, Nephi, said unto them that they should murmur no more against their father; neither should they withhold their labor from me, for God had commanded me that I should build a ship.

"And I said unto them: If God had commanded me to do all things I could do them. If he should command me that I should say unto this water, be thou earth, it should be earth; and if I should say it, it would be done.

"And now, if the Lord has such great power, and has wrought so many miracles among the children of men, how is it that he cannot instruct me, that I should build a ship?" (1 Nephi 17:49–51).

This is a great model for families in Zion as they struggle with accomplishing the difficult responsibilities they are given. We can say, as did Nephi, "If the Lord has such great power, and has wrought so many miracles among the children of men, how is it that he cannot instruct me, that I should raise my family in righteousness?" Or, "If the Lord has such great power, and has wrought so many miracles among the children of men, how is it that he cannot instruct me, that I should discipline my children in greater love?" Or, "If the Lord has such great power, and has wrought so many miracles among the children of men, how is it that he cannot instruct me, that I should show greater love and respect to my spouse?"

A response to the former questions—What "great things" is the Lord showing me? Why is he showing me this? How can knowing this benefit my family?—must at least be: he is showing us that he is a God of mercy and grace, full of good works and quick to do all things for the benefit of his children. By this we are able to come to the "correct idea of his character, perfections, and attributes"[3] which is necessary for us to exercise our faith in him and thus have hope in Christ. We have the assurance, in Christ, of receiving his mercy and grace in the protection and salvation of ourselves and our families.

Knowing

What covenants is the Lord helping me to know? Why is he helping me to know them? How can knowing the covenants of the Lord benefit my family?

Perhaps the greatest message of truth restored through the Book of Mormon is that which pertains to covenants. Our Heavenly Father is a covenant-making being. By virtue of the covenants he makes, he has an obligation to do all in his power for the salvation of his children. There cannot be a greater message, a greater truth restored, a greater declaration of the Lord, than that which he has spoken pertaining to his promise to save us from our lost and fallen state—the promise that we "are not cast off forever."

The Book of Mormon restores many of the plain and precious truths surrounding the covenants and ordinances of the gospel; for example, the Abrahamic covenant (see 1 Nephi 15:14; 17:40; 19:15; 2 Nephi 10:7; 29:14; 3 Nephi 20:11–46). Through the Book of Mormon, we know that Abraham's seed will be a tool in the Lord's hands in blessing all the inhabitants of the earth with the priesthood. We also know through this book that he will gather the seed of Abraham from the four quarters of the earth, giving them certain lands for an everlasting inheritance. In addition, through the Book of Mormon, our knowledge is restored concerning the covenants of baptism and the sacrament (see Mosiah 18:13; 3 Nephi 18:1–14; Moroni 4–5).

Through the Book of Mormon, the Lord has restored the lost truth that he operates with his children through ordinances and covenants. It is because of covenants that Lehi and Nephi, a father and son, struggled throughout their lives to save their wayward family members, despite those members' continued rejection of the gospel and family values. Likewise, it is because of covenants that our own Heavenly Father and his Son struggle to save their wayward family members, despite their family's continual rejection of the gospel and family values. These covenants are the binding link of salvation that brings our Redeemer continually to seek after us.

As a marriage binds a husband to his wife, so too has Christ bound himself to us through covenant. Has he not said, "Have I put thee away, or have I cast thee off forever? For thus saith the Lord: Where is the bill of your mother's divorcement? To whom have I put thee

Showing, Knowing, and Convincing

away, or to which of my creditors have I sold you? Yea, to whom have I sold you? Behold, for your iniquities have ye sold yourselves, and for your transgressions is your mother put away" (2 Nephi 7:1). He will continue, because of his covenantal relationship, to stretch out his gathering arm in power:

"How oft have I gathered you as a hen gathereth her chickens under her wings, and have nourished you.

"And again, how oft would I have gathered you as a hen gathereth her chickens under her wings, yea, O ye people of the house of Israel, who have fallen; yea, O ye people of the house of Israel, ye that dwell at Jerusalem, as ye that have fallen; yea, how oft would I have gathered you as a hen gathereth her chickens, and ye would not.

"O ye house of Israel whom I have spared, how oft will I gather you as a hen gathereth her chickens under her wings, if ye will repent and return unto me with full purpose of heart" (3 Nephi 10:4–6).

Indeed, it is the power of covenants, restored through the Book of Mormon, that gives one hope to draw on the power of heaven for salvation. Elder Henry B. Eyring taught this principle when he told the following story that illustrates the power of covenants. He said:

"I saw again the power of keeping covenants through a chance conversation with a man I sat down next to on a trip. I had never met him before, but apparently he had seen me in the crowd because his first words after I introduced myself were, 'I've been watching you.' He told me about his work. I told him about mine. He asked about my family, and then he told me something about his. He said that his wife was a member of the Church and that he was not.

"After he came to trust me, he said something like this: 'You know, there is something in your church you should fix. You need to tell your people when to quit.' He explained that he and his wife had been married for 25 years. She had been a member of the Church since childhood. In their years of marriage she had only once stepped into a building of the Church, and that was to tour a temple before its dedication, and then only because her parents had arranged it.

"Then he told me why he thought we ought to make a change. He said that in those 25 years of married life, in which his wife showed no interest in the Church, visiting teachers and home teachers had never stopped coming to their home. He told of one evening when he went out to walk his dog alone only to find the home teacher happening by with his dog, eager to visit with him.

"He told, with a touch of exasperation, of another night when he came home from a long business trip, put his car in the garage, and then came out to find his home teachers standing there, smiling. He said to me something like, 'And there they were, right in my face, with another plate of cookies.'

"I think I understood his feelings. And then I tried, as best I could, to tell him how hard it would be to teach such teachers to quit. I told him that the love that he had felt from those many visitors and their constancy over the years in the face of little response came from a covenant they had made with God."[4]

Just as these dedicated, covenant members of the Church continue to reach out to save others—even with little response for their efforts—our Heavenly Father, because of his integrity to his covenants, will continue to seek us out, even amidst little response. He is our Father, and he has not relinquished that responsibility.

President Gordon B. Hinckley has said: "Never forget that these little ones are the sons and daughters of God and that yours is a custodial relationship to them, that He was a parent before you were parents and that He has not relinquished His parental rights or interest in these His little ones."[5]

This idea God desires to plant in our minds is the essence of the Book of Mormon message. He has even declared the doctrine and set the example for us. When the Redeemer came to the temple in Bountiful, he spoke to the covenant people of their obligations to be as he was in ministering to their straying brothers and sisters. He said, "Unto such shall ye continue to minister; for ye know not but what they will return and repent, and come unto me with full purpose of heart, and I shall heal them; and ye shall be the means of bringing salvation unto them" (3 Nephi 18:32). Can there be more inspiring language than this? Can there be any greater hope than that which comes as a result of pondering those wonderful words of the Son of God?

Consider, as well, the example set forth in the *Lectures on Faith:*

"Not only was there a manifestation made unto Adam of the existence of a God; but Moses informs us, as before quoted, that God condescended to talk to Cain after his great transgression in slaying his brother, and that Cain knew that it was the Lord that was talking with him, so that when he was driven out from the presence of his brethren, he carried with him the knowledge of the existence of a God; and, through this means, doubtless, his posterity became acquainted with the fact that such a Being existed.

"From this we can see that the whole human family in the early age of their existence, in all their different branches, had this knowledge disseminated among them; so that the existence of God became an object of faith in the early age of the world. And the evidences which these men had of the existence of a God, was the testimony of their Fathers in the first instance.

"The reason why we have been thus particular on this part of our subject, is that this class may see by what means it was that God became an object of faith among men after the fall; and what it was that stirred up the faith of multitudes to feel after him—to search after a knowledge of his character, perfections and attributes, until they became extensively acquainted with him, and not only commune with him and behold his glory, but be partakers of his power and stand in his presence."[6]

This doctrine is found in the story of Enos, who, after reflecting on his father's testimony, decided to "feel after" the Savior and petition for his healing power. Enos wrote, "The words which I had often heard my father speak concerning eternal life, and the joy of the saints, sunk deep into my heart" (Enos 1:3). The same is the case of Alma the Younger. He recounted, "I remembered also to have heard my father prophesy unto the people concerning the coming of one Jesus Christ, a Son of God, to atone for the sins of the world" (Alma 36:17).

These examples give hope to LDS families in at least two ways. First, they inspire parents to begin at the earliest opportunity to bear witness of Christ and his power, to share with their sons and daughters the joy that comes from being in the Lord's kingdom, and to help their children know that they can always pray to their Heavenly Father. Second, these examples inspire the hope that someday, those children will remember and treasure the testimonies of their faithful parents and turn again to the Lord so that he may heal them.

The Lord uses this process in another example found in Helaman 5:35–52. Here, the Lord uses one who had strayed from the faith to help draw others unto him. Consider Aminidab, of whom the scripture reads, "Now there was one among [the Lamanites] who was a Nephite by birth, who had once belonged to the church of God but had dissented from them" (v. 35). In a moment of divine manifestation, he calls to his friends, "You must repent, and cry unto the voice, even until ye shall have faith in Christ, who was taught unto you by Alma, and Amulek, and Zeezrom; and when ye shall do this, the cloud of darkness shall be removed from overshadowing you" (v. 41). Think of it—an "inactive" member of the Church becomes the means of pointing a multitude to the true and living Church. What about Aminidab's parents? Where were they? Who knows but that they were back home among the "active" members, praying day and night and in their hearts that the Lord would one day bring their son back to the Church. What a message of hope! Knowing the Lord is covenantly bound to us as our Redeemer is a great truth restored through the Book of Mormon that gives great hope to Latter-day Saint families.

Our original questions may now be answered. What covenants of the Lord is he showing unto us? The covenants of the new and everlasting covenant of the gospel. Why is the Lord helping us to know the covenants? It is done that we might know that we are not cast off forever. We know that he continues to minister unto his children, even the sinner, with the hope that someday they will "return and repent, and come unto [him] with full purpose of heart" (3 Nephi 18:32). How can knowing this benefit my family? There is great hope in knowing there is power in the covenants between Heavenly Father and his children. There is also a great duty to live those covenants, thereby assisting our Father in the bringing about of the salvation of his children.

CONVINCING

What is the Lord doing to convince me that Jesus is the Christ? Why is he convincing me that Jesus is the Christ? How does being convinced that Jesus is the Christ benefit my family?

To convince us that Jesus is the Christ, the Book of Mormon contains teachings about Christ, teachings from Christ, and many testimonies regarding Christ. Add to this list the restoration of the doctrine of Christ, including the first principles and ordinances of the gospel, the restoration of truth concerning the power of the priesthood and the purpose of authorized servants, and the ministering of angels and the role they play in helping the "residue of men . . . have faith in Christ" (Moroni 7:32) and come to a knowledge of him and his plan of happiness.

All of these things and more constitute what the Lord is doing to convince us that he is the "Eternal God, manifesting himself unto all nations." He is doing everything he can. We know that at some future day, "The knowledge of a Savior shall spread throughout every nation, kindred, tongue, and people" (Mosiah 3:20). In addition, we know that "Every knee shall bow, and every tongue confess before him. Yea, even at the last day, when all men shall stand to be judged of him, then shall they confess that he is God" (Mosiah 27:31). Eventually all of Heavenly Father's children will be convinced that Jesus is the Christ, the Eternal God. The purpose of the Book of Mormon is to help move that convincing process along.

A good example of how the Lord is "manifesting himself" is found in the symbolism of the sacrament, its proper prayer, and in the manner of its administration. This is a profound truth, restored by the Book of Mormon, that churches of the world have tampered with for generations.

I live next door to a widow who is in poor health. She has a long driveway, and during the winter months it requires constant shoveling. One day, she informed me that she was going to move. At first I was gladdened with the prospect that I might not have to shovel the snow for her anymore. Then I remembered the joy both of us had felt as a result of the service. As I pondered over this, I decided I would give her my shovel when she moved—not to enable her to do the work herself, but instead, to give her a token of my love for her. The shovel had become a symbol of the hours of work and service I had rendered to her. The shovel now represented a Christlike love that was the motivation for the service I had given. I had even decided to burn into the wooden handle these words: "As the cross has become a symbol of God's love for his children, may this shovel come to represent the love of a friend extended toward you."

As I thought about this, I decided that during my life I had been too critical of the Catholics and Protestants of the world. I used to find fault with their seemingly "vain" display of the cross. I have since realized that in the sacrament we remember Christ's death and sufferings with symbols that are even more plain and revealing than the cross. I realized that the broken bread represents the broken body of the Savior and that the water is a representation of the blood that he sweat in our behalf. These symbols remind me that his sacrifice was motivated by love, and as I had wished to burn that message into the handle of my shovel, the Savior desires to burn the message of his atoning sacrifice into our souls. He, because of his great love for us, has shed his precious blood and has allowed his innocent body to be broken and mangled. He, in essence, is manifesting himself unto us through the sacrament, and convincing us that he is God. Everything God does is to manifest himself unto us, for "all things denote there is a God" (Alma 30:44; see also Moses 6:63).

Why is it so important that we become convinced "that Jesus is the Christ, the Eternal God"? The answer is: because he is both "the author and the finisher of [our] faith" (Moroni 6:4)—meaning, he is at the beginning of our faith, the middle of our faith, and he is at the end of our faith. If we are to have faith sufficient unto salvation, it must be in him. He is the great prototype. He is God. He manifests himself unto us, that we might know what we must do to become saved as he is saved.

The *Lectures on Faith* teach us why we must become convinced that Jesus is the Christ: "Where shall we find a prototype into whose likeness we may be assimilated, in order that we may be made partakers of life and salvation? or, in other words, where shall we find a saved being? for if we can find a saved being, we may ascertain without much difficulty what all others must be in order to be saved. We think that it will not be a matter of dispute, that two beings who are unlike each other cannot both be saved; for whatever constitutes the salvation of one will constitute the salvation of every creature which will be saved; and if we find one saved being in all existence, we may see what all others must be, or else not be saved. We ask, then, where is the prototype? or where is the saved being? We conclude, as to the answer of this question, there will be no dispute among those who believe the bible, that it is Christ: all will agree in this, that he is the prototype or standard of salvation; or, in other words, that he is a saved being."[7]

Becoming convinced of the divinity of his mission, that he has passed through the second estate and is now clothed with immortality and eternal life, and that he is the great saved prototype, a person is enabled to exercise faith in him. As one continues in this path of faith in Christ, he or she will discover that not only is Christ the author, or the beginning of their faith, but he is also the end, or finisher, as well. The ultimate goal of the faithful in Christ is to enter into his presence, or, as the Book of Mormon phrases it, enjoy the Son of God "manifesting himself unto all nations" (Book of Mormon title page).

Elder Bruce R. McConkie taught this plainly. He wrote: "Any person who will [search the scriptures, keep the commandments, and ask in faith] will get his heart so in tune with the Infinite that there will come into his being, from the 'still small voice,' the eternal realities of religion. And as he progresses and advances and comes nearer to God, there will be a day when he will entertain angels, when he will see visions, and the final end is to view the face of God."[8]

How then can becoming convinced that Jesus is the Christ benefit my family? Or, what does becoming convinced have to do with families? The answer can be found in the words of Elder Howard W. Hunter when he said, "Whatever Jesus lays his hands upon lives. If Jesus lays his hands upon a marriage, it lives. If he is allowed to lay his hands on the family, it lives."[9] Because he is God, the Eternal God, and had the power to save himself, he must also possess the power to save all of his creations, including individuals and families. Because the earth is his footstool and he has all things under his feet, he possesses the power to protect us from the evils of the world that try to destroy us. His power to save and protect is greater than his whose power is used to hurt and destroy. Isaiah taught that eventually the Lord's people would overcome the world. He wrote relative to the power of the evil one and the worldliness and sin that would encompass the Saints, but which they would eventually overcome through Christ.

"And [the house of Israel] shall take them captives unto whom they were captives; and they shall rule over their oppressors.

"And it shall come to pass in that day that the Lord shall give thee rest, from thy sorrow, and from thy fear, and from the hard bondage wherein thou wast made to serve" (2 Nephi 24:2–3; see also Isaiah 60:14).

Conclusion

For many Latter-day Saint families, the last days appear ominous. The idea of raising a faithful family can become overwhelming. Some even lose hope. The Book of Mormon restores and rejuvenates hope. By showing us "what great things the Lord hath done," by helping us to "know the covenants of the Lord, that [we] are not cast off forever," and through convincing us "that Jesus is the Christ, the Eternal God," the Book of Mormon creates hope.

In October 1998 general conference, Elder Richard G. Scott said that some "are pessimistic about the future. They justify that erroneous position by what they see around them and what is occurring in the world. They perceive their future threatened by worsening trends in divorce rates, escalating crime, drugs, terrorist acts, and other atrocities that cripple or destroy life." He responds to these concerns by telling us that we "are living in the most exciting period of time in history. Many reasons could be cited for that optimism. Yet your greatest source of hope and assurance is that you have the fulness of the teachings of the Master. They will show you how to live a good life. You can receive ordinances and covenants that, when righteously lived, ensure true happiness and significant attainment."[10]

Elder Neal A. Maxwell, in that same conference, echoed those same sentiments and truths when he said, "Ultimate hope is . . . tied to Jesus and the blessings of the great Atonement, blessings resulting in the universal Resurrection and the precious opportunity provided thereby for us to practice emancipating repentance, making possible what the scriptures call 'a perfect brightness of hope' (2 Nephi 31:20)."[11]

Of the truths surrounding the teachings of the Master, the great Atonement, and the blessings that flow therefrom, the Book of Mormon stands preeminent. The restoration of these truths by the Book of Mormon provides the families of the last days with greater faith and hope for enduring the challenges of this final dispensation.

Notes

1. Joseph Smith, *Lectures on Faith* (Salt Lake City: Deseret Book, 1985), 38.

2. My thanks to Joel R. Wiest, president of the Anoka Minnesota

Showing, Knowing, and Convincing 147

Stake, for the organization of this chapter. During a recent stake conference, he instructed members on how to invite inspiration while worshiping in the temple. With gratitude, I take from his instructions two of my questions: "What is the Lord showing me?" and "Why is the Lord showing me this?"

3. Smith, *Lectures on Faith,* 38.

4. Henry B. Eyring, Conference Report, Oct. 1996, 40; or *Ensign,* Nov. 1996, 30.

5. Gordon B. Hinckley, "Parental Duties," *Church News,* 1 Mar. 1997, 2.

6. Smith, *Lectures on Faith,* 17–18.

7. Smith, *Lectures on Faith,* 75–76.

8. Bruce R. McConkie, "How to Get Personal Revelation," *New Era,* June 1980, 50.

9. Howard W. Hunter, Conference Report, Oct. 1979, 93; or Ensign, Nov. 1979, 65.

10. Richard G. Scott, Conference Report, Oct. 1998, 86; or *Ensign,* Nov. 1998, 68.

11. Neal A. Maxwell, Conference Report, Oct. 1998, 77; or *Ensign,* Nov. 1998, 61.

CHAPTER TWELVE

THE RIGHTEOUSNESS OF THE REDEEMER

DANIEL K JUDD

A careful study of the Book of Mormon reveals a doctrinal framework described as "the great plan of the Eternal God" (Alma 34:9). While the Lord's plan is composed of many glorious doctrines, at the very center is the atonement of Jesus Christ. The primary intent of this chapter is to discuss the teachings found in the Book of Mormon concerning the Atonement, specifically the significance of the "righteousness of [the] Redeemer" (2 Nephi 2:3). In addition to discussing the necessity of redemption through the "merits, and mercy, and grace of the Holy Messiah" (2 Nephi 2:8), I will also discuss the role of mankind's "good works" (Alma 5:41) in "the plan of redemption" (Alma 12:25), as well as Satan's counterfeit representations of these doctrines.

RELYING WHOLLY UPON CHRIST

The Book of Mormon is a prophetic account of the creation, fall, and redemption of individuals, families, and entire nations. While some reached the zenith of a Zion society, others "wandering in strange roads" (1 Nephi 8:32) descended to the depths of hell. From beginning to end, the Book of Mormon is the story of a fallen people; some were able to reconcile with God and their fellowmen, and others were not. Those who were able to transcend their fallen conditions and receive the blessings of God had one thing in common—they knew of, looked to, and relied on Jesus Christ as their Redeemer.

Daniel K Judd is an associate professor of ancient scripture at Brigham Young University.

Representative of all of the Book of Mormon prophets, Helaman pleaded with his sons to remember the necessity of founding their lives on Christ: "And now, my sons, remember, remember that it is upon the rock of our Redeemer, who is Christ, the Son of God, that ye must build your foundation; that when the devil shall send forth his mighty winds, yea, his shafts in the whirlwind, yea, when all his hail and his mighty storm shall beat upon you, it shall have no power over you to drag you down to the gulf of misery and endless wo, because of the rock upon which ye are built, which is a sure foundation, a foundation whereon if men build they cannot fall" (Helaman 5:12).

Similarly, the prophet Lehi instructed his family: "Wherefore, all mankind were in a lost and in a fallen state, and ever would be save they should rely on this Redeemer" (1 Nephi 10:6). Speaking to members of the Church who had already entered the "strait and narrow path" (2 Nephi 31:18) by repenting and being baptized, Lehi's son Nephi reminded them that they could not have come as far as they had "save it were by the word of Christ with unshaken faith in him, relying wholly upon the merits of him who is mighty to save" (2 Nephi 31:19). Nephi continued his council to the former-day Saints by stating that they "must press forward with a steadfastness in Christ" (2 Nephi 31:20).

The Book of Mormon clearly teaches that founding our lives on Christ, relying upon the sacrifice he made, and drawing from the righteousness of his sinless life are not optional alternatives to leisurely consider; they are imperative if we ever hope to have peace in this life and eternal life in the world to come. King Benjamin recorded, "There shall be no other name given nor any other way nor means whereby salvation can come unto the children of men, only in and through the name of Christ, the Lord Omnipotent" (Mosiah 3:17).

Scientific knowledge and technology, as blessed as we are to have them, cannot save us; neither can politicians, philosophers, physicians or therapists. As important as these people are—as well as the scriptures, our families, and the prophets—none of them can save us. President Joseph F. Smith once stated: "I cannot save you; you cannot save me; we cannot save each other, only so far as we can persuade each other to receive the truth, by teaching it."[1]

Alma counseled his son Shiblon, "And now, my son, I have told you this that ye may learn wisdom, that ye may learn of me that there is no other way or means whereby man can be saved, only in and through Christ. Behold, he is the life and the light of the world. Behold, he is the word of truth and righteousness" (Alma 38:9). Moroni taught that salvation would come by "relying alone upon the merits of Christ, who was the author and the finisher of their faith" (Moroni 6:4).

The Book of Mormon teaches that redemption does not come to mortal man in his own name nor through his own righteousness, or the righteousness or wisdom of some other being, but is found only through the merits of Christ. From the previous texts cited, note that Nephi taught that salvation comes by "relying wholly upon the merits of him who is mighty to save" (2 Nephi 31:19). Moroni describes this same principle by stating that redemption is experienced by relying "alone upon the merits of Christ" (Moroni 6:4).

While some might interpret these verses to mean that mankind's own personal righteousness is not a part of the redemptive process, the Book of Mormon offers clarification. While redemption is found only through Christ, to realize and receive the full significance of his sacrifice we must make the Atonement infinitely operative by repenting of our sins and recognizing our own inability to save ourselves. From the words of Lehi we read:

"Wherefore, redemption cometh in and through the Holy Messiah; for he is full of grace and truth. Behold he offereth himself a sacrifice for sin, to answer the ends of the law, *unto all those who have a broken heart and a contrite spirit;* and unto none else can the ends of the law be answered" (2 Nephi 2:6–7; italics added).

Jesus Christ is indeed the only means by which we may gain salvation, but redemption comes through him as we repent of our sins. Aaron taught King Lamoni's father: "Since man had fallen he could not merit anything of himself; but the sufferings and death of Christ atone for their sins, through faith and repentance, and so forth" (Alma 22:14).

From these prophets we learn that man does have a part to play if he hopes to realize the full blessings of the Atonement. Mankind's humility, faith, and repentance are all a part of our fully partaking of "the righteousness of [the] Redeemer" (2 Nephi 2:3), but we must remember that salvation of any kind comes through the grace of God made possible by the atoning sacrifice of Jesus Christ.

GRACE AND WORKS

The scriptural text Latter-day Saints often cite to explain to themselves and to others the proper relationship between the works of man and the grace of God comes from the writings of Nephi: "For we labor diligently to write, to persuade our children, and also our brethren, to believe in Christ, and to be reconciled to God; for we know that it is by grace that we are saved, after all we can do" (2 Nephi 25:23).

Depending upon the reader's prior understanding (and in some cases, personal agenda), this profound verse is interpreted in various ways. Perhaps two of the most common satanic scenarios concerning the relationship of grace and works are what I have chosen to identify as "humanism" and "salvationism." Salvation cannot be found in either of these false philosophies nor in a "balance" between the two.

HUMANISM (LEGALISM)

Religious humanism, sometimes called legalism, places man and not God at the center of salvation. From a humanistic perspective, salvation is the reward of a righteous life and the grace of God is at best supplementary. It has been my experience—personally, ecclesiastically, and professionally—that many Latter-day Saints have a humanistic interpretation of the gospel. Note the following observations written by an editor from *Newsweek* magazine concerning his perceptions of a Latter-day Saint perspective on the Atonement:

"'Unlike orthodox Christians, Mormons believe that men are born free of sin and earn their way to godhood by the proper exercise of free will, rather than through the grace of Jesus Christ. Thus Jesus' suffering and death in the Mormon view were brotherly acts of compassion, but they do not atone for the sins of others. For this reason, Mormons do not include the cross in their iconography nor do they place much emphasis on Easter.' [*Newsweek*, 1 September 1980, 68]." When Bruce C. Hafen "read this statement, I was appalled that a writer as sophisticated as *Newsweek's* religion editor would miss the point of our core doctrine."[2]

However, Brother Hafen later discovered that the journalist had indeed tried to understand the doctrine of the Church and that his article and the statement in question were based on interviews with a representative sample of LDS Church members. Personally, I wasn't surprised by the statement in *Newsweek*, because of what my own views of grace and the Atonement had once been and what was the understanding of many of my students.

As a missionary I was constantly at battle with those of other faiths who wanted to assert the preeminence of the doctrine of grace. My companions and I even had a name for them—"gracers." Though some of these people had a distorted view of the doctrine of grace and believed that their acceptance of Jesus meant he would "save them in their sins" (Alma 11:37), I have come to understand that there were others who had a much better understanding of the saving power of the grace of Christ than I was willing to acknowledge. As I look back on my missionary experiences, I am ashamed of my attitudes toward this later group because, in reality, I hadn't done my "homework" and didn't properly teach them "the plan of salvation" (Jarom 1:2), as it is taught in the Book of Mormon. Because of my inadequate understanding of the relationship between the doctrines of grace and works, I wasn't able to teach my investigators properly nor comprehend and experience for myself the full blessings of the atonement of Jesus Christ.

A clear example of this humanistic approach to salvation is found in the Book of Mormon account of the anti-Christ Korihor. Korihor's approach to salvation of any kind asserted that "every man fared in this life according to the management of the creature; therefore every man prospered according to his genius, and that every man conquered according to his strength" (Alma 30:17). Korihor obviously believed that reliance upon anyone but oneself is foolishness. Notice how consistent Korihor's teachings are with a declaration endorsed by some of the world's leading scholars:

"They [secular humanists] reject the idea that God has intervened miraculously in history or revealed himself to a chosen few, or that he can save or redeem sinners. They believe that men and women are free and are responsible for their own destinies and that they cannot look toward some transcendent Being for salvation. We reject the divinity of Jesus, the divine mission of Moses, Mohammed, and other latter-day prophets and saints of the various sects and denominations. . . .

" . . . The problems that humankind will face in the future, as in the past, will no doubt be complex and difficult. However, if it is to prevail, it can only do so by enlisting resourcefulness and courage. Secular humanism places trust in human intelligence rather than in divine guidance. Skeptical of theories of redemption, damnation, and reincarnation, secular humanists attempt to approach the human situation in realistic terms: human beings are responsible for their own destinies."[3]

In addition to teaching the self-sufficiency of man, Korihor also taught that a remission of sins was unnecessary: "Ye look forward and say that ye see a remission of your sins. But behold, it is the effect of a frenzied mind; and this derangement of your minds comes because of the traditions of your fathers, which lead you away into a belief of things which are not so" (Alma 30:16).

From what we have already read, it is clear to see that the Book of Mormon contradicts Korihor's arguments (and the arguments of others) for the centrality of man and the irrelevance of Christ. Addressing another anti-Christ (Sherem) who taught a similar form of humanism, the prophet Jacob taught: "If there should be no atonement made all mankind must be lost" (Jacob 7:12). Jacob also taught that without the atonement of Christ "our spirits must have become . . . devils, angels to a devil" (2 Nephi 9:9).

Although it is important to live a righteous life, our own personal righteousness is not enough. Salvation is not to be found in the casseroles we bake, the temple excursions we take, or the home or visiting teaching visits we make; salvation is found in the "righteousness of [the] Redeemer" (2 Nephi 2:3). In the words of Elder Dallin H. Oaks, "We can forget that keeping the commandments, which is necessary, is not sufficient"[4] to salvation.

SALVATIONISM

The British philosopher C. S. Lewis taught that the adversary "sends errors into the world in pairs—pairs of opposites. And he always encourages us to spend a lot of time thinking which is the worse. You see why, of course? He relies on your extra dislike of the one error to draw you gradually into the opposite one."[5] Those who are not deceived by the hoax of humanism are often blind to the deception of salvationism.

Even though we have established that mankind cannot "merit anything of himself" (Alma 22:14) and is redeemed through "the righteousness of [the] redeemer" (2 Nephi 2:3), it is also possible to take the doctrine of grace beyond what the Lord and his servants have intended. Just as there are many Latter-day Saints who have been deceived by the humanistic approach to salvation, I believe that there is also an increasing number who are being seduced by the snare of salvationism. Again, a careful reading of the Book of Mormon provides clarification.

During Alma the Younger's first year as chief judge, he faced Nehor and his nefarious doctrine of universal salvation. From Mormon's abridgement we read:

"And he [Nehor] testified unto the people that all mankind should be saved at the last day, and that they need not fear nor tremble, but that they might lift up their heads and rejoice; for the Lord had created all men, and had also redeemed all men; and, in the end, all men should have eternal life" (Alma 1:4).

Salvationism can be defined as the belief that all mankind will unconditionally inherit eternal life, without regard to their own righteousness or sinfulness. The deceptiveness of this doctrine arises from the fact that it contains some elements of truth. Samuel the Lamanite taught that through the grace of Christ (made possible through his atoning sacrifice) all mankind will be resurrected and all mankind will be brought back into the presence of God:

"Yea, behold, this death bringeth to pass the resurrection, and redeemeth all mankind from the first death—that spiritual death; for all mankind, by the fall of Adam being cut off from the presence of the Lord, are considered as dead, both as to things temporal and to things spiritual.

"But behold, the resurrection of Christ redeemeth mankind, yea, even all mankind, and bringeth them back into the presence of the Lord" (Helaman 14:16–17; see also Alma 11:40–44; 42:23).

Everything that is lost in the fall of Adam is regained through the atonement of Christ.[6] Most Latter-day Saints understand that the fall of Adam and Eve brought both physical and spiritual death into the world (see Alma 42:9). The majority of us also know that the

The Righteousness of the Redeemer

Resurrection is an unconditional blessing of the Atonement—saint and sinner alike will be resurrected (see Alma 11:44). But the point of doctrine many of us miss is that the Atonement also addresses everyone's spiritual death as well. It has been my experience that most Latter-day Saints have a limited view of the Atonement and do not understand that the atonement of Jesus Christ enables everyone to be brought back into the presence of God regardless if we have lived righteous or sinful lives.

Up to this point, Nehor's teachings are consistent with the teachings of Book of Mormon prophets, for the Lord has indeed "redeemed all men" from both physical and spiritual death (Alma 1:4), but it is the next tenet of Nehor's philosophy that is spurious. Nehor also taught that "in the end, all men should have eternal life" (Alma 1:4). While it is doctrinally correct to say that all men will be resurrected, and that all men will return to God's presence for judgment, it is not correct that all men will have eternal life, for "eternal life is life in the presence of the Father and the Son."[7]

Writing of the Savior's atonement and resurrection, Samuel the Lamanite taught: "Yea, and it bringeth to pass the condition of repentance, that whosoever repenteth the same is not hewn down and cast into the fire; but whosoever repenteth not is hewn down and cast into the fire; and there cometh upon them again a spiritual death, yea, a second death, for they are cut off again as to things pertaining to righteousness" (Helaman 14:18; see also Mormon 9:13–14).

In other words, while the sacrifice and "righteousness of [the] Redeemer" (2 Nephi 2:3) brings everyone back into the presence of God, whether we are allowed to remain (or dwell) in the presence of the Father depends upon the degree to which we have accepted the sacrifice of the Son and have been willing to keep his commandments. The Prophet Mormon teaches us:

"Know ye that ye must . . . repent of all your sins and iniquities, and believe in Jesus Christ. . . .

"And he bringeth to pass the resurrection of the dead, whereby man must be raised to stand before his judgment-seat.

"And he hath brought to pass the redemption of the world, whereby he that is found guiltless before him at the judgment day hath it given unto him to dwell in the presence of God in his kingdom, to sing ceaseless praises with the choirs above, unto the Father, and unto the Son, and unto the Holy Ghost . . . in a state of happiness which hath no end" (Mormon 7:5–7).

To "*dwell* in the presence of God" (v. 7; italics added) denotes a continued existence with God following the time when the individual is brought "to *stand* before his judgment-seat" (v. 6; italics added). The Prophet Nephi explained that "the final state of the souls of men is to dwell in the kingdom of God, or to be cast out because of that justice of which I have spoken" (1 Nephi 15:35). Concerning the status of those who are judged to be wicked, the Prophet Helaman taught:

"And I would that all men might be saved. But we read that in the great and last day there are some who shall be cast out, yea, who shall be cast off from the presence of the Lord;

"Yea, who shall be consigned to a state of endless misery, fulfilling the words which say: They that have done good shall have everlasting life; and they that have done evil shall have everlasting damnation" (Helaman 12:25–26).

The Book of Mormon describes the judgments of those who inherit "eternal life" (2 Nephi 2:27) and those who suffer the "second death" (Helaman 14:18). We can only speculate as to why there is no mention made of the gradations of glory that are detailed in the Doctrine and Covenants (see D&C 76:50–98). If "eternal life" can be defined as dwelling in the presence of God, what does it mean to suffer "second death"? Elder Orson Pratt explained: "Second death, What is that? After you have been redeemed from the grave, and come into the presence of God, you will have to stand there to be judged; and if you have done evil, you will be banished everlastingly from His presence—body and spirit united together; this is what is called the second death. Why is it called the second death? Because the first is the dissolution of body and spirit, and the second is . . . a banishment—a becoming dead to the things of righteousness."[8]

Modern revelation teaches us that those who suffer "second death" are also known as "sons of perdition" (see D&C 76:31–38). The Book of Mormon describes these individuals as those who "deny the Holy Ghost when it once has had place in [them], and [they] know that [they] deny it" (Alma 39:6).

The salvationistic doctrine that "all men should have eternal life"

The Righteousness of the Redeemer 157

(Alma 1:4) regardless of their righteousness or wickedness, may bring both its teachers and its believers a sense of security, but their hope of eternal happiness will eventually turn to the reality of eternal misery if they are not able to come to a correct understanding of the necessity of personal accountability: "And in one year were thousands and tens of thousands of souls sent to the eternal world, that they might reap their rewards according to their works, whether they were good or whether they were bad, to reap eternal happiness or eternal misery, according to the spirit which they listed to obey, whether it be a good spirit or a bad one" (Alma 3:26).

INDIVIDUALISM

Another satanic deception that is closely linked to both the counterfeit philosophies of humanism and salvationism is the philosophy of individualism. Elder John A. Widtsoe taught that "man must not go through his earth-life independently, doing as he pleases, living apart from his fellowmen and accepting the Great Plan in his own way. . . . The Church is the community of those who, having accepted the Plan, desire unitedly to work out their mutual salvation under the settled authority of God."[9] Eternal life in the presence of God cannot be accomplished alone. Not only are we dependent upon Christ and his atoning sacrifice, we are also dependent upon one another.

As mentioned earlier, the Book of Mormon is a story about a covenant people—families, communities, and nations. There is no doubt in my mind that one of the reasons Lehi had his sons return to Jerusalem and bring Ishmael and his family to join their journey was because he understood that "in order to obtain [celestial glory], a man must enter into . . . marriage" (D&C 131:2). Lehi understood that a man cannot be saved without the woman nor can woman obtain eternal life without the man. While the doctrine of eternal family relationships is not explicitly outlined in the Book of Mormon, there is evidence that it was understood. Mormon writes: "And the day soon cometh that your mortal must put on immortality, and these bodies which are now moldering in corruption must soon become incorruptible bodies; and then ye must stand before the judgment-seat of Christ, to be judged according to your works; and if it so be that ye are righteous, then are ye blessed with your fathers who have gone before you" (Mormon 6:21).

There is also another sense in which the Book of Mormon teaches against an individualistic interpretation of salvation. We aren't simply individuals who have made covenants with God and our partners, we as a people are "the covenant people of the Lord" (2 Nephi 30:2) with the Abrahamic mandate to bless "all the kindreds of the earth" (1 Nephi 15:18). God has promised the house of Israel great blessings if we are true to the covenants we have made:

"Wherefore, the Lord God will proceed to make bare his arm in the eyes of all the nations, in bringing about his covenants and his gospel unto those who are of the house of Israel.

"Wherefore, he will bring them again out of captivity, and they shall be gathered together to the lands of their inheritance; and they shall be brought out of obscurity and out of darkness; and they shall know that the Lord is their Savior and their Redeemer, the Mighty One of Israel" (1 Nephi 22:11–12).

The Lord God of Israel has and will continue to be true to the promises he has made to his people. It now remains for us to be faithful to the covenants we have made with him. For it is by "having [our] hearts knit together in unity and in love one towards another" (Mosiah 18:21) that we are able to unitedly work out our salvation as individuals, families, nations, and a covenant people.

Conclusion

The prophet Nephi taught that "all nations, kindreds, tongues, and people shall dwell safely in the Holy One of Israel if it so be that they will repent" (1 Nephi 22:28). Nephi's statement underscores the doctrine that has been the thesis of this chapter—salvation is found in Christ if we come unto him through repentance. While the Book of Mormon clearly teaches that "it is by grace that we are saved, after all we can do" (2 Nephi 25:23), some have "wrested the scriptures" (Alma 41:1) and distort the relationship of the grace of Christ and what is expected of mankind in the process of salvation. With the exception of "little children" who die in infancy (Moroni 8:20) and others who are without the law (see 2 Nephi 9:25), good works are necessary but not sufficient to gain eternal life—for salvation is truly dependent upon the "righteousness of [the] Redeemer" (2 Nephi 2:3).

In describing the covenant he and his followers had made with the Lord and each other to repent of their past sins, the Lamanite king, Anti-Nephi-Lehi stated:

"And I also thank my God, yea, my great God, that he hath . . . taken away the guilt from our hearts, through the merits of his Son.

"And now behold, my brethren, since it has been *all that we could do* (as we were the most lost of all mankind) to repent of all our sins and the many murders which we have committed, and to get God to take them away from our hearts, *for it was all we could do to repent* sufficiently before God that he would take away our stain" (Alma 24:10–11; italics added).

While there are a myriad of interpretations of what Nephi meant when he stated "it is by grace that we are saved, after all we can do" (2 Nephi 25:23), perhaps these words by the Lamanite king can assist us in arriving at a correct interpretation. In each case when the phrase "all we could do" is mentioned, it is linked to the principle of repentance.

President Spencer W. Kimball taught that it is through repentance that we access the grace of Christ: "The principle of repentance—of rising again whenever we fall, brushing ourselves off, and setting off again on that upward trail—is the basis for our hope. It is through repentance that the Lord Jesus Christ can work his healing miracle, infusing us with strength when we are weak, health when we are sick, hope when we are downhearted, love when we feel empty, and understanding when we search for truth."[10]

In his sermon to the Saints of Zarahemla, the prophet Alma asked some penetrating questions concerning salvation. Among the forty crucial queries are the following:

"And now behold, I ask of you, my brethren of the church, have ye spiritually been born of God? Have ye received his image in your countenances? Have ye experienced this mighty change in your hearts?

"Do ye exercise faith in the redemption of him who created you?" (Alma 5:14–15).

Repentance is not simply a change of behavior, it is a change in our hearts made possible through the atonement of Jesus Christ. Faith in an alternative form of salvation may bring mankind "joy in their works for a season, [but] by and by the end cometh, and they are hewn down and cast into the fire, from whence there is no return" (3 Nephi 27:11). Prophets, both living and dead, have taught that the only permanent answer to the problems of our day and days to come is found in exercising faith in Christ.

President Howard W. Hunter once stated: "Please remember this one thing. If our lives and our faith are centered upon Jesus Christ and his restored gospel, nothing can ever go permanently wrong. On the other hand, if our lives are not centered on the Savior and his teachings, no other success can ever be permanently right."[11]

The prophet Moroni concluded that our salvation is found in Christ as we have faith in him and repent of our sins:

"Yea, come unto Christ, and be perfected in him, and deny yourselves of all ungodliness; and if ye shall deny yourselves of all ungodliness, and love God with all your might, mind and strength, then is his grace sufficient for you, that by his grace ye may be perfect in Christ; and if by the grace of God ye are perfect in Christ, ye can in nowise deny the power of God.

"And again, if ye by the grace of God are perfect in Christ, and deny not his power, then are ye sanctified in Christ by the grace of God, through the shedding of the blood of Christ, which is in the covenant of the Father unto the remission of your sins, that ye become holy, without spot" (Moroni 10:32–33).

Notes

1. Joseph F. Smith, *Gospel Doctrine,* 5th ed. (Salt Lake City: Deseret Book, 1939), 2.

2. Bruce C. Hafen, *The Broken Heart* (Salt Lake City: Deseret Book, 1989), 2.

3. Charles W. Dunn, ed., *American Political Theology: Historical Perspective and Theoretical Analysis* (New York: Praeger, 1984), 114, 116–17.

4. Dallin H. Oaks, Conference Report, Oct. 1988, 77; or *Ensign,* Nov. 1988, 67.

5. C. S. Lewis, *Mere Christianity* (New York: Macmillan, 1960), 160.

6. For a more complete treatment of the need for an atonement, see Robert J. Matthews, *A Bible! A Bible!* (Salt Lake City: Bookcraft, 1990), 191.

7. Joseph Fielding Smith, *Doctrines of Salvation,* comp. Bruce R. McConkie, 3 vols. (Salt Lake City: Bookcraft, 1954–56), 2:9; see also D&C 19:10–12.

8. Orson Pratt, *Journal of Discourses*, 1:288.

9. John A. Widtsoe, *A Rational Theology* (Salt Lake City: Deseret Book, 1937), 90.

10. Spencer W. Kimball, *The Teachings of Spencer W. Kimball*, ed. Edward L. Kimball (Salt Lake City: Bookcraft, 1982), 106.

11. Howard W. Hunter, "'Fear Not, Little Flock,'" in *BYU 1988–89 Devotional and Fireside Speeches* (1989), 112.

CHAPTER THIRTEEN

SICKLE OR SWORD? CONVERSION VERSUS COMPULSION IN THE BOOK OF ALMA

MICHAEL L. KING

From the time of our premortal existence, a war has been waged as to whether man should be compelled to obey or whether he should be taught correct principles and then be allowed to choose for himself. In the premortal existence, Satan sought power to compel the human family to do his will by suggesting that the agency of man be inoperative. President David O. McKay commented that had Satan's plan of force been accepted, "human beings would have become mere puppets in the hands of a dictator."[1]

Man's freedom and agency were maintained and vindicated by the war in heaven, and man became free to choose his course through the eternities. Yet the war continues here on earth. Societies, families, and individuals are all affected by this conflict. In governments as well as homes, the battle between compulsion and conversion rages in the hearts of God's children (2 Nephi 28:20). This battle can be vividly seen in the pages of the Book of Mormon, particularly in the book of Alma.

Many Saints have wondered why the Lord inspired Mormon to include so many pages regarding war in a book that is supposed to bring men to Christ, the author and Prince of Peace (see 2 Nephi

---

Michael L. King is an instructor of religion in the Idaho East Area of the Church Educational System.

19:6). Much of the book of Alma reads more like a manual for war than a spiritual record. Yet nowhere in scripture is the battle between conversion and compulsion more vividly described than in Alma. It is not mere coincidence that of the thirty-four times the words *force, compel,* or *compelled* appear in the Book of Mormon, thirty of those are in the book of Alma, where war and bloodshed occupy many of its pages. Through its pages, the Lord teaches us the critical lesson that forced compliance is not sufficient to bring about a lasting change and a godly character. In the midst of the great wars, we see the result of those who are compelled by force to comply, contrasted with examples of those who are truly converted to righteousness through the power of the word.

THE POWER OF THE SWORD

One of the most colorful examples of this forced compliance is found in Alma 44. Zerahemnah was brought to obedience at the point of a sword by Captain Moroni. Reluctantly, Zerahemnah "came forth and delivered up his sword and his cimeter, and his bow into the hands of Moroni" (Alma 44:8), but he refused to make an oath to not return against the Nephites in war. Though he had been compelled at the point of the sword to throw down his weapons, no change had taken place in his heart regarding his feelings about the Nephites and their God. Moroni returned his sword and stated that they "would end the conflict" (Alma 44:10). The battle resumed and Moroni's forces were successful in defeating the Lamanites, to the point that Zerahemnah eventually entered into a covenant of peace with the Nephites.

But the conflict did not end with that battle. Less than two years later, the Lamanites once again came out to subject the Nephites to bondage. Led this time by Amalickiah, who had become king of the Lamanites by treachery, murder, and deceit, the Lamanites returned to wage war against the Nephites (see Alma 48:1–8). The earlier Nephite victory with the sword had proven to have a very short-term effect in maintaining peace in their land. Though the Nephites were reluctant to fight, and their cause was truly just, their righteous motives did not change the fact that victory by force had not changed the hearts of the Lamanites.

Five years later, in the twenty-fifth year of the reign of the judges, the Nephites were preparing for another attack from the Lamanites. Conflict arose within the Nephite kingdom between the kingmen and the freemen. Captain Moroni, knowing of the Lamanites' preparations for war and the need for unity among the Nephites, petitioned the governor of the land for power to *compel* those dissenters to defend their country or to be put to death (see Alma 5:15). Thus, the dissenters were either killed or "compelled to hoist the title of liberty" (Alma 51:20). Forcing the kingmen to comply would have serious ramifications to the Nephite nation in later battles.

The wars between Amalickiah and Captain Moroni continued for several years. Following numerous battles and much bloodshed, Teancum, a faithful Nephite captain, tried to put an end to the conflict by killing Amalickiah (see Alma 51:33–37). Though he had killed the torchbearer, the flame of hatred continued to burn in the hearts of the Lamanites. All of the war, bloodshed, defeat, and death had not changed their hearts, nor had it softened the hearts of the kingmen who now waged their own war deep in the center of the Nephite kingdom. While they had complied with the law when compelled by Moroni, they turned and fought against their own people when the threat of their own destruction appeared to have been removed. Then, with the Lamanites keeping the main armies of the Nephites occupied, they proceeded to take control of the city of Zarahemla (see Alma 61:2–8). Eventually they were defeated by Moroni and were forced once again to comply with the rule of law and to fight for freedom (see Alma 62:1–11).

In each of the above instances, force and compulsion seem to have been the only methods available to the Nephites in defending their people. They did not glory in the use of the sword, but were compelled to do so by those who were in opposition to their freedom. Captain Moroni epitomizes this attitude regarding the use of force and compulsion when he cried to Zerahemnah:

"We do not desire to be men of blood. Ye know that ye are in our hands, yet we do not desire to slay you.

"Behold, we have not come out to battle against you that we might shed your blood for power; neither do we desire to bring anyone to the yoke of bondage. But this is the very cause for which ye have come against us" (Alma 44:1–2).

Later in the book of Alma, Mormon describes Moroni as "a man of perfect understanding; yea, a man that did not delight in bloodshed; a man whose soul did joy in the liberty and the freedom of his country, and his brethren from bondage and slavery" (Alma 48:11).

Captain Moroni did not desire to use force and compulsion to bring about compliance, yet he himself was compelled to defend his people. While ineffective in changing the hearts of their enemies, the use of force by the Nephites did prove effective to deter the aggression and disobedience of their foes for a short period of time. Ironically, the only way the Nephites had to maintain their freedom was to use force and compulsion upon their enemies and dissenters. President David O. McKay stated that "force . . . emanates from Lucifer," but also admitted that "force rules in the world today; consequently, . . . government must keep armies . . . to protect itself from threatened aggression of a nation which seems to listen to no other appeal but compulsion."[2]

While there may be times when force and compulsion are the only recourse for a society to maintain its freedoms, no enduring society of peace can be established upon the principle of force.

Ernest L. Wilkinson, a former president of BYU, stated: "No great society can ever be created by political action; . . . it must be founded upon religious premises and conviction. The one emanates from the power and compulsion of Caesar; the other is premised on the love and voluntary action of Christ."[3]

Though the Nephites were compelled to defend their freedom by force, it becomes evident from the Alma account that force is not effective in bringing about lasting change and a society of peace. In his epistle to Captain Moroni, Pahoran, the chief judge, offers an appropriate pattern for bringing people to obedience: "Therefore my beloved brother, Moroni, let us resist evil, and whatsoever evil we cannot resist with our words, yea such as rebellions and dissensions, let us resist them with our swords, that we may retain our freedom, that we may rejoice in the great privilege of our church, and in the cause of our Redeemer and our God" (Alma 61:14).

THE POWER OF THE WORD

Pahoran understands that the first line of defense for preserving freedom and bringing about obedience is through the word of God. Just as the Lord uses the book of Alma to show the ineffectiveness of compulsion as a method of bringing about long-term change, he uses the same book to show the lasting effect that is wrought by the power of his word.

Alma the Younger knew and understood the power of the word in bringing about a change in people when he went to teach the apostate Zoramites. Fearing that the Zoramites would "enter into a correspondence with the Lamanites, and that it would be the means of great loss on the part of the Nephites," Alma thought "it was expedient that they should try the virtue of the word of God," as the "preaching of the word had a great tendency to lead the people to do that which was just—yea, it had had more powerful effect upon the minds of the people than the sword or anything else" (Alma 31:4–5). Rather than turn to the sword to force the Zoramites into compliance, Alma understood that a more permanent and inward change could be brought about through the teaching of the gospel. Those Zoramites who listened to the word were converted and remained faithful to the cause of freedom, while those who refused to listen were eventually destroyed when the Lamanites invaded their land. Without the change of heart, the people perished by the sword.

Not only had Alma experienced this kind of change of heart within himself by coming to a knowledge of Christ, but he also witnessed how the message of the Redeemer had changed the lives of his friends, the sons of Mosiah. These four men experienced such a change that "they could not bear that any human soul should perish" (Mosiah 28:3). They were so convinced by the power of the word that Mosiah's sons chose to go and teach the Lamanites, who were described as "a wild and a hardened and a ferocious people; a people who delighted in murdering the Nephites, and robbing and plundering them; and their hearts were set upon riches, or upon gold and silver, and precious stones; yet they sought to obtain these things by murdering and plundering, that they might not labor for them with their own hands" (Alma 17:14).

Even these wild and ferocious people were "brought to behold the marvelous light of God" through the teaching of the word (Alma 26:3). When Ammon, the senior of the sons of Mosiah, taught King Lamoni and his people, "as many as heard his words believed, and were converted unto the Lord. . . . Their hearts had been changed; that they had no more desire to do evil" (Alma 19:31, 33).

This same change was also experienced by the father of King Lamoni when he was taught by Aaron about the plan of redemption and the coming of the Messiah. Following his conversion, the king of the Lamanites sent a proclamation throughout all the land that the Lamanites were to allow Ammon, Aaron, and their brethren free access to their houses, temples, and sanctuaries, that "they might go forth and preach the word according to their desires," that the preaching of the word might convince the people "concerning the wicked traditions of their fathers, and that they might be convinced that they were all brethren" (Alma 23:1–3).

As a result of the teachings of the sons of Mosiah, "thousands were brought to the knowledge of the Lord," and "they became a righteous people; they did lay down the weapons of their rebellion, that they did not fight against God any more, neither against any of their brethren" (Alma 23:5, 7). As a symbol of their permanent change, these people changed their names to Anti-Nephi-Lehies (see Alma 23:17–18). They were no longer Lamanites, following the traditions of rebellion passed down from Laman, but people of God, following in the ways of Nephi and Lehi. They had not been compelled by the sword, but had been taught by the word of God, which had wrought a change in their very nature. In another powerful symbolic gesture, they took all their weapons of war and buried them in the earth (see Alma 24:17).

The word had indeed had power over the sword in bringing a people to peace, and the change was not just temporary. Even when threatened with death, these people would not return to their old pattern of war, hatred, and disobedience to God's commandments. Many, in fact, gave their lives to seal their testimonies that they had changed, and "praised God even in the very act of perishing under the sword" (Alma 24:23). The powerful spirit of their sacrifice brought a mighty change to those who had wielded the sword of destruction upon them. "The people of God were joined that day by more than the number who had been slain" (Alma 24:26). No greater evidence could be given that the word has power over the sword.

Further evidence of the permanent nature of the change brought to these Lamanites comes to light some twenty years later when they still chose not to take up arms against the enemy. Around the year 64 B.C., Helaman, in an epistle to Moroni, says that he has "somewhat to say concerning the people of Ammon, who, in the beginning, were Lamanites; but . . . by the power and word of God, they had been converted unto the Lord" (Alma 53:10). Helaman states that these people were moved to compassion because they were not helping the Nephites in their war with the Lamanites. Some were desirous to take up their swords to help their brethren due to the gravity of the conflict, yet because of their oath, they maintained their covenant to never return to their old ways of war.

The Lamanite conversion had lasted a lifetime, and they had instilled it into the hearts of their children. The Lamanite youth demonstrated the power of the teachings of their parents when they "did think more upon the liberty of their fathers than they did upon their lives; yea, they had been taught by their mothers, that if they did not doubt, God would deliver them" (Alma 56:47). They now took up arms to fight in behalf of the Nephites and the cause of freedom. They had been taught by their parents to have faith in God, and to fight for his just cause. The converting power of the word had stretched down into a second generation.

While the torch of hatred seems to be passed on naturally from generation to generation by those who have been compelled to obey, the light of the gospel must be rekindled within the heart of each individual of the coming generation. Once converted, parents must teach and pass on the legacy of faith and truth to their children. Future generations of converted Lamanites learned the lesson of the power of the word even better than most of the Nephites. Several years after the battles contained in the book of Alma had ended, the Gadianton robbers came among both the Lamanites and the Nephites. It was the Lamanites who "did hunt the band of robbers of Gadianton; and they did preach the word of God among the more wicked part of them, insomuch that this band of robbers was utterly destroyed from among the Lamanites" (Helaman 6:37).

The Lamanites had learned that the word of God is more powerful than the sword in bringing about a change to the individual hearts of men, which in turn helps to shape a society. Samuel the Lamanite confirmed that "as many of [the Lamanites] as are brought to the knowledge of the truth, . . . and are led to believe the holy scriptures, . . . are firm and steadfast in the faith, and in the thing wherewith they have been made free" (Helaman 15:7–8).

A Lesson for Our Day

We have been told by modern prophets that the Book of Mormon was written for our day. In a world where force and compulsion are used on every side to bring about compliance and obedience, the lesson of the book of Alma should serve to teach us a better way. The wars of the book of Alma clearly show the ineffectiveness of force as a means of bringing about a change to an individual's heart so they can progress to be as God. The book of Alma also illustrates how the converted soul experiences a lifelong change by recording some of the greatest conversion stories found in scripture. The Lord includes both concepts within the same setting to teach us by contrast the way to bring about change within an individual and within a society.

As the Book of Mormon continues on from Alma, the Lord shows us that the power of the word can convert entire civilizations. Following the visit of the Savior, the people "taught, and did minister one to another; and they had all things common among them" until "the people were all converted unto the Lord, upon all the face of the land." There was "no contention," and there "could not be a happier people among all the people who had been created by the hand of God" (see 3 Nephi 26:19; 4 Nephi 1:2, 15–16).

Modern prophets confirm the idea that force and compulsion will not produce a godly person or a godly society. The only way to bring about an enduring change of behavior in either the society or the individual is through conversion to righteous principles through the teaching of the word of God. President David O. McKay stated, "Force and compulsion will never establish the ideal society. This can come only by a transformation within the individual soul—a life redeemed from sin and brought in harmony with the divine will."[4] The conversion of the soul to righteous principles is the key to bringing about obedience. Only as an individual understands and believes in divine truths will he use his agency to choose to be obedient without compulsion or force.

The Battle in Our Homes

The challenge that faces all parents is to apply these principles in the home. The battle in the home is fought on two levels. First, the parents themselves must be converted to the Lord so that their obedience to him is motivated out of love for the Lord and the principles he taught. Second, they must teach these principles to their children so that they too become converted to doing what is right without being forced or compelled. If the parents themselves are to be converted, they must apply the power of the word in their own lives by coming to know the doctrine for themselves. Just as the converted Lamanites, parents must also listen to God's chosen servants as they teach the doctrines of the gospel by the power of the Spirit. We learn from Alma, Ammon, and Aaron that we must learn, understand, and be converted to the basic doctrines of the gospel: the existence of God, the Creation, the Fall, the Atonement, and the saving ordinances of the gospel (see Alma 18:22–40; 22:7–18; 33:12–23).

Once converted to these principles, parents must teach them in the home to insure that the lamp of truth will light the path for the rising generation. In the Book of Mormon, it is the rising generation who strays from the inspired teachings of King Benjamin, which had been the major cause of the conversion and faithfulness of an entire generation (see Mosiah 26:1). Later, after the powerful conversions of the Lamanites in Alma's record, it is the rising generation of Lamanite youth who "became for themselves" and "began to decrease as to their faith and righteousness" (3 Nephi 1:29–30).

In our modern day, President Boyd K. Packer expressed concern that young people are growing up "without values on which to base their conduct." He continued, "I have long believed that the study of the doctrines of the gospel will improve behavior quicker than talking about behavior will improve behavior." According to President Packer, the primary doctrine of the gospel that the youth need to learn is that the influence of the atonement of Christ is "individual, very personal, and very useful." He comments that even the beginner must learn that "an understanding of the Atonement is of immediate and very practical value in everyday life."[5]

What youth need, to become more obedient to parents and to gospel principles, is not necessarily more discipline, but more discipleship to Christ. The Savior himself was the perfect example of obedience to his Father. Without compulsion or force, he willingly submitted to the will of the Father. When faced with the agony of the garden and the cross, the will of the Son was swallowed up in the will of the Father (see Mosiah 15:7). He chose not his own will, but that of the Father. No one could have forced him to perform such a task, and no one could have taken his life from him. All this he had to do willingly. He alone had power to give his life. As he told the Nephites, "I have laid down my life, and have taken it up again" (3 Nephi 9:22).

Christ emulated perfectly the words of his servant King Benjamin when he told us that we must be "willing to submit to all things which the Lord seeth fit to inflict upon [us], even as a child doth submit to his father" (Mosiah 3:19).

In order to motivate both our youth and ourselves to willingly do that which is good and be obedient, we must learn from the Savior by studying and applying his divine truths. Truly we must become, and must help our youth to become, more obedient as a result of a higher vision of our relationship to God. The Book of Mormon is the divine record of these higher truths that will bring us closer to God than any other book (see Book of Mormon introduction). Elder Boyd K. Packer once observed:

"Latter-day Saints are not obedient because they are compelled to be obedient. They are obedient because they know certain spiritual truths and have decided, as an expression of their own individual agency, to obey the commandments of God. . . .

" . . . There is an obedience that comes from a knowledge of the truth that transcends any external form of control. We are not obedient because we are blind, we are obedient because we can see."[6]

Conclusion

The book of Alma allows us to see through contrasting examples of compulsion and conversion that the word of God is more effective than the sword in bringing about the kind of change that leads to the development of a godly character. Through the power of the word of God, we are able to see and understand divine truth that allows us to be obedient, not out of compulsion or external control, but out of a love for our Heavenly Father and our fellowman. It is obedience born of love that is the fruit of the converted soul. The Nephites enjoyed a blessed and happy society because of the "love of God which did dwell in the hearts of the people" (4 Nephi 1:15). This is the kind of obedience that Elder Packer said "transcends any external form of control" and "comes from a knowledge of the truth."[7]

For this reason, Moroni taught in the closing chapters of the Book of Mormon that we should "pray unto the Father with all the energy of heart, that ye may be filled with this love" (Moroni 7:48). When we love God, we willingly perform all that he asks us to do. The Lord desires that we obey him because we love him; and because he loves us, he has made us free to choose. He will not force our obedience. As taught in the inspiring words of one of our hymns:

> Know this, that ev'ry soul is free
> To choose his life and what he'll be;
> For this eternal truth is giv'n:
> That God will force no man to heav'n.
> He'll call, persuade, direct aright,
> And bless with wisdom, love, and light,
> In nameless ways be good and kind,
> But never force the human mind.[8]

The Book of Mormon clearly demonstrates the power of teaching correct principles to inspire obedience born of love. The book of Alma in particular teaches us again and again to use the word of God as a means to foster obedience. Whether in dealing with a society as a whole, as Alma did in the case of the erring Nephites and Zoramites (see Alma 4:19; 31:1–5), or in dealing with a wayward son, as in the case of Corianton (see Alma 39–42), Alma continually relied on the converting power of the word of God to change the hearts of the people so that they would seek the mighty change through the power of Christ. It is the Book of Mormon that will bring us closer to God so that we will, out of our own agency and love, obey him and return home to be as he is.

"And now, as the preaching of the word had a great tendency to lead the people to do that which was just—yea it had had more powerful effect upon the minds of the people than the sword, or anything else, which had happened unto them—therefore Alma thought it was expedient that they should try the virtue of the word of God" (Alma 31:5).

Notes

1. David O. McKay, Conference Report, Apr. 1950, 34.
2. Ibid., 34–35.
3. Ernest L. Wilkinson, introduction to Marion G. Romney, *Socialism*

and the United Order Compared, Brigham Young University Speeches of the Year (1 Mar. 1966), 1.

4. McKay, Conference Report, Oct. 1962, 8.

5. Boyd K. Packer, Conference Report, Apr. 1997, 8; or *Ensign,* May 1997, 9.

6. Boyd K. Packer, Conference Report, Apr. 1983, 89–90; or *Ensign,* May 1983, 66.

7. Ibid., 90; or 66.

8. Anonymous, "Know This, That Every Soul Is Free," *Hymns* (Salt Lake City: The Church of Jesus Christ of Latter-day Saints, 1985), no. 240.

CHAPTER FOURTEEN

Conflict in the Book of Mormon: Types and Shadows of Spiritual Battle Today

John P. Livingstone

From the first page to the last, death, destruction, challenges, wars, battles, contentions, and adversity abound in the Book of Mormon. Some people have wondered[1] at the seeming abundance and graphic portrayal of violence and terror in the record. Themes of bondage[2] and deliverance[3] are woven throughout the narrative. Striking word-picture phrases, such as "chains of hell" and "chains of death," allude to principles arising from spiritual conflict. Many articles dealing with Book of Mormon warfare describe military tactics that confirm the internal consistency of an ancient record. Others focus on the morality of conflict and the implications for Latter-day Saint military personnel and general membership.[4] Can individuals and families deal better with conflict by learning from these stories of warfare, battle, intrigue, and strategy? Are there underlying purposes for the preservation of these accounts? Is it possible that answers for today's spiritually perplexing problems and convolutions are quietly embedded or encoded in the Book of Mormon?

Moroni said: "Behold, the Lord hath shown unto me great and marvelous things concerning that which must shortly come, at that

---

John P. Livingstone is an associate professor of Church history and doctrine at Brigham Young University.

day when these things [the Book of Mormon] shall come forth among you.

"Behold, I speak unto you as if ye were present, and yet ye are not. But behold, Jesus Christ hath shown you unto me, and I know your doing" (Mormon 8:34-35).

It seems clear that the Book of Mormon compilation was geared for modern times and is applicable to our spiritual needs.

Today the forces of evil do not necessarily come in the form of enemy soldiers bent on physical death and destruction. They usually appear as subtle or direct influences set to offer temptation of all kinds, like a great tantalizing smorgasbord of sin, with the dreadful consequences tastefully hidden from immediate view. Perhaps everyone has a weakness that requires vigilance in order to keep it under control within the bounds of righteous living (see Ether 12:27). Turning to the Book of Mormon in the "battle" to overcome these weaknesses and temptations may bring important insights for Latter-day Saints. This chapter proposes that Book of Mormon strategies, defenses, fortifications, and other reactions to conflict represent principles and practices that can bolster individuals, families, and communities under spiritual siege.

Symbolism of "Chains of Hell" and "Chains of Death"

Such common Book of Mormon phrases as "chains of hell," and "chains of death" can typify addictions, abuses, and other evils permeating contemporary society. Today's news reports highlight a world where evil runs rampant, with desperate people bent on desperate courses. We can learn from similar circumstances in the Book of Mormon.

Lehi worried about his two oldest sons and their rebellious, self-centered attitudes. They became cankered, violent, and even homicidal (see 1 Nephi 7:16-17; 17:48). Lehi rebuked his sons with sharpness: "O that ye would awake; awake from a deep sleep, yea, even from the sleep of hell, and shake off the awful chains by which ye are bound, which are the chains which bind the children of men, that they are carried away captive down to the eternal gulf of misery and woe" (2 Nephi 1:13).

The "sleep" alluded to seems to denote an inattentive, careless, or detached cognizance of danger. He calls it a deep sleep, which further projects the image of a groggy negligence—a blasé recklessness that has fallen upon his older sons. In his mind, Laman and Lemuel were clearly unaware of impending perils, and perhaps blind to their diminishing ability to extract themselves from looming spiritual doom.

As their father, Lehi was troubled with this sleepy stupor that captivated them. He seemed to see his sons as spiritually "drugged." Yet, his warnings were clear and consistent, lovingly and longingly delivered. He tried to reach them "with all the feeling of a tender parent, that they would hearken to his words, that perhaps the Lord would be merciful to them, and not cast them off" (1 Nephi 8:37).

Lehi used, for the first time in the Book of Mormon, the powerful metaphor of "chains" that bind and captivate—those subsequently conveyed into spiritual bondage. Chains here suggest imprisonment or confinement against one's volition. Lehi clearly saw his sons as constrained or restricted in some way. His admonition to "shake off" those chains suggests an inherent ability or power to rid themselves of those compulsions to a certain point, beyond which spiritual captivation would be inevitable (see 2 Nephi 1:13).

Later, Alma gave a scriptural definition of these chains (referred to thirteen separate times in the Book of Mormon—2 Nephi 1:13, 23; 9:45; 28:19, 22; Alma 5:7, 9–10; 12:6, 11; 13:30; 26:14; 36:18): "And they that will harden their hearts, to them is given the lesser portion of the word until they know nothing concerning his mysteries; and then they are taken captive by the devil, and led by his will down to destruction. Now this is what is meant by the chains of hell" (Alma 12:11).

The imagery of being leashed and dragged or compelled by Satan is powerful. No one appreciates even mild pushiness or prodding by someone with ulterior motives, obvious or subtle, much less by the adversary, Satan, who is interested only in promoting human misery (see 2 Nephi 2:27). President Joseph Fielding Smith referred to modern issues relative to these "chains of hell":

"He has made the promise that if the inhabitants of this land, choice above all other lands, would humble themselves and give heed to his commandments, he would fortify this land and give us divine protection.

"Unfortunately the people of this land have not been willing to do this thing. They have turned from righteous ways and the keeping of their bodies clean to ways of evil. Immorality rages, drunkenness prevails from sea to sea, the filthiness of tobacco has debased both men and women, and the stench thereof has ascended to high heaven. *By the practice of these evils humanity is binding itself by the chains of hell.*"[5]

Violations of the Word of Wisdom are by no means the only addictive sins. While the ravages of alcohol and drug abuse have touched many families, small and great, rich and poor, educated and uninformed, considerable new knowledge is being discovered about such topics as anger, food addiction, sexual addiction, Internet addiction, and a host of other habitual disorders.[6] Acting to end the inuring causes and effects of certain substances, events, and procedures that control thoughts, words, and actions is critical to avoiding temporal and eternal misery. Alma explained clearly that Satan can ultimately achieve full control over people (see Alma 12:6, 11, 17), which was his obsession even from before the foundations of the world (see Moses 4:1–4).

Elder Bruce R. McConkie further outlined the cumulative effect of being baited and hooked by the tempting wiles of the evil one. He also mentions a possible escape: "When persons are thus finally bound, there is no longer hope of reprieve; they suffer the second death and are 'chained down to an everlasting destruction' (Alma 12:17), 'from whence there is no deliverance.' (2 Ne. 28:19, 22.) But as these chains begin to encircle the mind, closing out light and truth degree by degree, there is still the chance of escape through repentance and righteousness. (2 Ne. 1:13, 23; 9:45; Alma 5:7, 9; 13:30; 26:14.)"[7]

Joseph Smith made a similar point when he said, "All beings who have bodies have power over those who have not. The devil has no power over us only as we permit him. The moment we revolt at anything which comes from God, the devil takes power."[8]

Spiritual Bondage

One of the overriding themes of the Book of Mormon is that of bondage, both physical and spiritual. In 1 Nephi, Nephi was bound and threatened by his brothers. His miraculous escape from their tormenting (see 1 Nephi 7:17–18) sets the stage for a series of events throughout the narrative, showing how enduring faithfulness consistently overthrows bondage, threat, and trouble. We can see a contemporary spiritual corollary in all of this. The parallels are striking as modern society tries to cope with an onslaught of temptation affecting youth and adults alike. We have all witnessed someone close to us become enslaved to their own cravings and hungers, seeking pleasure or imagined liberation in that which only enslaves them and brings misery. Invariably they only succeed in becoming physiologically or psychologically addicted and potentially "sealed up" (Alma 34:35) spiritually unto a miserable, compulsive existence.

Many parents have struggled to help their addicted or near-addicted children "shake off" the powerful effects of substances and behaviors that "chain" them to unhappy, miserable circumstances that the youths themselves may have trouble sensing. In other cases the situation is reversed, where children realize the foreboding peril of a parent who is drinking or drugging himself or herself into alienation from family members. Addiction-associated behaviors by the troubled father or mother thrust children into embarrassing and abusive conditions from which both parent and child manufacture compensating evasive maneuvers, attempting to cover and conceal deteriorating home conditions from the outside world, and especially from those whose acceptance they seek or need. What can be done to help? The admonition of King Limhi is as applicable now as in Book of Mormon times: "But if ye will turn to the Lord with full purpose of heart, and put your trust in him, and serve him with all diligence of mind, if ye do this, he will, according to his own will and pleasure, deliver you out of bondage" (Mosiah 7:33).

Many scholars have noted the sacred purposes ascribed to ancient warfare.[9] The Book of Mormon justified warfare on principles of right versus wrong and on moral defense. The help of the Lord was usually sought prior to (see Mosiah 9:17; 10:10; Alma 2:28; 43:23; 46:13, 16–17; 58:10; 3 Nephi 3:20, 25; 4:8) and during battle (see Alma 2:30; 16:5; 24:21; 43:49), with gratitude generally expressed following successful campaigns (see Alma 28:6; 45:1; 49:28; 62:51; 3 Nephi 4:30–32). Readers today can see the importance of prayer and reliance on the Lord for Book of Mormon writers and leaders.

Nephi admonished his brothers, "O, my beloved brethren, turn away from your sins; shake off the chains of him that would bind you fast; come unto that God who is the rock of your salvation" (2 Nephi 9:45). The most effective way to "shake off the chains" or effects of addiction is to "come unto" the Lord. This can happen through a pointed and diligent study of the Book of Mormon's portrayals of physical or spiritual captivity and escape. Following are several examples.

RELIANCE ON THE LORD

At the outset of the Book of Mormon, Nephi and his brothers came face to face with evil incarnate as they tried to obtain the brass plates from the wicked Laban. Their efforts to obtain the plates were evolutionary. First was the initial, direct request by Laman for the desired plates (see 1 Nephi 3:11–14). There appeared to be little preparation prior to the bold inquiry. In retrospect, it is little wonder the plates were not surrendered upon simple request. Laban's accusation that Laman was a robber worthy of death caused Laman to flee and the brothers were forced to consider another suggestion made by Nephi (see 1 Nephi 3:16, 22–26). He proposed an appeal to trade valuables for the plates. Laban was affected by their offer, but soon hailed his servants to chase off the young men and retain the goods anyway. Laman and Lemuel's ensuing assault on Nephi, curbed by an angel, confirmed the difficulty and importance of their divinely appointed mission.

Nephi, of course, was fully committed, having himself sworn with an oath to fulfill the will of the Lord (undoubtedly to his older brothers' dismay) in obtaining the plates (see 1 Nephi 3:15). With determination he risked his life by returning to the city at night for that purpose. His great faith qualified him to receive spiritual promptings and impressions in accomplishing the God-given goal (see 1 Nephi 4:6). Readers become riveted as spiritually driven Nephi creeps into the darkened city to find a drunken Laban fallen to the ground. Nephi was prompted to kill the man, dress in his clothes, and feign his way into having Zoram retrieve the plates and carry them outside the city walls. These events certainly attest to the innovative and ingenious ways the Spirit of the Lord can assist the truly faithful in solving near-insurmountable problems. The importance of relying ultimately on the Lord, while otherwise doing all that can be done to solve problems, is clear. This lesson is repeated throughout the Book of Mormon.[10]

Direct Leader Involvement

Many great leaders in the Book of Mormon personally led their people into battle. Kings Mosiah and Zeniff, as well as such leaders as Moroni, Helaman, and Mormon, fought at the head of their people (see Words of Mormon 1:13; Mosiah 9:16–17; Alma 52:35; 56:9; Mormon 6:11–12). Alma led out in mortal hand-to-hand combat with Amlici (see Alma 2:29–31). Such direct personal involvement of leaders portrayed an exemplary, participatory leadership, as opposed to an aloof conducting of battle by back-room strategists. The inference is that important battles often require the presence and direct involvement of leaders. The profound trust, confidence, and love that developed between Helaman and his stripling warriors seems to confirm the value of being directly and personally involved with youth (see Alma 53, 56–57).

Parents, too, can note the example of being "on site" and involved in their children's activities, particularly when spiritual battles may be waged. Parents attending dances, parties, and other events as chaperones or leaders, clearly involved and appropriately interacting with youth, send a caring, committed message to their own children as well as others. After all, Mormon editorialized that the Nephite motivation to war was primarily for the benefit of the family (see Alma 43:9).

Councils

Counsel and strategy form an important element of Book of Mormon warfare. When difficult circumstances presented themselves, and especially when conditions seemed to stymie leaders, they would often gather to consult: "And in the commencement of the twenty and eighth year, Moroni and Teancum and many of the chief captains held a council of war—what they should do to cause the Lamanites to come out against them to battle; or that they might by some means flatter them out of their strongholds, that they might gain advantage over them and take again the city of Mulek" (Alma 52:19; see also 24:5).

Whether as parents or as leaders, wrestling with difficult decisions and circumstances by counseling with priesthood leaders or participating in family and other councils as exemplified in the Book of Mormon seems a worthy means of pooling wisdom and obtaining insight and help from God (see Alma 37:37; see also 2 Nephi 9:28; 15:19; 27:27; 28:30; Jacob 4:10; Alma 29:8; 37:12; 37:37). Resulting strategy and action usually enjoy the support of more than just one person's opinion and inspiration. A wonderful side effect is also portrayed in the Book of Mormon: "And Moroni went to the city of Mulek with Lehi, and took command of the city and gave it unto Lehi. Now behold, this Lehi was a man who had been with Moroni in the more part of all his battles; and he was a man like unto Moroni, and they rejoiced in each other's safety; yea, they were beloved by each other, and also beloved by all the people of Nephi" (Alma 53:2).

Individuals working together on common problems or crises seem to develop a great bonding of love and respect for each other as well as for those for whom they labor. A husband and wife, or an entire family, may feel greater warmth and love for each other, as illustrated by Moroni and Lehi, when they work in council together to solve significant problems.

BURYING TEMPTATION

Another type and pattern is seen in instances of abject surrender. The capitulation of self-will to the will of God or his servants, and the consequences of such a surrender, are found in the Book of Mormon. Perhaps a well-known example is that of the Lamanites under Ammon who took upon themselves the name of Anti-Nephi-Lehi (see Alma 23:17). They considered themselves possibly guilty of murder and made a sacred oath to shed blood no more (see Alma 24:6–18). They sealed their promise symbolically and ritually by burying their weapons of war, thus putting the armaments beyond ready reach should they be tempted under duress to kill again. Later, many kept the oath but lost their lives when they were attacked by angry fellow Lamanites.

Their willingness to keep their commitment at all costs, and the burying of the swords and weapons, becomes a type for contemporary souls seeking to overcome serious, repetitive sin. "Burying" that which tempts points to the usefulness of somehow separating one's self from that which can trigger a return to former vices. The young man who determines to avoid walking down the magazine aisle in stores and shops is trying to "bury" the temptation to view even the covers of lewd publications. Avoiding former friends and associates who were cohorts in sin would fall into the same category.

The traveler who conscientiously decides to keep the hotel television off also "cuts off at the pass" his temptation to prurient viewing. Likewise, the man who decides to stop watching late-night television alone may be "burying" the habit of seeking the titillation of sleazy entertainment by ensuring that by staying in the presence of other family members, he will not be lured into watching that which inappropriately attracts him. And, as with the Anti-Nephi-Lehis, one can expect to encounter further testing of new resolves. Their willingness to lay down life itself rather than break their commitment serves as an example to all.

PRIORITIES

Another precedent may be observed from the great Captain Moroni. In his development of defenses for the Nephites, he first sought to protect his soldiers personally with breastplates, arm shields, headgear, and thick clothing (see Alma 43:19). Moroni later progressed to defending towns and cities by the construction of defensive battlements that served to protect larger groups of people (see Alma 48:8). Simultaneously, he also placed larger numbers of soldiers in the weaker positions. He finally succeeded in fortifying the entire nation by establishing a defensive line between his nation and the enemy (see Alma 50:11–13).

This progressive defensive action suggests a pattern of primary concern with individuals first, followed by efforts with groups, communities, and, finally, entire nations. Ranking our spiritual defensive efforts to meet challenges as Captain Moroni did helps to clarify the order in which we might place our priorities. Fortifying family members in the home (which is perhaps where spiritual strengthening is most easily and economically accomplished) comes first. Personal and family efforts cannot be replaced effectively by social services (family home evening takes precedence over church or community service). Building stronger church units and neighborhoods seems an essential prelude to strengthening and fortifying the nation.

Deliverance through Patience and Submission to God

When one has sinned to the point where he or she feels helpless in the face of a particular temptation, insight and solace and strength may come from reviewing the accounts of escape or deliverance from bondage found in the Book of Mormon. Consider the dilemma of Limhi and his followers. The immoral behavior of King Noah had created serious problems for them. The abduction of the Lamanite daughters by Noah's former "cabinet" of fugitive priests compounded the problem by providing the dominant Lamanites a reason to break their nonaggression pact and attack Limhi's people. Their attack was barely repulsed. When the wounded Lamanite king was discovered during an interim body count, Gideon proposed that Limhi straightaway inform the injured king who the real abductors were. This resulted in the captured king calming his warriors at the outset of the second attack and stemmed future invasions. While the Lamanites then honored their former oath not to slay the Nephites, Limhi and his people were assessed a burdensome 50 percent tax, as well as indiscriminate corporal punishment at the hand of their captors. The complaining citizenry then resolved upon a strategy to counterattack the oppressive Lamanites. Three successive attacks resulted in their not only being soundly repulsed, but losing a large number of men, which their small population could ill afford. They finally faced their seemingly immutable bondage with resignation and humility.

Their resignation and the following events are instructive: "And they did humble themselves even to the dust, subjecting themselves to the yoke of bondage, submitting themselves to be smitten, and to be driven to and fro, and burdened, according to the desires of their enemies.

"And they did humble themselves even in the depths of humility; and they did cry mightily to God; yea, even all the day long did they cry unto their God that he would deliver them out of their afflictions" (Mosiah 21:13–14).

The Lord did not relieve their suffering readily, but seemed to give time for them to comprehend the consequences of their aggressive behavior. Slowly, they once again began to prosper. Their suffering brought perspective, progress, and a unity that seemed absent earlier (see Mosiah 21:15–18). So it can be with one struggling to overcome an overriding weakness that may have affected a significant portion of his or her life. Deliverance requires an abject submission to the commandments of God, his servants, and his word.

Scripture: The Text Itself and Reading between the Lines

When reading these scriptural accounts, one who is wrestling to overcome a weakness or temptation (and feeling impatient for relief) may see or feel somewhat beyond what is actually written in black and white on the page. This spiritual "reading between the lines" begins to bring (in due time) hope, comfort, and direction. This was suggested by Alma when he compared scripture study to the early use of the Liahona in the Book of Mormon. When instructing his son Helaman, Alma said:

"For behold, it is as easy to give heed to the word of Christ, which will point to you a straight course to eternal bliss, as it was for our fathers to give heed to this compass, which would point unto them a straight course to the promised land.

"And now I say, is there not a type in this thing? For just as surely as this director did bring our fathers, by following its course, to the promised land, shall the words of Christ, if we follow their course, carry us beyond this vale of sorrow into a far better land of promise" (Alma 37:44–45).

On at least two other occasions, the effectiveness of the word of the Lord in delivering peoples from bondage was noted. In the first instance, we see the literal word of God spoken to the hearts of Alma and his people at the time Amulon and his fellows (the fugitive priests and the Lamanite military) were exercising onerous authority over them: "And behold, after that, they were brought into bondage by the hands of the Lamanites in the wilderness; yea, I say unto you, they were in captivity, and again the Lord did deliver them out of bondage by the power of his word; and we were brought into this land, and here we began to establish the church of God throughout this land also" (Alma 5:5).

Ammon, in his grateful pronunciation at the end of a prolonged mission to the Lamanites, noted, "Behold, how many thousands of our brethren has he loosed from the pains of hell; and they are brought to sing redeeming love, and this because of the power of his word which is in us, therefore have we not great reason to rejoice?"

(Alma 26:13). The power of scripture to not merely inspire, but to liberate, is affirmed. The Book of Mormon also notes the relative simplicity of this "scriptural deliverance" immediately following the parallel drawn to the Liahona: "O my son, do not let us be slothful because of the easiness of the way; for so was it with our fathers; for so was it prepared for them, that if they would look they might live; even so it is with us. The way is prepared, and if we will look we may live forever" (Alma 37:46).

Conclusion

The Book of Mormon offers great spiritual insight in avoiding conditions that lead to trouble—individually, within a family, or within a nation. Mormon concluded, "And those who were faithful in keeping the commandments of the Lord were delivered at all times, whilst thousands of their wicked brethren have been consigned to bondage, or to perish by the sword, or to dwindle in unbelief" (Alma 50:22). Those who struggle with problems of spiritual bondage can take advantage of the principle of spiritual deliverance by reading these Book of Mormon accounts. The Lord promised, "And I will also be your light in the wilderness; and I will prepare the way before you, if it so be that ye shall keep my commandments; wherefore, inasmuch as ye shall keep my commandments ye shall be led towards the promised land; and ye shall know that it is by me that ye are led" (1 Nephi 17:13). The "promised land" is undoubtedly where relief from spiritual suffering is found. The Lord inspired Book of Mormon writers to provide food for the spiritually malnourished and balm for the afflicted. There is power in the scriptures to relieve spiritual bondage and pain. Healing may be initiated by looking for answers and principles for today's complexities embedded in the Book of Mormon. They are there, albeit perhaps written in scriptural "code," to be broken by those willing to prayerfully "*search* the scriptures" (see John 5:39; Alma 14:1; 33:2).

Notes

1. See H. Dean Garrett, "Inspired by a Better Cause," in Kent P. Jackson, ed., *Studies in Scripture: Volume Eight, Alma 30 to Moroni* (Salt Lake City: Deseret Book, 1988), 69–70.

2. See 1 Nephi 17:24–25; 19:10; 2 Nephi 24:3; Mosiah 7:15–33;

11:23; 23:23; 24:21; 27:16; Alma 5:5; 36:2; 61:12. The word *bondage* occurs sixty-six times in the Book of Mormon.

3. See 1 Nephi 1:20; 2 Nephi 4:31; 7:2; 28:19, 22; Mosiah 9:17; 22:11; 24:9, 13, 19–21. The words *deliver* and *deliverance* appear 114 times in the Book of Mormon.

4. See Stephen D. Ricks and William J. Hamblin, eds., *Warfare in the Book of Mormon* (Salt Lake City: Deseret Book, 1990).

5. Joseph Fielding Smith, *Doctrines of Salvation,* comp. Bruce R. McConkie, 3 vols. (Salt Lake City: Bookcraft, 1954–56), 3:277.

6. See John W. Santrock, Ann M. Minnett, and Barbara D. Campbell, *The Authoritative Guide to Self-Help Books* (New York: Guilford Press, 1994), 2–3.

7. Bruce R. McConkie, *Mormon Doctrine,* 2d ed. (Salt Lake City: Bookcraft, 1966), 120.

8. Joseph Smith, *Teachings of the Prophet Joseph Smith,* sel. Joseph Fielding Smith (Salt Lake City: Deseret Book, 1976), 181.

9. See R. Douglas Phillips, "Why Is So Much of the Book of Mormon Given Over to Military Accounts?"; Richard Dilworth Rust, "Purpose of the War Chapters in the Book of Mormon"; Stephen D. Ricks," "'Holy War': The Sacral Ideology of War in the Book of Mormon and in the Ancient Near East," in Ricks and Hamblin, *Warfare in the Book of Mormon,* 25–32, 103–17.

10. Others include obtaining food (see 1 Nephi 16:18–31), escaping murder (see 2 Nephi 5:1–7), escaping bondage (see Mosiah 24:16–25; Alma 14:4–28), discovering the whereabouts of the Lamanites (see Alma 16:6; 43:23–24; 48:16), and preparing light for submarine-like barges (see Ether 2:17–3:6).

CHAPTER FIFTEEN

REPENTANCE IN THE BOOK OF MORMON

ROBERT L. MARROTT

At least four general aspects of repentance are clarified and verified in the Book of Mormon. First, the Book of Mormon teaches that repentance is a gift from God and requires divine involvement. Second, implications and inferences arise from other terms related to the word *repentance* in the Book of Mormon. Third, the Book of Mormon teaches about the result of delaying or ignoring repentance for those who have made covenants with God through ordinances. Fourth, the Book of Mormon defines repentance and correlates it with the threefold mission of the Church.

A GIFT FROM GOD

A businessman conceived the manufacture and marketing of a wonderful product. He assembled an excellent group of employees and provided marvelous benefits for them. He obtained quality components and materials. The product became very successful. Customers were satisfied with the use and quality of the product. The employees shared in the wealth the product produced. The businessman reaped a surprising reward. He soon realized, however, that his profits could greatly increase if he froze the benefits to his employees and cut the quality of the materials used in manufacturing his product. As he expected, profits rose dramatically, and he envisioned himself among the elite of entrepreneurs.

After a while, things began to unravel. Discontent among his

Robert L. Marrott is a professor of religious education at Ricks College.

employees began to rise. Some of his best people quit the firm. Others campaigned for an adversarial union organization. Customers began to realize that product reliability had dropped. The quality just was not there anymore. Profits began to drop to the point that the businessman wondered if he would lose everything.

He recognized the error of his ways. The remorse he felt for his loss of reputation and profit was deep and painful. He acknowledged his greedy errors before his employees and the press. He resolved never to make such mistakes again. He renegotiated contracts with his employees so that they again shared in the wealth of the company. He offered replacement products at no cost to customers. Once again only top-quality components and materials were purchased to manufacture the product. In a short time, the great decline leveled off and began a reversal. Soon the company became very profitable again. Employees and customers were content. Oh yes, and by the way, the businessman was an atheist.

This story illustrates the application of the traditional five *R*s of repentance that has often been taught: First, we must *recognize* that we have committed a sin. Second, we must feel *remorse* for it. Third, we must *repay or restore* the damage done. Fourth, we must *relate or confess* it. And fifth, we *never repeat* it. One, two, three, four, five—and boom! We have repented!

The problem is that these steps can be accomplished without any need for God or acknowledgment of him. Paul refers to godly sorrow and sorrow of the world (see 2 Corinthians 7:9–10). Godly sorrow brings true repentance and forgiveness. The sorrow of the world does not. The story of the businessman symbolizes the sorrow of the world. One can go through the traditional five *R*s of repentance, accomplish every step, and be a full-fledged, 100 percent atheist. God is not needed to go through the traditional five *R*s, and yet positive results may occur, from the world's perspective.

The Book of Mormon teaches that repentance requires divine involvement. Indeed, the Book of Mormon shows that repentance is a gift dispensed from God to man—that repentance is impossible from the mortal perspective alone. Although the word *repentance* itself may mean "change one's mind or direction," when placed in gospel context as presented most clearly in the Book of Mormon, repentance requires a dependence upon, and the involvement of, the Savior.

President Ezra Taft Benson wrote in a First Presidency message in the *Ensign:* "Godly sorrow is a gift of the Spirit. It is a deep realization that our actions have offended our Father and our God. It is the sharp and keen awareness that our behavior caused the Savior, He who knew no sin, even the greatest of all, to endure agony and suffering. Our sins caused Him to bleed at every pore. This very real mental and spiritual anguish is what the scriptures refer to as having 'a broken heart and a contrite spirit.'"[1] So, even the desire to repent comes from God.

Elder Marion G. Romney said: "It is clear that our ability to repent, as well as the efficacy of our repentance, comes as a gift from the Redeemer. . . . This gift men reject at their peril. Unless they exercise it, they remain spiritually dead, just as dead as if there had been no redemption made."[2]

Although the Bible informs us that repentance is a gift from God, the Book of Mormon emphasizes the gift more strongly. The headnote to Acts 11 in the LDS edition of the King James Bible reads, "God grants the gift of repentance to Gentiles." The text reads, "Then hath God also to the Gentiles granted repentance unto life" (Acts 11:18). That is virtually the only reference in the Bible of the principle that repentance is a gift granted of or from God.

To the people of Ammonihah, Alma said, "There was a space granted unto man in which he might repent" (Alma 12:24). He continued, "And may the Lord grant unto you repentance" (Alma 13:30). King Anti-Nephi-Lehi, a Lamanite convert, in speaking to his people, said, "And I also thank my God, yea, my great God, that he hath granted unto us that we might repent of these things" (Alma 24:10). To the Zoramites, Amulek said, "Therefore may God grant unto you, my brethren, that ye may begin to exercise your faith unto repentance" (Alma 34:17). In explaining justice and punishment to his son Corianton, Alma stated: "There was a time granted unto man to repent, yea, a probationary time, a time to repent and serve God. . . .

"But there is a law given, and a punishment affixed, and a repentance granted; which repentance mercy claimeth" (Alma 42:4, 22).

Mormon, in concluding his discourse on mankind's slowness in hearkening to God and man's being less than the dust, stated: "And may God grant, in his great fulness, that men might be brought unto repentance and good works" (Helaman 12:24). And finally, Mormon, in the closing days of the Nephite nation, spoke against the self-sufficient, positive mental attitude of his people and wrote: "And I did cry unto this people, but it was in vain; and they did not realize that it was the Lord that had spared them, and granted unto them a chance for repentance" (Mormon 3:3).

The word *grant* connotes something offered, allowed, or dispensed. The inference is that true repentance requires the involvement of God in its availability.

Elder James E. Talmage wrote: "Repentance is a means of pardon and is therefore one of God's great gifts to man. It is not to be had for the careless asking; it may not be found upon the highway; nevertheless it is given with boundless liberality unto those who have brought forth works that warrant its bestowal. That is to say, all who prepare themselves for repentance will be led by the humbling and softening influence of the Holy Spirit to the actual possession of this great gift."[3]

The nature of repentance being a gift granted by God has at least two dimensions. One is the general notion that repentance is part of the plan of salvation, which was established before the foundations of the world. The plan itself, conceived before the creation of this world, is a glorious gift to us from God. The second dimension of repentance being a gift is that it is a day-to-day granting that enables our efforts to be coupled to the grace of God. It is acknowledging that we need God's assistance in our repentance. Consider the difference in attitude and actions between a person who self-sufficiently tries to repent on his own and a person who acknowledges his dependence upon God for the desire, the understanding, and the ability to repent.

King Benjamin shows that fallen man is incapable of true repentance unless and until he understands something of the holiness and goodness of Christ and the contrasting states of man's own fallen nature and that of a sinless God. Man must recognize that Christ is the source of all good (see Moroni 7:12–16). Mankind is dependent upon that goodness and mercy and healing for repentance to occur. Merely recognizing that we have sinned is not sufficient in the recognition aspect of repentance; we have to recognize God for who he is and what he does.

King Benjamin's people "viewed themselves in their own carnal state, even less than the dust of the earth. And they all cried aloud with one voice, saying: O have mercy, and apply the atoning blood of Christ that we may receive forgiveness of our sins, and our hearts may be purified" (Mosiah 4:2).

We are sad not just because we did something wrong, or because we got caught, but because of what sin does to us and to our relationship with the perfect being who is our God. We want to end the discomfort caused by our sins and mistakes and weaknesses and transgressions and stupidity. We contributed to the agony Christ suffered in accomplishing the Atonement. That realization is humbling; it causes one to feel less than the dust of the earth.

We realize that we are incapable of saving ourselves. Even though we may keep the commandments, even though we may change our minds and behavior, even though we *do* things, only the power of Christ makes what we do count, or makes it work. We have to learn to rely upon him for all things. Not only does God preserve you "from day to day, by lending you breath, that ye may live and move and do according to your own will, and even supporting you from one moment to another" (Mosiah 2:21), but "the natural man is an enemy to God, and has been from the fall of Adam, and will be, forever and ever, unless he yields to the enticings of the Holy Spirit, and putteth off the natural man and becometh a saint through the atonement of Christ the Lord, and becometh as a child, submissive, meek, humble, patient, full of love, willing to submit to all things which the Lord seeth fit to inflict upon him, even as a child doth submit to his father" (Mosiah 3:19).

King Benjamin advises his people to "always retain in remembrance, the greatness of God, and your own nothingness, and his goodness and long-suffering towards you, unworthy creatures, and humble yourselves even in the depths of humility" (Mosiah 4:11). Nephi reminds us that we "have not come thus far save it were by the word of Christ with unshaken faith in him, relying wholly upon the merits of him who is mighty to save" (2 Nephi 31:19; see also 1 Nephi 10:6).

With a resolution to come unto him and reliance upon him, we find ourselves on the path to being reconciled to Christ through our obedience and the charity he grants to us, charity being a gift of the Spirit (see Moroni 8:25–26; 7:48; 10:18–20). Charity is a cause of pure motives. The reconciliation with Christ causes us to want to be reconciled with our fellowmen, to restore things to a rightful state. King Benjamin talks of retaining a remission of sins through attitudes and behaviors related to members of one's family, to the poor and needy, through doing things in order, and even through returning things borrowed (see Mosiah 4:12–28).

King Benjamin's people, after repenting, had no more disposition to do evil (see Mosiah 5:2). They were changed. God changed them as they qualified for the change. Alma discourses about this principle in Alma 5: "Behold, he [God] changed their hearts. . . .

" . . . A mighty change was also wrought in their hearts, and they humbled themselves and put their trust in the true and living God" (Alma 5:7, 13). Again the involvement of God in our change of nature and disposition is evident from the Book of Mormon.

The Book of Mormon not only confirms the principles that repentance is a gift from God and that God must be involved in our repentance, but it also contains other interesting aspects related to repentance. These aspects tie the principle of repentance to other principles of the gospel. These aspects surface in certain terms and phrases that are used in conjunction with the word *repentance*.

OTHER TERMS USED WITH *REPENTANCE*

The Book of Mormon uses interesting terminology with the word *repentance:* "faith unto repentance" (Alma 34:15–17); "baptizing unto repentance" (3 Nephi 1:23). What could these terms mean?

Amulek's context in Alma 34 for the term "faith unto repentance" concerns the power of the atonement of Christ to bring about mercy. Once we have faith in and from Christ, meaning trust and confidence in him and power from him, we want to repent. Once we have knowledge revealed to us about the role of the Savior and we choose to accept and act upon it, we wish to repent. This is a relatively simple concept and flows from the usual order where the first principles and ordinances of the gospel are presented. For example, the fourth Article of Faith: "first, Faith in the Lord Jesus Christ; second,

Repentance." In other words, by trusting in the Lord, we have a change of mind.

The second phrase, "baptizing unto repentance," is more curious. We normally think of the process as: first, we have faith in Christ, then we repent, and then we are baptized. We would probably prefer to think "repentance unto baptism" rather than "baptizing unto repentance."

This Book of Mormon phrase could mean, based on the context in which the more part of the people believed and were converted to the gospel and experienced a "great remission of sins," that repentance, which precedes baptism, also continues on throughout life. One continues to improve one's life even after baptism. Baptism symbolizes, among other things, the new man, the new way of life. Even after one is born again, there is still more spiritual growth ahead. One's future repentance is validated by baptism.

The idea could be that not only does our baptism symbolize the remission of past sins, which in reality are remitted by keeping the commandments (see Moroni 8:25–26), but that our baptismal covenant includes the remission of future sins from which we repent. That covenant is renewed by worthily partaking of the sacrament.

At least nine references to a variation of the phrase "baptism unto repentance" are presented in the Book of Mormon. The phrase "baptized unto repentance" is found in Mosiah 26:22; Alma 5:62; 6:2; 7:14; 9:27; 48:19; 49:30; Helaman 5:17, 19; and 3 Nephi 7:26. The phrase appears in the King James Version of the Bible in Matthew 3:11, in which John the Baptist states, "I indeed baptize you with water unto repentance." The words "unto repentance" are from the Greek *eiv metanoian (eis metanoian). Eiv* is a preposition used as a function word indicating motion; it can mean "toward, to, into,[4] in order to, with a view to, with reference to, as far as, to the extent of, till, until, against, before, in the presence of, for, in accordance with, and for the use or service of."[5] *Metanoia* means "a change of mind."[6]

The most interesting of these Book of Mormon passages is Alma 7:14: "Now I say unto you that ye must repent, and be born again; for the Spirit sayeth if ye are not born again ye cannot inherit the kingdom of heaven; therefore come and be baptized unto repentance, that ye may be washed from your sins, that ye may have faith on the Lamb of God, who taketh away the sins of the world, who is mighty to save and to cleanse from all unrighteousness."

Notice that the order is different, showing that the gospel process is not simply a step-by-step mechanical process of do "A," then do "B," then do "C," and bingo—you are done. Here we find (1) repent (2) be born again, which includes baptism and the gift of the Holy Ghost, (3) be "baptized unto repentance," (4) so that sins are washed away, (5) so that one can have faith in Christ, (6) who takes away sin and (7) can save, and (8) cleanse from all unrighteousness. Obviously, faith is more than just a beginning step; it continues throughout man's progression toward God, and repentance occurs more than just before baptism.

Following baptism comes the bestowal of the Holy Ghost. We are given the gift of the Holy Ghost by the laying on of hands. Only with this gift can we see things anew. In fact, our ability to have faith in Christ, which was the initial step in being born again, also comes after having this new change of mind. This illustrates how intertwined and how interdependent these principles of the gospel are. We trust in God, so we attempt to change; this change qualifies us for baptism (see D&C 20:37); once we are baptized we receive the Holy Ghost, which really enables us to change and see things anew, which enables us to increase our faith in Christ. In fact, one cannot have the pure love of Christ without baptism and the gift of the Holy Ghost (see Moroni 8:25–26).

If we acknowledge that repentance is a gift from God and if we have agreed and promised through religious covenants and ordinances to subscribe to faith in Christ, repentance, baptism, the gift of the Holy Ghost, and obedience or enduring to the end, what happens if we then ignore or rebel against God and his gospel?

THE CONSEQUENCES OF PROCRASTINATING THE DAY OF OUR REPENTANCE

The Book of Mormon is very specific in addressing the consequences of not repenting, of putting it off, or of procrastinating repentance. Although the opportunity and the desire and the power to repent may be a gift from God, man has a direct responsibility in implementing that gift. If he does not implement the gift once he has made covenants to do so, dire consequences result.

Amulek's famous warning about not procrastinating the day of repentance, in Alma 34:32–35, illustrates this principle. The people he spoke to were not unfamiliar with the doctrines of the gospel. They were dissenters from the truth. What is said to them may not be said to those who have never heard the truths of the gospel. He reminds them that "if we do not improve our time while in this life, then cometh the night of darkness wherein there can be no labor performed" (Alma 34:33). The Savior used the same phraseology in 3 Nephi 27:33. After stating that "strait is the gate, and narrow is the way that leads to life, and few there be that find it," he said, "Wide is the gate, and broad the way which leads to death, and many there be that travel therein, until the night cometh, wherein no man can work."

Apparently those who have had access to the plan of salvation and have made covenants therein, yet die unrepentant, will be denied the opportunity to repent in the spirit world, as far as gaining their exaltation is concerned. As long as we are in the attitude and behavior of repentance while in this life, we will be allowed to continue to do so in the spirit world. But for those who procrastinate their repentance until it is too late and they are dead, they will not be able to labor or work toward following the Savior in fulness. The Book of Mormon provides some of the strongest scriptural evidence against the notion of a second chance for salvation in the spirit world if we ignore repenting in this life when we know we should.

Both President Joseph Fielding Smith and Elder Bruce R. McConkie have addressed the issue of not having a second chance to obtain exaltation if we do not accept and live up to our first chance here in mortality.

President Smith said: "If men do not receive this privilege [of repentance] here, they will receive it in the spirit world, for it must come to all. If they reject it here, they may not receive the fulness in eternity. . . .

" . . . The privilege of exaltation is not held out to those who have had the opportunity to receive Christ and obey his truth and who have refused to do so. . . .

"Those who have the opportunity here, those unto whom the message of salvation is declared, who are taught and who have this truth presented to them in this life—yet who deny it and refuse to receive it—shall not have a place in the kingdom of God. They will not be with those who died without that knowledge and who yet accepted it in the spirit world."[7]

Elder McConkie wrote: "*There is no such thing as a second chance to gain salvation* [exaltation and eternal life] *by accepting the gospel in the spirit world after spurning, declining, or refusing to accept it in this life.* It is true that there may be a second chance to hear and accept the gospel, but those who have thus procrastinated their acceptance of the saving truths will not gain salvation in the celestial kingdom of God."[8]

Amulek's remarks, again, are not made to those who may never have heard the gospel or who heard the gospel but rejected it, not having made any covenants or participated in any ordinances. People who do not have a first chance to understand and accept the gospel in this life can have that opportunity in the spirit world and be candidates for the celestial kingdom if they would have accepted the gospel in mortality with all their hearts (see D&C 137:7–8). People who heard the prophets and rejected them in mortality are allowed to accept the gospel—if they will repent in the spirit world and be candidates for the terrestrial kingdom, which is the middle of the three degrees of glory (see D&C 76:73–75; 138:28–32, 57–59).

Our mission is to be involved in the attitude and behavior of repentance while here in mortality. If that is the case, we may continue on that path in the spirit world. If, however, we who should, while knowing better, procrastinate the day of our repentance, then comes the night of darkness in which no labor, no repentance, can be performed toward exaltation.

Amulek's passage also contains an appositive to the word *repentance* that provides a very positive understanding about repentance in contrast to the negative connotation that procrastination carries. This principle will be the last we shall consider about repentance.

To "Come unto Christ" Is to Repent

One of the grandest and most glorious principles of repentance is found in a speech by Amulek. He said, "Ye cannot say, when ye are brought to that awful crisis, that I will repent, that I will return to my God" (Alma 34:34). The meaning of the clause "that I will repent" is "that I will return to my God."

How wondrously simple! To repent is to return to God. To return to God is to repent. The Church of Jesus Christ of Latter-day Saints has expounded a threefold mission: proclaim the gospel, redeem the dead, and perfect the Saints. These three assignments culminate in bringing people to Christ. That is the mission of the Church: to bring people to Christ. To have Latter-day Saints involved in the threefold mission to bring people to Christ is to preach repentance.

All of the conditions, elements, steps, benefits, and principles related to repentance can be summed up in this all-inclusive, simple statement of "return to God" or "come unto Christ." When the Lord states, "Say nothing but repentance unto this generation" (D&C 11:9) and "Preach naught but repentance" (D&C 19:21), he is directing his servants to invite people to come unto him.

This is a marvelous way to look upon the broad principle of repentance. I may have faith, trust, or revelation from Christ; I may have been baptized worthily and by proper authority; I may have been commanded to receive the Holy Ghost—but unless and until I am in the attitude and behavior of repentance, of coming to the Savior, even having these other gifts, in Paul's language in the English translation, I would be "as sounding brass, or a tinkling cymbal . . . nothing" (1 Corinthians 13:1, 3).

Of course, this aspect of repentance is no secret. The Greek words for *repent*—*metanoian* (*metanoian*, noun) and *metanoew* (*metanoeo*, verb)—as found in the New Testament are translated as "return, or change directions in mind, thought, or action." The following passages in the Book of Mormon also link repentance with returning to God:

- "I will be merciful unto them, saith the Lord God, if they will repent and come unto me" (2 Nephi 28:32).
- "That ye would repent, and come with full purpose of heart, and cleave unto God as he cleaveth unto you" (Jacob 6:5).
- "Except this people repent and turn unto the Lord their God, they shall be brought into bondage; and none shall deliver them, except it be the Lord the Almighty God" (Mosiah 11:23).
- "They should repent and come unto our God" (Alma 29:2).
- "O repent ye, repent ye! Why will ye die? Turn ye, turn ye unto the Lord your God. Why has he forsaken you?" (Helaman 7:17).

- "Therefore, whoso repenteth and cometh unto me as a little child, him will I receive" (3 Nephi 9:22).

None of these passages put the terms in apposition, a restatement of the idea itself as is found in Alma 34:34. These other passages use a conjunction to tie the words together and can make it appear as two separate things: to return and also to repent. But I take Amulek's passage to be a key in interpreting all the others. To repent and to return are the same thing. The culmination of constantly coming unto Christ, of continually having the attitude and behavior of repentance is eventually to become reconciled with him and to be able to reap the blessings of sanctification.

The phrase about doing things with an eye single to God's glory, rather than for our own glory, takes on a deeper meaning when repentance is thought of as coming to Christ. No longer is repentance merely a sequence of requirements and steps to accomplish. If I am coming to Christ, nothing else should get in the way of focusing on the Master. All I do is done to make him happy, to please him, to bring him joy. It is his glory I am interested in, not mine. If I lose my life for his sake, I find it. If I seek my own life, then I lose eternal life (see Matthew 10:39).

Summary

The Book of Mormon clarifies, emphasizes, and establishes some particular ideas and principles about repentance. Repentance is a gift from God. Man is incapable of truly repenting without God's involvement. We have to trust in him and expect his help, from the initial desire through to perfection.

Terminology such as "baptism unto repentance" and "faith unto repentance" cause us to reflect on the word *repentance* and see additional application and understanding. The context of these phrases enables us to see the interconnections of the principles of the gospel. The elements of repentance include remorse, resolution, restoration, and confession.

Joseph Smith said: "Repentance is a thing that cannot be trifled with every day. Daily transgression and daily repentance is not that which is pleasing in the sight of God."[9] Using the elements of repentance to overcome a particular sin is something we get through, get over, and stop. One cannot repent of being a thief if he returns to thievery every day. But the *attitude* of repentance is coming unto Christ. That is something that is always pleasing in the sight of God.

The Book of Mormon uniquely presents the consequences of not repenting, or of delaying repentance; it speaks of the night of darkness wherein no labor or work can be performed. Nehor, one of the Book of Mormon anti-Christs, taught that God would save us all (see Alma 1:4). The inference is that there would be nothing about which to worry or repent. Nehor, in effect, invites us to procrastinate our repentance. Elder McConkie concludes his "Second Chance Theory" entry in *Mormon Doctrine* with the following: "Thus the false and heretical doctrine that people who fail to live the law in this life (having had an opportunity so to do) will have a further chance of salvation in the life to come is a soul-destroying doctrine, a doctrine that lulls its adherents into carnal security and thereby denies them a hope of eternal salvation."[10]

Our joy comes in the realization that repentance, broadly defined as coming unto Christ or returning to God, is portrayed with the greatest force in the Book of Mormon. All aspects, requirements, and conditions of repentance can be summed up in the simple phrase of "come unto Christ."

The Book of Mormon not only teaches us aspects and elements about repentance that are not available as plainly elsewhere, but it also clarifies and verifies principles about repentance that are found elsewhere. The Book of Mormon provides intelligence that causes us to ask questions and ponder about the principle of repentance.

Notes

1. Ezra Taft Benson, "A Mighty Change of Heart," *Ensign,* Oct. 1989, 4.

2. Marion G. Romney, *Look to God and Live,* comp. George J. Romney (Salt Lake City: Deseret Book, 1973), 99.

3. James E. Talmage, *The Articles of Faith,* 12th ed. (Salt Lake City: The Church of Jesus Christ of Latter-day Saints, 1924), 114.

4. See Walter Bauer, trans., *A Greek-English Lexicon of the New Testament and Other Early Christian Literature,* 2d ed. (Chicago: University of Chicago Press, 1979), 228.

5. See G. V. Wigram, *Analytical Greek Lexicon of the New Testament* (Wilmington, Del.: Associated Publishers and Authors, n.d.), 119.

6. See Bauer, *A Greek-English Lexicon of the New Testament,* 512; Wigram, *Analytical Greek Lexicon of the New Testament,* 266.

7. Joseph Fielding Smith, *Doctrines of Salvation,* comp. Bruce R. McConkie, 3 vols. (Salt Lake City: Bookcraft, 1954–56), 2:181–83.

8. Bruce R. McConkie, *Mormon Doctrine,* 2d ed. (Salt Lake City: Bookcraft, 1966), 685.

9. Joseph Smith, *Teachings of the Prophet Joseph Smith,* sel. Joseph Fielding Smith (Salt Lake City: Deseret Book, 1976), 148.

10. McConkie, *Mormon Doctrine,* 687.

CHAPTER SIXTEEN

ABINADI, MOSES, ISAIAH, AND CHRIST: "O HOW BEAUTIFUL UPON THE MOUNTAINS ARE THEIR FEET"

DAVID ROLPH SEELY

Abinadi is one of the most eloquent witnesses in all of scripture of the coming of the Messiah and his mission. Not only did he prophesy the coming of Christ, but he explained the doctrinal significance of his mortal ministry. The story of Abinadi in Mosiah 12–17 is one of the most memorable of all of the Book of Mormon stories. On the surface it is a very simple story—a confrontation between a prophet of the Lord and a proud and wicked king and his priests. Abinadi condemns them for their iniquity and teaches them the true doctrine of the coming of the Messiah—"that God himself shall come down among the children of men, and shall redeem his people" (Mosiah 15:1). The wicked priests become angry, they accuse Abinadi of blasphemy, and then they kill him—scourging him to death with fire. As we read and ponder this story, it becomes clear that there is much in this narrative beyond the simple storyline, for from Abinadi's discourses and through his martyrdom we find that the coming of the Messiah will involve each of us in a very profound way.

Throughout the story, Abinadi explains that what will happen to

---

David Rolph Seely is an associate professor of ancient scripture at Brigham Young University.

him "shall be as a type and a shadow of things which are to come" (Mosiah 13:10). The fabric of scripture is woven with types and shadows. One of the keys to understanding scriptural stories is to learn to recognize and explore the types and shadows of these stories. Certain individuals in the scriptural narrative loom so large as to cast a shadow into the future. Men like Adam, Enoch, Melchizedek, Abraham, and Moses lived exemplary lives that pointed the children of the covenant toward the central event in history—the coming of Christ. The accounts of their lives were monumental and served as beacons to those in the future, pointing all who emulated them toward Christ.

The story of Abinadi is full of types and shadows. Its meaning is brought sharply into focus as we look to scriptural history for the types it represents and as we explore the shadows it projects into the future. The story of Abinadi looks back to the type of Moses, the prophet like unto Christ (see Deuteronomy 18:15–18), and to Isaiah's prophecies of the coming of God to earth as the Messiah (see Isaiah 52–53). Abinadi's life and death foreshadow the coming of Jesus Christ. Abinadi, through the type of Moses, explains the law and, through his interpretation of Isaiah, explains the prophets. In short, this remarkable Book of Mormon prophet explains to us the meaning of the Old Testament as it would be fulfilled in Christ. Most importantly, Abinadi explains in great doctrinal detail the significance of the mortal ministry of Jesus Christ and his atonement. He explains to us what Isaiah meant when he said that the Messiah would "see his seed" (Isaiah 53:10) and invites us to become the seed of Christ.

ABINADI: A PROPHET LIKE UNTO MOSES

The story of Abinadi is framed with elements of the story of Moses and his confrontation with Pharaoh. It begins with the reign of King Noah—the epitome of a wicked king: immorality, idolatry, taxation, drunkenness, and riotous living. Noah surrounds himself with a select group of priests who share his values and support him in his wickedness. Through taxation, Noah has put his people in bondage (see Mosiah 11:1–15). In spite of their wickedness, King Noah and his people win a great victory in battle against the Lamanites, begin to boast in their own strength, and delight in the shedding of blood (see Mosiah 11:16–19).

To this people, the Lord called Abinadi to be prophet and to proclaim to the people that unless they repented the Lord would visit them in his anger, they would be delivered into the hands of their enemies, and they would be brought into bondage (see Mosiah 11:20–21). Abinadi went forth, reciting to his people the same words that Moses had spoken centuries before to the children of Israel warning them about idolatry: "And it shall come to pass that they shall know that I am the Lord their God, and am a jealous God, visiting the iniquities of my people" (Mosiah 11:22; see also Exodus 20:5; Deuteronomy 5:9; cf. Mosiah 13:13). When Noah heard of these words, he was enraged. The first words spoken by King Noah in the Book of Mormon echo the words first spoken by Pharaoh to Moses and Aaron: "Who is Abinadi, that I and my people should be judged of him, or who is the Lord, that shall bring upon my people such great affliction" (Mosiah 11:27; see also Exodus 5:2; cf. Moses 5:16). Further, the Book of Mormon records that Noah, like Pharaoh, hardened his heart (see Mosiah 11:29; JST Exodus 7:13).

Abinadi fled for his life but returned after two years with the same message and enumerated a list of signs that would occur if the people did not repent, signs reminiscent of the plagues of Moses: afflictions, famine, pestilence, bondage, hail, the east wind, insects (see Mosiah 12:3–7; Exodus 7–10), and even the death of Noah, whose life "[should] be valued even as a garment in a hot furnace" (Mosiah 12:3). For these prophecies Abinadi was arrested and brought before the king and his priests for cross-examination with the intent of making a formal and legal accusation against him. Finally, one of the priests asked him to interpret the passage in Isaiah 52:7–10 that begins "How beautiful upon the mountains are the feet of him that bringeth good tidings" and that ends "the Lord hath made bare his holy arm in the eyes of all the nations, and all the ends of the earth shall see the salvation of our God" (Mosiah 12:24).

Abinadi responded to this question with a series of questions of his own. He addressed the priests: "Are you priests, and pretend to teach this people . . . ?" (Mosiah 12:25); "What teach ye this people?" (v. 27); "If ye teach the law of Moses why do ye not keep it?" (v. 29). He then challenged them by reading the first of the Ten

Commandments and asked them why they did not obey them. By this time the king had had enough and ordered his priests to take Abinadi away and kill him. The Lord intervened and Abinadi was transfigured before him, "for the Spirit of the Lord was upon him; and his face shone with exceeding luster, even as Moses' did while in the mount of Sinai, while speaking with the Lord" (Mosiah 13:5; cf. Exodus 34:29–35). Under divine protection, Abinadi then finished reading the Ten Commandments to the priests. Having represented Moses as the lawgiver, Abinadi compared the priests of Noah with the children of Israel, who were stiffnecked and quick to do iniquity, and invoked Moses as prophet, "for behold, did not Moses prophesy unto them concerning the coming of the Messiah?" (Mosiah 13:33).

ABINADI QUOTES ISAIAH 53 AS A PROPHECY OF THE COMING OF JESUS CHRIST

Abinadi taught that the law of Moses was "a law of performances and of ordinances" that were "types of things to come" (Mosiah 13:30–31) and that "there could not any man be saved except it were through the redemption of God" (v. 32). He testified that this redemption was taught and prophesied by all the prophets since the world began and that Moses the Lawgiver prophesied "unto them concerning the coming of the Messiah, and that God should redeem his people" (v. 33). The center of Abinadi's message to Noah and his priests is the fulfilment of the law of Moses and the prophecies of all the prophets in the future coming of God to earth as the Messiah.

In Mosiah 13:34–35, Abinadi identifies five specific teachings about the Messiah taught by all of the prophets: "Have they not said that [1] God himself should come down among the children of men, and [2] take upon him the form of man, and [3] go forth in mighty power upon the face of the earth?

"Yea, and have they not said also that he should [4] bring to pass the resurrection of the dead, and [5] that he, himself, should be oppressed and afflicted?"

Abinadi then proceeds to recite Isaiah 53 in its entirety in Mosiah 14 as evidence for these doctrines. Isaiah 53 is a poetic description of the earthly ministry of Jesus Christ, the Messiah, who would come as a Suffering Servant. It should be noted that the entire chapter of Isaiah 53 in Mosiah 14 is a poem in four stanzas of three

Abinadi, Moses, Isaiah, and Christ

verses each (vv. 1–3, 4–6, 7–9, 10–12), constructed with well-known Hebrew parallelism. Much of Isaiah's figurative language is open to various interpretations. Following his recitation of Isaiah 53 in Mosiah 14, Abinadi then explains with great clarity in chapter 15 the mission of the Messiah by quoting, paraphrasing, and explaining some of the important phrases and images from Isaiah.

As the earthly ministry of the Savior unfolded in the meridian of time, most, if not all, of those who followed him did not completely understand the significance of his mission as it was described in Isaiah 53. After his crucifixion, resurrection, and ascension, however, early Christians were able to see clearly the meaning of many of Isaiah's prophecies about the Messiah. As Nephi said, "Nevertheless, in the days that the prophecies of Isaiah shall be fulfilled men shall know of a surety, at the times when they shall come to pass" (2 Nephi 25:7).[1] Jews, on the other hand, have continued to read Isaiah 53 as a prophecy directed to the Suffering Servant as the house of Israel.[2] While it is clear the whole of chapter 53 is about the mortal ministry of the Messiah, even among Latter-day Saints there are various interpretations of the particulars in Isaiah's prophecy.[3] Abinadi's interpretation of Isaiah 53 precedes the coming of the Christ by almost 150 years and yet remains the most clear and full interpretation of this prophetic chapter anywhere in scripture.

Let us review this important Isaiah chapter using Abinadi's five statements as a guide. We will note the passages that might be interpreted in the light of these statements and then quote some important phrases from Abinadi's sermon in Mosiah 15 that explain the content of these passages.

"God Himself Should Come Down among the Children of Men"

The first verse of Mosiah 14:1 is intriguing:

> Who hath believed our report,
> and to whom is the arm of the Lord revealed?

The first six verses of Mosiah 14 are in the voice of a first person plural narrator; the last six verses appear to be the Lord speaking. So, who is this narrator? A close reading of the text suggests that the narrators of this section are those among covenant Israel who witnessed his ministry in the flesh.

The opening lines of this chapter pose two questions: Who will believe what will be recounted here? and To whom is the "arm of the Lord" revealed? The sense of the first question can be taken in several different ways. Most obviously it appears to be a rhetorical question—expecting a negative answer—that no one has or will believe this incredible report of God coming to earth as a mortal. On the other hand, it may be an invitation to all who hear the report to consider it and to accept and believe it.

The "arm of the Lord" is a central image in the second question. The "arm of the Lord" is a commonly used metaphor for the power of God in the Bible in the context of creation (see Jeremiah 32:17), in the redemption of Israel from Egypt (see Exodus 15:16; Deuteronomy 4:34), and in his deliverance of Israel in the last days (see Isaiah 40:10; 52:10).[4] In the Book of Mormon, the image of the "arm of the Lord" occurs in the context of the restoration of the gospel and the coming forth of the Book of Mormon (see 1 Nephi 22:10–11; Enos 1:13), and the "arm of mercy" is associated with the power of the Atonement on behalf of the repentant (see Jacob 6:5; Mosiah 29:20; Alma 19:36).[5]

In this passage, the "arm" may have a sense more literal than that of the metaphor. The biblical and Book of Mormon association of this image with creation, redemption, latter-day restoration, and especially with the Atonement, all point toward the power of God manifested to the world through his Son Jesus Christ. Perhaps it is in this image that Abinadi would have us see that God himself, Jesus Christ, will reveal himself as the "arm of the Lord."

The question "To whom is the arm of the Lord revealed?" (see Isaiah 52:10) is posed in the passage the wicked priests asked Abinadi to interpret (see Mosiah 12:20–24). At the end of his description of the coming of Christ and his death and resurrection, Abinadi explained by reading this passage of Isaiah: "The Lord hath made bare his holy arm in the eyes of all the nations; and all the ends of the earth shall see the salvation of our God" (Mosiah 15:31). It is interesting to note that the Hebrew word for *salvation* (*yeshua*ʿ) is the same root as the name *Jesus* from the shortened form of *Yehoshua*ʿ.[6]

Perhaps it is Mosiah 14 that Abinadi has in mind when he says,

"I would that ye should understand that God himself shall come down among the children of men, and shall redeem his people" (Mosiah 15:1).

"Take upon Him the Form of Man"

> For he shall grow up before him as a tender
>   plant,
> and as a root out of dry ground;
> He hath no form nor comeliness;
> and when we shall see him there is no beauty
>   that we should desire him.
>
> He is despised and rejected of men;
> a man of sorrows, and acquainted with grief;
> and we hid as it were our faces from him;
> he was despised, and we esteemed him not.
>   (Mosiah 14:2–3)

This imagery graphically portrays Abinadi's second statement that God will take upon himself the form of a man. The Messiah will grow and mature as a plant, growing out of the dry ground. This may be an allusion to the fact that the Messiah was born of a mortal woman, was placed in a manger as Mary's baby, and grew to adulthood in a way similar to other mortals.

The statements that he had "no form nor comeliness" nor "beauty that we should desire him" describe the Messiah as coming in plainness with none of the royal outward trappings that many expected of the Davidic Messiah. The phrases "he is despised and rejected of men; a man of sorrows, and acquainted with grief; and we hid as it were our faces from him; he was despised, and we esteemed him not" describe his mortal life as one in which he experienced a full range of the experiences of mortality." Chief among these was rejection—he came into the world and was ignored, despised, and not esteemed by those he had come to save.

In chapter 15 Abinadi explains: "And because he dwelleth in flesh he shall be called the Son of God" (v. 2); "and thus the flesh becoming subject to the Spirit . . . suffereth temptation, and yieldeth not to the temptation, but suffereth himself to be mocked, and scourged, and cast out, and disowned by his people" (v. 5).

"Go Forth in Mighty Power upon the Face of the Earth"

> Surely he has borne our griefs,
> and carried our sorrows;
> yet we did esteem him stricken,
> smitten of God, and afflicted . . .
>
> All we, like sheep, have gone astray;
> we have turned every one to his own way;
>
> And the Lord hath laid on him
> the iniquities of us all.
>
> He was oppressed, and he was afflicted,
> yet he opened not his mouth;
> He is brought as a lamb to the slaughter,
> and as a sheep before her shearers is dumb,
> so he opened not his mouth.
> (Mosiah 14:4–7)

The first two lines may well be intended to be a description of the Savior's ministry to heal the sick and to cast out devils. This is the way it is interpreted by Matthew in his Gospel: "When the even was come, they brought unto him many that were possessed with devils: and he cast out the spirits with his word, and healed all that were sick: That it might be fulfilled which was spoken by Esaias the prophet, saying, Himself took our infirmities, and bare our sicknesses" (Matthew 8:16–17). In addition, these images are an apt description of the suffering of the Savior in the Garden of Gethsemane and the cross when he took the sins and the afflictions of the world upon himself as described by Alma: "And he will take upon him their infirmities, that his bowels may be filled with mercy, according to the flesh that he may know according to the flesh, how to succor his people according to their infirmities" (Alma 7:12).

Abinadi explains: "And after all this, after working many mighty miracles among the children of men, he shall be led, yea, even as Isaiah said, as a sheep before the shearer is dumb, so he opened not his mouth" (Mosiah 15:6).

Abinadi, Moses, Isaiah, and Christ

"Bring to Pass the Resurrection of the Dead" and "He, Himself, Should Be Oppressed and Afflicted"

There are a host of dramatic images in Isaiah 53 that describe these aspects of the ministry of the Messiah. These two themes are woven together both in Isaiah's prophecy as well as Abinadi's interpretation:

> He is despised and rejected of men;
> a man of sorrows,
> and acquainted with grief. . . .
>
> Surely he has borne our griefs,
> and carried our sorrows. . . .
>
> But he was wounded for our transgressions,
> he was bruised for our iniquities;
> the chastisement of our peace was upon him;
> and with his stripes we are healed. . . .
>
> He was taken from prison and from judgment;
> and who shall declare his generation?
> For he was cut off out of the land of the living;
> for the transgressions of my people was he stricken.
>
> And he made his grave with the wicked,
> and with the rich in his death;
> Because he had done no evil,
> neither was any deceit in his mouth.
>
> Yet it pleased the Lord to bruise him;
> he hath put him to grief;
> When thou shalt make his soul an offering for sin
> he shall see his seed,
> He shall prolong his days,
> and the pleasure of the Lord shall prosper in his hand.
>
> He shall see the travail of his soul,
> and shall be satisfied;

> by his knowledge shall my righteous servant
>   justify many;
> for he shall bear their iniquities.
>
> Therefore will I divide him a portion with the
>   great,
> and he shall divide the spoil with the strong;
> Because he hath poured out his soul unto
>   death;
> and he was numbered with the transgressors;
> and he bore the sins of many,
> and made intercession for the transgressors."
>   (Mosiah 14:3–5, 8–12)

These verses describe the judgment and the death of the Savior, that he was executed with the wicked and buried with the rich. It is possible that the phrase "he shall prolong his days" is a reference to the resurrection of the Messiah and his seed.

Abinadi answers the question "And who shall declare his generation?" with a description of Jesus Christ as the spiritual father of those who accept and follow him. Abinadi says: "Behold, I say unto you, that when his soul has been made an offering for sin he shall see his seed. And now what say ye? And who shall be his seed?" (Mosiah 15:10). One of the most important contributions of Abinadi's prophetic commentary on Isaiah is to explain that the reference to the seed of the Messiah is a reference to those who will accept and follow him. Abinadi used this reference to the seed of the Messiah in his explanation of the passage in Isaiah 52:7–10 to the priests of Noah: "How beautiful upon the mountains are the feet of him that bringeth good tidings" (Mosiah 15:18).

Abinadi explains all of these verses as foreshadowing the rejection, death, and resurrection of the Messiah and his power to give to his followers eternal life. He says the following:

"Yea, even so he shall be led, crucified, and slain, the flesh becoming subject even unto death, the will of the Son being swallowed up in the will of the Father.

"And thus God breaketh the bands of death, having gained the victory over death; giving the Son power to make intercession for the children of men—

"Having ascended into heaven, having the bowels of mercy; being filled with compassion towards the children of men; standing betwixt them and justice; having broken the bands of death, taken upon himself their iniquity and their transgressions, having redeemed them, and satisfied the demands of justice" (Mosiah 15:7–9).

"When Thou Shalt Make His Soul an Offering for Sin He Shall See His Seed" (Mosiah 14:10)

The story of Abinadi first entices and then entraps the reader. We, the audience, are drawn at first to the story by our sympathy for this man of God and his unpleasant and painful task of calling a wicked king to repentance. As Abinadi strides onto the stage in the robes of Moses, he meets King Noah as Pharaoh, and we are reminded that the story of Moses and Pharaoh is a type of the timeless conflict between prophets proclaiming the need for humility and repentance and hard-hearted, proud, and wicked leaders of iniquitous yet successful people. As members of the covenant, we are challenged by Abinadi's reading of the law to the priests of Noah. We must put ourselves in their places and ask ourselves hard questions, If we believe and teach the law, then why don't we live it? And do we remember that salvation comes through the redemption of Christ and not only through the law?

Then, incredibly, Abinadi draws us further into the story as covenant Israel. We become the narrators who ask the question, "Who hath believed our report?" (Mosiah 14:1). We describe the mortal ministry of the Messiah: "When we shall see him there is no beauty that we should desire him"; "and we hid as it were our faces from him"; "surely he has borne our griefs, and carried our sorrows"; "he was wounded for our transgressions, he was bruised for our iniquities"; "and with his stripes we are healed" (vv. 2–5). Finally, we, as Israel, betray ourselves: "All we, like sheep, have gone astray; we have turned every one to his own way; and the Lord hath laid on him the iniquities of us all (v. 6).

The Lord then addresses each individual among us: "When thou shalt make his soul an offering for sin he shall see his seed, he shall prolong his days, and the pleasure of the Lord shall prosper in his hand" (v. 10). We, of course, want to know what this individual challenge means. And Abinadi does not disappoint us. When he finishes his citation of Isaiah 53, he immediately turns to the question of the seed of the Messiah and explains in plain language that God himself (Jesus Christ) will come down to earth to redeem his people and that he will be both the Son and the Father—the Son because he "dwelleth in the flesh" and subjects the will of the flesh to the will of the Father" (Mosiah 15:2), and the Father because he is God (v. 1) and "because he was conceived by the power of God" (v. 3). In this way we come to understand the full import of the image of the seed of the Messiah.

The prophet then describes the way in which the Messiah will "justify many," will "divide the spoil with the strong," and make "intercession for the transgressors" (Mosiah 14:11–12). He teaches that redemption comes through the death, resurrection, and ascension of the Messiah with the following language: "And thus God breaketh the bands of death, . . . giving the Son power to make intercession for the children of men—

"Having ascended into heaven, having the bowels of mercy; being filled with compassion towards the children of men; standing betwixt them and justice; having broken the bands of death, taken upon himself their iniquity and their transgressions, having redeemed them, and satisfied the demands of justice" (Mosiah 15:8–9).

Abinadi teaches, "When his soul has been made an offering for sin he shall see his seed. . . . And who shall be his seed? . . .

" . . . Whosoever has heard the words of the prophets, . . . have hearkened unto their words, and believed that the Lord would redeem his people, . . . these are his seed, or they are the heirs of the kingdom of God" (vv. 10–11).

Finally, Abinadi turns to answer the original question posed by the priests of Noah about the identity of him who stands on the mountain to publish peace and proclaim the good tidings. Abinadi first identifies this entity as the seed of the Messiah—the prophets and those who have hearkened unto their words: "And these are they who have published peace. . . .

"And O how beautiful upon the mountains were their feet" (vv. 14–15).

He then identifies the Messiah: "O how beautiful upon the mountains are the feet of him that bringeth good tidings, . . . even the Lord, who has redeemed his people" (v. 18).

With this comparison, Abinadi has dramatically presented us with a powerful type and shadow of the Messiah—for even as he will proclaim the good tidings from the mountain, so will those who follow him (his seed) proclaim the tidings from the mountain. This typology explains a very important part of the Abrahamic covenant. The Lord promised Abraham, "In thy seed shall all the nations of the earth be blessed" (Genesis 22:18). This, of course, was fulfilled in a very specific way with the coming of the Messiah through the lineage of Abraham to bless the nations of the earth through the Atonement (as attested by the genealogies in Matthew 1 and Luke 3). Further, the Abrahamic covenant promises that the seed of Abraham, including all that accept the Gospel (Abraham 2:10; cf. D&C 84:34) "shall bear this ministry and Priesthood unto all nations" (Abraham 2:9) and through this seed of Abraham "shall all the families of the earth be blessed, even with the blessings of the Gospel, which are the blessings of salvation, even of life eternal" (Abraham 2:11).

In the end, we sorrow as Abinadi's message is rejected and we are powerless to save him from the priests of Noah. Abinadi was killed by fire for his testimony of the iniquities and of the coming of God to earth. His rejection is in the type of the ministry of Moses, who delivered the law to a hard-hearted people and who finally was taken from their midst (see D&C 84:25). Abinadi's death is a type and shadow of the coming, rejection, and death of the Messiah. He fulfills his calling as one of the holy prophets who have opened their mouths, testifying of the Messiah and thus becoming the seed of Christ, one "who [has] published peace, who [has] brought good tidings of good, who [has] published salvation; and said unto Zion: Thy God reigneth!

"And O how beautiful upon the mountains were their feet!" (Mosiah 15:14–15).

Abinadi's death also foreshadowed the burning deaths of King Noah and the Lamanite converts who died at the hands of descendants of King Noah's wicked priests (see Mosiah 19:20; Alma 25:9–12). In the Exodus story, Pharaoh and his armies, ironically, suffered death in the waters of the Red Sea (see Exodus 14)—the same death that Pharaoh had decreed upon the Hebrew male children—to be cast into the water.

"But There Was One among Them Whose Name Was Alma" (Mosiah 17:2)

But Abinadi did not die in vain. For in declaring repentance, he had brought one soul unto Christ (see D&C 18:15), and this one soul would bring many, many more. One of Noah's priests, a man named Alma, heard the words of the prophet "and he believed the words which Abinadi had spoken, for he knew concerning the iniquity which Abinadi had testified against them" (Mosiah 17:2). Just as Abinadi is a type of Moses and a shadow of Jesus Christ—who delivered his message and then was rejected and killed—so Alma becomes a type and shadow for us, the readers. When his defense of the prophet failed, he fled for his life into the wilderness, where he hid and wrote down the words of Abinadi (see Mosiah 16:3–4). We next see Alma in the wilderness, where he "repented of his sins and iniquities" and went among the people "and began to teach the words of Abinadi" (Mosiah 18:1). Indeed, Alma's words resonate with those of Abinadi, for he taught "concerning that which was to come, and also concerning the resurrection of the dead, and the redemption of the people, which was to be brought to pass through the power, and sufferings, and death of Christ, and his resurrection and ascension into heaven" (Mosiah 18:2).

And thus we see that Alma, following in the footsteps of Abinadi, also became the seed of Christ: "Whosoever has heard the words of the prophets, yea, all the holy prophets who have prophesied concerning the coming of the Lord . . . , that all those who have hearkened unto their words, and believed that the Lord would redeem his people, and have looked forward to that day for a remission of their sins, I say unto you, that these are his seed, or they are the heirs of the kingdom of God. . . .

"And these are they who have published peace, who have brought good tidings of good, who have published salvation; and said unto Zion: Thy God reigneth!

"And O how beautiful upon the mountains were their feet!" (Mosiah 15:11, 14–15).

Not only did Alma become the seed of Christ, but also his posterity after him, for he became the ancestor of generations of prophets who kept the sacred records and served the Nephites as ecclesiastical and political leaders for the next four hundred years.[7]

And so, at the end of the story, we find ourselves with Alma in the wilderness. There he instructs us how, through baptism, we can, like him, become the seed of Christ and how we can become, with him, one "of those who shall hereafter publish peace, yea from this time henceforth and forever!" (Mosiah 15:17).

We may apply Alma's words to those who were about to be baptized: "And now as ye are desirous to come into the fold of God, and to be called his people, and are willing to bear one another's burdens, that they may be light;

"Yea, and are willing to mourn with those that mourn; yea, and comfort those that stand in need of comfort, and to stand as witnesses of God at all times and in all things, and in all places that ye may be in, even until death, that ye may be redeemed of God, and be numbered with those of the first resurrection, that ye may have eternal life" (Mosiah 18:8–9).

And while we may not be called like Moses to confront Pharaoh, or Isaiah to prophesy the coming of the Messiah, or Abinadi to die as a witness of his message, and while we cannot take upon ourselves the sins of the world as did the Messiah, we can follow Alma and take upon ourselves the burdens of others, to mourn with those that mourn, and stand as witnesses of God in all times, things, and places that we may have eternal life.

Notes

1. For a review of Christian interpretations of Isaiah 53, beginning with the New Testament, see M. Hooker, *Jesus and the Servant: The Influence of the Servant Concept of Deutero-Isaiah in the New Testament* (London: SPCK, 1959); M. H. Bellinger Jr. and W. R. Farmer, eds., *Jesus and the Suffering Servant: Isaiah 53 and Christian Origins* (Harrisburg, Penn: Trinity Press International, 1998).

2. See S. R. Driver and A. Neubauer, *The Fifty-third Chapter of Isaiah According to the Jewish Interpreters* (New York: Ktav, 1969); J. Rembaum, "The Development of a Jewish Exegetical Tradition Regarding Isaiah 53," in *Harvard Theological Review* no. 75 (1982): 289–310.

3. See John W. Welch, "Isaiah 53, Mosiah 14, and the Book of Mormon," in Donald W. Parry and John W. Welch, eds., *Isaiah in the Book of Mormon* (Provo, Utah: Foundation for Ancient Research and Mormon Studies, 1998), 293–312; John S. Thompson and Eric Smith, "Isaiah and the Latter-day Saints: A Bibliographic Survey," 445.

4. See R. Laird Harris, Gleason L. Archer Jr., and Bruce K. Waltke,

eds., *Theological Wordbook of the Old Testament* (Chicago: Moody Press, 1980), s.v., "zeroa^c," 1:253–54.

5. See David Rolph Seely, "The Image of the Hand of God in the Book of Mormon and the Old Testament," in John L. Sorenson and Melvin J. Thorne, eds., *Rediscovering the Book of Mormon* (Salt Lake City: Deseret Book, 1991), 141–43.

6. See F. C. Grant, "Jesus Christ," *Interpreters Dictionary of the Bible* (Nashville: Abingdon, 1962), 2:869.

7. See Robert J. Matthews, "Abinadi: The Prophet and Martyr," in Monte S. Nyman and Charles D. Tate Jr., eds., *The Book of Mormon: Mosiah, Salvation Only through Christ* (Provo, Utah: Brigham Young University, 1991), 91–111.

CHAPTER SEVENTEEN

THE DOCTRINE OF GOD THE FATHER IN THE BOOK OF MORMON

ANDREW C. SKINNER

No other ancient record does what the Book of Mormon does. When it comes to testifying of Jesus as the Messiah, the Book of Mormon is unparalleled. It boldly proclaims to a modern world that Jesus was the Great Jehovah before he came to earth (see 3 Nephi 15:5), that as the Messiah he was born into mortality a real flesh and blood being (see Mosiah 3:5–7), that he was literally the Son of God and son of a mortal woman named Mary (see Mosiah 3:8, Alma 7:9–10), and that through his suffering and sacrifice an infinite and eternal atonement was made for all humankind (see Alma 34:8–15; 3 Nephi 11:10–15). While secular scholarship ofttimes tries to allegorize or explain away these truths, the Book of Mormon restores to both Jew and Gentile descriptions of the Atonement that were lost for centuries. And it places the Atonement at the very center of our understanding of God's plan *and* our religion itself. But the Book of Mormon also does something else in a profound and unrelenting way: it stands as a pivotal witness of God the Eternal Father.

A WITNESS OF GOD THE FATHER

Perhaps we do not reflect a great deal on the notion that the Book of Mormon stands as a premier witness of God the Father. This may be so precisely because we spend so much time emphasizing the

---

Andrew C. Skinner is chair of the Department of Ancient Scripture at Brigham Young University.

Book of Mormon as a witness of Christ (and rightly so). But if we are not vigilant, we may miss the significance of the foundational corollary doctrine restored by the ancient record—the Messiah had a literal divine Father, and the prophets of the Book of Mormon knew it! No matter how carefully, how often, or how long one studies the Book of Mormon, its message is constantly hammered home: Jesus the Messiah is the literal son of God the Father, who also figures prominently in its pages. We cannot ignore this, wish it away, or twist it into something that does not square with the Prophet Joseph Smith's first vision.

Joseph Smith translated and pondered the doctrines of the Book of Mormon through the lenses of the Sacred Grove. He said he saw and interacted with "two Personages, whose brightness and glory defy all description" (JS–H 1:17). Everything in the Book of Mormon fits perfectly with, and ultimately supports, the Prophet's experience and understanding. There is no confusion over this or shred of evidence to the contrary in the Book of Mormon. In fact, there is evidence to indicate that the Prophet Joseph Smith carefully reviewed the text of the Book of Mormon with the doctrine of the Fatherhood of God specifically in mind. For example, the first edition (1830) of 1 Nephi 11:21 contained the words, "Behold the Lamb of God, yea, even the Eternal Father!" By the time of the 1837 edition, Joseph Smith had inserted a clarifying phrase so that the verse then read, "Behold the Lamb of God, yea, even *the Son of* the Eternal Father!" The Prophet also inserted this same clarifying phrase in verse 32 of chapter 11 so that the 1837 edition read, "And I looked and beheld the Lamb of God, that he was taken by the people; yea, *the Son of* the everlasting God was judged of the world."

Without question, these two verses were doctrinally correct as they stood in the original 1830 edition of the Book of Mormon. Jesus Christ is indeed the Eternal Father and the Everlasting God, as is explained by the prophet Abinadi in Mosiah 15. But Joseph Smith Jr., prophet, seer, and revelator of the Lord in this modern (and last) dispensation, also knew the doctrine of the Godhead (from firsthand experience, we might add), and also knew that the Book of Mormon was to stand as a sure and clear witness of that doctrine *in* the latter days and *among* the Latter-day Saints. The changes he made to the texts of 1 Nephi 11:21, 32 are appropriate, appreciated, and much

The Doctrine of God the Father in the Book of Mormon 219

needed in our day to clear up misunderstandings. The fundamental truth that there exists a divine Father, separate from other beings, is taught no less powerfully in the Book of Mormon than the doctrine that there exists a divine Son, whom we worship as our Messiah and Savior. Therefore, let us explore two of the seminal ways in which the reality of God the Father is taught in the Book of Mormon.

NUMEROUS EXPLICIT VERSES

First of all, the doctrine of God the Father is taught in the Book of Mormon through explicit references to Jesus Christ as Son of an Eternal Father. The language used to teach the divine Sonship of Jesus is plentiful and varied, as well as obvious and subtle. He is called "the Son" (2 Nephi 31:18), the "Beloved Son" (2 Nephi 31:11), the "Son of God" (1 Nephi 10:17), the "Holy Child" (Moroni 8:3), the "Son of the most high God" (1 Nephi 11:6), the "Son of the living God" (Mormon 5:14), "Son of our great God" (Alma 24:13), "Son of the everlasting God" (1 Nephi 11:32), "Son of the Eternal Father" (1 Nephi 11:21; 13:40), the "Only Begotten of the Father" (Alma 5:48), the "Only Begotten Son" (Jacob 4:5, 11; Alma 12:33), "Christ the Son" (Alma 11:44), and the "Son of Righteousness" (3 Nephi 25:2). One would be hard pressed to find a more explicit and consistent list of titles that testifies of the obvious: Jesus is regarded as the Son of a divine Father.

The phrase "Son of God" alone is used fifty-one times throughout the Book of Mormon text, with variations of this phrase occurring several more times. The phrase "Only Begotten Son" is used five times, "Only Begotten of the Father" four times, and "Son of the living God" four times. The prophets Mormon and Moroni use this very powerful and expressive phrase (i.e., "Son of the living God)" always in tandem with the specific mention of the name of Jesus (see 3 Nephi 30:1; Mormon 5:14; 9:29). And Nephi uses it when discussing the baptism of Christ (see 2 Nephi 31:16).

Here are Mormon's words in describing the purpose of the doctrines and teachings of the Book of Mormon: "And behold, they shall go unto the unbelieving of the Jews; and for this intent shall they go—that they may be persuaded that Jesus is the Christ, the Son of the living God; that the Father may bring about, through his most Beloved, his great and eternal purpose, in restoring the Jews, or all the house of Israel, to the land of their inheritance, which the Lord their God hath given them, unto the fulfilling of his covenant" (Mormon 5:14).

As inferred in this verse, Jesus, the earthly Messiah or Anointed One, who was the first born of all of our Heavenly Father's spirit sons and daughters (see D&C 93:21), and who became the literal son of that same divine Father, was also the designated agent of his Father's plan, the one chosen to carry out and put into effect his Father's will—all of his Father's aims and desires for this earth and the people who live upon it. This even included the Father's desire that the earthly family known as Israel be established in lands appointed for their habitation and use while living on this earth. Thus, Abinadi could teach that the will of the Son was "swallowed up" in the will of the Father (Mosiah 15:7).

It is instructive to note that the phrase "Son of God" often appears in certain chapters of the Book of Mormon that focus especially on aspects of the Atonement. The Book of Mormon prophets understood well that the Atonement, brought about by the matchless sacrifice of God's earthly Son, was the central feature of the Father's plan for his children from the beginning. As Alma testifies, "God did call on men, in the name of his Son, (this being the plan of redemption which was laid) saying: If ye will repent, and harden not your hearts, then will I have mercy upon you, through mine Only Begotten Son" (Alma 12:33).

Those chapters where mention of the "Son of God" figures prominently include 1 Nephi 11; Alma 11; Alma 33; Alma 34; Helaman 8; and Helaman 14. In 1 Nephi 11 Nephi describes his vision of the birth and ministry of the Son of God, who was himself God before he came to earth as a mortal being. In Alma 11, Amulek teaches that a universal resurrection comes through the Son of God. In Alma 33 Zenos and Zenock teach that mercy is bestowed because of the Son of God. In Alma 34, Amulek teaches that the Son of God would become the great and last sacrifice, an infinite and eternal atonement for all. In Helaman 8, Nephi teaches that Abraham, Moses, Zenos, Zenock, Ezias, Isaiah, Jeremiah, Lehi, and Nephi all testified that the Son of God would come to earth as the Messiah and bring salvation. And Helaman 14 recounts the prophesies of Samuel the Lamanite,

The Doctrine of God the Father in the Book of Mormon 221

wherein he testified of the mortal birth of the Son of God who would redeem human beings from temporal and spiritual death.

Even after only a cursory reading of the Book of Mormon, it becomes apparent that the most consistent and persistent teaching by Book of Mormon prophets about the Savior-Messiah is that he was the Son of God. What Amulek said specifically to one of his audiences could well be said to every soul after they have read the Book of Mormon: "My brethren, I think that it is impossible that ye should be ignorant of the things which have been spoken concerning the coming of Christ, who is taught by us to be the Son of God" (Alma 34:2).

EPISODES DESCRIBING THE FATHER AS DISTINCT FROM THE SON

The doctrine of God the Father is taught in specific, unique episodes in the Book of Mormon, where the Father and the Son are described as separate divine personages. One of the most powerful and impressive of these is found in Nephi's prophetic discourse regarding the baptism of Christ in 2 Nephi 31. Nephi was shown in vision both the ministry of John the Baptist, "that prophet . . . that should baptize the Lamb of God" (2 Nephi 31:4), as well as the actual baptismal scene of the Messiah (see 2 Nephi 31:17). The text makes clear that Nephi was also given an explicit and detailed understanding of the doctrinal basis of the ordinance of baptism, and the reason for Christ's baptism (see 2 Nephi 31:5–10). But what also comes out of a careful reading of 2 Nephi 31 is the unmistakable conclusion that Nephi had a profound understanding of, and encounter with, the Godhead. In stunning detail, Nephi tells his readers that he was privileged to hear the voices of both the Father and the Son.

As a way of introducing his Son, God the Father commanded Nephi to repent, "and be baptized in the name of my Beloved Son" (2 Nephi 31:11). The Son, our Savior, then told Nephi that those who would follow the Father's command would be given the Holy Ghost, just as the Father had given the Holy Ghost to the Son (see 2 Nephi 31:12). After he presents some of his own words of exhortation, Nephi then relates how he heard the voice of the Savior a second time: "But, behold, my beloved brethren, thus came the voice of the Son unto me, saying: After ye have repented of your sins, and witnessed unto the Father that ye are willing to keep my commandments, by the baptism of water, and have received the baptism of fire and of the Holy Ghost, and can speak with a new tongue, yea, even with the tongue of angels, and after this should deny me, it would have been better for you that ye had not known me" (2 Nephi 31:14).

Immediately after this instruction from the premortal Savior, Nephi again heard the voice of God the Father bearing record of his Son, in a manner that fits the pattern established and repeated in the rest of the standard works: "And I heard a voice from the Father, saying: Yea, the words of my Beloved are true and faithful. He that endureth to the end, the same shall be saved" (2 Nephi 31:15). Only on certain special occasions have certain select humans on this earth had the privilege of hearing the voice of God the Father, and then it has been to hear him introduce and bear record of his Son, who is his executor and creator of those worlds he calls his own (see JST John 1:19; Moses 1:31–33).[1] These special occasions include, interestingly, the actual baptism of Christ (see Matthew 3:17), the Mount of Transfiguration (see Matthew 17:5), the Savior's appearance at the temple after his triumphal entry (see John 12:28), the Savior's appearance in the New World after his resurrection (see 3 Nephi 11:7), and the First Vision (see JS–H 1:17).

In each of these instances the sentiments expressed by God the Father are so similar to one another as to be considered virtually identical: "This is my Beloved Son, in whom I am well pleased; hear ye him." While it is possible that Nephi's encounter with the Father is an example of the premortal Savior (Jehovah) speaking as though he were God the Father, a more compelling case is made for this being the actual voice of God the Father. It fits the pattern of the Father bearing witness of the Son as seen elsewhere. It uses almost the same language, certainly the same sentiment, of the other examples. And it concerns the baptism of the Son, which we know did evoke the Father's voice when the Savior experienced the ordinance in the flesh.

If 2 Nephi recounts the actual utterance of God the Father, then it is unique in our scriptural library, for it is our only record of the Father's actual voice being heard by a mortal being *before* his Son, our Redeemer, was born into mortality. In other words, 2 Nephi 31 is the only recorded instance in scripture of the Father bearing testimony

The Doctrine of God the Father in the Book of Mormon 223

of the premortal Savior. Were we to judge the value of the Book of Mormon based on this episode alone, we would be compelled to label the sacred text not only unique, but truly invaluable.

Another invaluable contribution to our understanding of the doctrine of the Fatherhood of God is made by Alma in his discourse to the people of Gideon. He describes the context or background of Christ's birth into mortality in these words:

"And behold, he shall be born of Mary, at Jerusalem which is the land of our forefathers, she being a virgin, a precious and chosen vessel, who shall be overshadowed and conceive by the power of the Holy Ghost, and bring forth a son, yea, even the Son of God" (Alma 7:10).

Here we learn not only that the earthly name of the Savior's mortal mother was foreknown by prophets long before the actual events occurred, but also that Mary herself was specially chosen during her sojourn in our premortal existence to perform her special role of motherhood. (It will be remembered that the Prophet Joseph Smith taught that every man, and by implication every woman, who has a calling to minister to the inhabitants of this world was foreordained to that calling in the grand council before the world was created.[2] What greater calling could any individual have than to be the mother of the literal Son of God in mortality?) In addition, we understand from Alma's comment that the third member of the Godhead had a role in the mortal birth of the Son of God. On this point, Elder Melvin J. Ballard has offered the following commentary:

"Joseph Smith made it perfectly clear that Jesus Christ told the absolute truth, as did those who testify concerning him, the Apostles of the Lord Jesus Christ, wherein he is declared to be the very Son of God. And if God the Eternal Father is not the real Father of Jesus Christ, then are we in confusion; then he is not in reality the Son of God. But we declare that he *is* the Only Begotten of the Father in the flesh. Mary told the story most beautifully when she said that an angel of the Lord came to her and told her that she had found favor in the sight of God, and had come to be worthy of the fulfillment of the promises heretofore made, to become the virgin mother of the Redeemer of the world. She afterwards, referring to the event, said: 'God hath done wonderful things unto me.' 'And the Holy Ghost came upon her,' is the story, 'and she came into the presence of the highest.' No man or woman can live in mortality and survive the presence of the Highest except by the sustaining power of the Holy Ghost. So it came upon her to prepare her for admittance into the divine presence, and the power of the Highest, who is the Father, was present, and overshadowed her, and the holy Child that was born of her was called the Son of God."[3]

Perhaps the most compelling texts in the Book of Mormon that discuss God the Father are found in the section that details the postresurrection appearance of the Savior in the New World, namely 3 Nephi 11:3–28:15. These chapters contain the Savior's personal teachings and testimony given to his American Israelites, and give to us in modern times important insights regarding his relationship with his divine Father, as well as the Father's will concerning us. Of the eighteen chapters comprising this section, only two do not mention the Father: 3 Nephi 22 (which is the Savior's recitation of Isaiah 54) and 3 Nephi 25 (wherein the Savior quotes Malachi 4). A list of a few of the references to the Father in each of these chapters may be profitable.

3 Nephi 11

The voice of the Father introduces and bears witness of the Savior (see v. 7).

The Savior tells his disciples that he and the Father are one (see v. 27).

The Savior testifies that his doctrine was given to him by the Father; also he bears record of the Father, and the Father and Holy Ghost, in turn, bear witness of him (see vv. 31–32, 35–36).

3 Nephi 12

The Savior exhorts all to let their light shine and, thus, glorify their Father in Heaven (see v. 16).

The Savior exhorts all disciples to be perfect, just as he or their Father in Heaven is perfect (see v. 48).

3 Nephi 13

The Savior teaches the order of prayer, instructing his disciples to address their Father, who already knows all things they need before they ask (see vv. 8–9).

3 Nephi 14

The Savior describes the Father's concern for his children as being so much greater than mortal parents' concern for their children; thus the Father will give good things to those who ask (see v. 11).

The Savior declares that only those who actually do the will of their Father in heaven will be able to enter the kingdom of heaven (see v. 21).

3 Nephi 15

The Savior testifies that it is the Father who has given the house of Joseph their land of inheritance (see vv. 12–13).

The Savior explains that at no time did the Father give him a commandment to teach the Jerusalem disciples about the other tribes of the house of Israel, whom the Father led away out of their lands (see v. 15).

The Savior declares that he received commandments of the Father to teach some things and not others because of unbelief manifested by Israelites in the Old World (see vv. 15–18).

The Savior tells his disciples in the New World that they, as well as other tribes, were separated from the Old World Israelites by the Father (see vv. 19–20).

3 Nephi 16

The Savior again reiterates the point that he was commanded by the Father to give the American Israelites the land on which they were residing as their land of inheritance (see v. 16).

3 Nephi 17

The Savior commands the people to go to their homes and ask the Father in Jesus' name for understanding concerning the teachings that the Father commanded the Savior to give to them (see v. 3).

The Savior tells the multitude that he is going to the Father and then to the lost tribes of Israel (see v. 4).

The Savior speaks directly to the Father, calling him "Father" (see v. 14).

After calling out to the Father, the Savior kneels and prays to the Father, speaking words so great and marvelous they cannot be written (see vv. 15–18).

The Savior again prays to the Father on behalf of the little children (see v. 21).

3 Nephi 18

The Savior teaches his disciples to partake of the sacrament as a testimony to the Father that they do always remember the Savior and his sacrifice, and as a witness to the Father that they are willing to do the things the Savior has commanded (see vv. 1–11).

The Savior tells the Nephites that he must go unto his Father to fulfill other commandments that the Father has given him (see v. 27).

3 Nephi 19

The twelve special disciples divide the multitude into twelve groups and teach them to pray unto the Father in the name of Jesus (see vv. 5–9).

The Savior prays to the Father in a manner that resembles the great high priestly prayer he offered in Jerusalem (see vv. 20–23, 27–29; cf. John 17).

The Savior again prays to the Father in words that cannot be recorded (see vv. 31–32).

3 Nephi 20

The Savior speaks of the covenant he says the Father made with the house of Israel through Abraham and the patriarchs (see vv. 12–13, 25). It seems unlikely that he is speaking of himself acting in the role of the Father—when one considers a subsequent verse where he also declares that the Father raised him up and sent him to the Nephites to bless them because they are the children of the covenant (see v. 26).

The Savior teaches the people that the Father is behind the gathering of Israel and will fulfill the covenant he made with Abraham (see vv. 27–34).

The Savior declares that with the fulfillment of the covenant, all the ends of the earth shall see the salvation of the Father; he also reiterates that he and the Father are one (see v. 35).

3 Nephi 21

The Savior teaches the Nephites that the Gentiles will be established in their land and set up as a free people by the power of the

Father. Furthermore, the Gentiles will be instrumental in fulfilling the covenant of the Father with a remnant of the Nephite and Lamanite peoples (see v. 2–5).

The Savior speaks of the work of the Father (see v. 26).

3 Nephi 23

The Savior commands that certain things be added to their records, and says they will go forth to the Gentiles according to the time and will of the Father (see v. 4).

3 Nephi 24

The Savior commands the disciples to write down the words the Father had given to Malachi (see v. 1).

3 Nephi 26

The Savior tells the multitude that the Father commanded him to restore to them those scriptures they did not have in their possession because the Father wants the scriptures to go forth to future generations (see v. 2).

The narrative explains that the Savior did go back to the Father after the end of the second day that he was with the people (see v. 15).

3 Nephi 27

The Savior shows himself to the disciples as they were praying unto the Father in Jesus' name (see v. 2).

The Savior defines the gospel in its simplest form as his act of doing the will of the Father. He says his Father sent him into the world to be lifted up upon the cross. And just as men had lifted him up, so would men be lifted up by the Father because of his atoning act (see vv. 13–14).

The Savior declares that he will act as a mediator, holding men guiltless before his Father if they will endure in righteousness. He was given this power as mediator by his Father (see vv. 15–16).

3 Nephi 28

The Savior tells the Three Nephites that because of their selfless request to tarry on the earth and not taste death, just as the apostle John had requested, they shall have a fulness of joy, sit down in the kingdom of his Father, and shall be even as he is—like the Father. "I am even as the Father; and the Father and I are one" (v. 10).

CLARIFYING SOME POSSIBLE CONFUSION

Reflection on the Savior's references to the Father in 3 Nephi raises an interesting issue. From the Savior's statements, it would seem that the Father is much more involved than we may have previously thought in matters of salvation history usually ascribed to Jehovah. For example, the Savior said it is the Father who made the covenant with the house of Israel through Abraham (see 3 Nephi 20:12–13, 25). It is the Father who is intimately involved in the scattering and gathering of the house of Israel. And it is the Father who gave to the prophet Malachi the words recorded in Malachi 3:1 that he would send a messenger. Yet we know that the scriptures teach that it was Jehovah who covenanted with Abraham (see Abraham 1:16; 2:6–8); it was Jehovah who inspired the prophets of old, like Malachi; and only on rare occasions has God the Father been directly involved with mortals on this earth. Given those truths, it might almost sound like the Father being spoken of by the Savior in 3 Nephi is Jehovah, and that Jehovah is a being separate from Jesus Christ; or, on the other hand, if Jehovah and Jesus are one and the same, Christ in 3 Nephi is speaking to or about himself, praying to himself as Jehovah, that he suffered his own will on the cross, and that it was he himself who caused himself to be raised from the dead.

Resolution of the seeming confusion may be found by integrating the Savior's statements in 3 Nephi with other revelations of the Restoration. Through the Prophet Joseph Smith we know that the Father, Son, and Holy Ghost are separate and distinct personages from one another (see JS–H 1:17; D&C 130:22). From the Book of Mormon itself we know that Jesus Christ was the premortal Jehovah come to earth as the long awaited Messiah (see 3 Nephi 15:5). We also know that the plan of salvation was Heavenly Father's plan and that Jesus Christ put into effect, or executed, all the terms and conditions of his Father's plan (see Moses 4:1–4)—whether acting in premortality as Jehovah, or acting in mortality as Christ. We further know from the Savior's emphasis of the point he makes in 3 Nephi, as well as from modern revelation, that even though the Godhead is composed of individual beings, their unity in perfection is far more intertwined and intense than we mortals might comprehend.

The Savior himself told the Nephites several times that he and the Father are one—not in personage or physical form, but in purpose. But even more than that, says the Savior, "I am in the Father, and the Father in me, and the Father and I are one" (3 Nephi 11:27; cf. 3 Nephi 9:15; 19:23; 28:10). In other words, the Father and the Son, whether the Son is acting as Jehovah or Christ, are so unified in mind and will that what one thinks, says, and does, the other one thinks, says, and does exactly.

This concept has been described, in part, by modern prophets, as the principle of divine investiture of authority. President Joseph Fielding Smith taught:

"Christ is also our Father because his Father has given him of his fulness; that is, he has received a fulness of the glory of the Father. This is taught in Doctrine and Covenants 93:1–5, 16–17, and also by Abinadi in the 15th chapter of Mosiah. Abinadi's statement that he is 'the Father, because he was conceived by the power of God,' harmonizes with the Lord's own words in section 93 that he is the Father because he has received of the fulness of the Father. Christ says he is the Son because, 'I was in the world and made flesh my tabernacle, and dwelt among the sons of men.' Abinadi expresses this truth by saying he is 'the Son because of the flesh.'

"The Father has honored Christ by placing his name upon him, so that he can minister in and through that name as though he were the Father; and thus, so far as power and authority are concerned, his words and acts become and are those of the Father."[4]

Thus, when the Savior visited his American Israelites, he testified with perfect propriety of his Father's intimate involvement in those matters of salvation history (covenanting with Abraham, speaking through Old Testament and Book of Mormon prophets, and establishing laws and commandments on the earth) with which Jehovah was also intimately involved. And yet there are also some actions and sayings attributed to the Father in the text of 3 Nephi that are uniquely God the Father's. When his voice bears witness of his Beloved Son, in whom he is "well pleased," it is the Father's voice and no other (3 Nephi 11:7). When the Savior testifies that it was by the power of the Father that he was raised up, it is the power of God the Father and no other (see 3 Nephi 27:14–15). When the Savior declares that he will hold the righteous guiltless before the Father (acting as a mediator representing us to the Father), it is the Father before whom the Savior will stand and no other (see 3 Nephi 27:16; cf. D&C 45:3–5). And when the Savior declares that he received the doctrine he teaches from the Father, it is ultimately God the Father from whom all doctrine originates, for it was originally the Father's plan by which we live (see 3 Nephi 11:31–32; Moses 4:1–4).

Conclusion

The words of the Book of Mormon and modern prophets describe a doctrine of the Godhead, and a doctrine of God the Eternal Father, that is so much more profound, and yet at the same time so much simpler, than Trinitarian formulations. Joseph Smith said that he had "always declared God to be a distinct personage, Jesus Christ a separate and distinct personage from God the Father, and that the Holy Ghost was a distinct personage and a Spirit: and these three constitute three distinct personages and three Gods."[5] The Book of Mormon is a monumental witness of God the Father, as well as Joseph Smith's personal experience and teaching. How could it be otherwise? Would it not be unusual, at the very least, for the Book of Mormon to teach something different from what Joseph Smith said he had always taught about the Godhead, especially considering that the Book of Mormon is one of our most significant evidences of Joseph Smith's divine calling?

The Book of Mormon is not an elementary treatise on, nor does it contain a confused notion of, the doctrine of the Godhead. It does not display an evolving concept of the Godhead, where only later Book of Mormon prophets knew of three separate deities. Nor does it support the idea of a prophet-translator who only later in his ministry came to understand a clear picture of three distinct personages. From its beginning, the Book of Mormon teaches what Joseph Smith knew from the beginning: God the Father, God the Son, and God the Holy Ghost are separate and distinct personages, although they think, speak, and act as one God. And they testify of each other, as the Book of Mormon so powerfully demonstrates.

"And in the mouth of three witnesses shall these things be established; and the testimony of three, and this work, in the which shall be shown forth the power of God and also his word, of which the Father, and the Son, and the Holy Ghost bear record—and all this shall stand as a testimony against the world at the last day" (Ether 5:4).

NOTES

1. President Joseph Fielding Smith taught: "All revelation since the fall has come through Jesus Christ, who is the Jehovah of the Old Testament. In all of the scriptures, where God is mentioned and where he has appeared, it was Jehovah who talked with Abraham, with Noah, Enoch, Moses and all the prophets. . . . The Father has never dealt with man directly and personally since the fall, and he has never appeared except to introduce and bear record of the Son. Thus the *Inspired Version* records that 'no man hath seen God at any time, except he hath borne record of the Son'" (*Doctrines of Salvation,* comp. Bruce R. McConkie, 3 vols. (Salt Lake City: Bookcraft, 1954–56), 1:27.

2. See Joseph Smith, *Teachings of the Prophet Joseph Smith,* sel. Joseph Fielding Smith (Salt Lake City: Deseret Book, 1976), 365.

3. Bryant S. Hinckley, ed., *Sermons and Missionary Services of Melvin Joseph Ballard* (Salt Lake City: Deseret Book, 1949), 166–67.

4. Smith, *Doctrines of Salvation,* 1:29–30.

5. Smith, *Teachings of the Prophet Joseph Smith,* 370.

CHAPTER EIGHTEEN

LOST AND FOUND: THE PLAIN AND PRECIOUS THINGS

BRIAN L. SMITH

Several years ago, I was in a meeting with some Latter-day Saint religious educators where a non-LDS Bible scholar was sharing some of his theological beliefs. We had an interesting biblical discussion, after which he asked about our belief concerning the "many plain and precious things" taken from the Bible. He first stated, "As a scholar of biblical languages, I am aware that there are over five thousand different New Testament fragments and documents now in existence. Very few of them are identical, yet because we can cross-reference the similarities in a large number of these manuscripts, scholars can confidently say that the Bible, as currently translated, is reasonably accurate." He further explained, "With the preponderance of manuscripts, scholars have determined a common source and what doctrines it contained." He then asked, "What are some of the plain and precious parts referred to by Latter-day Saints that have been taken from the biblical text? Can you give me some specific examples?" The group appeared somewhat stunned as each of us thought about how to best answer the scholar's question. Time had slipped away and we were forced to dismiss almost immediately after the question. After pondering what happened, I felt that I had failed to bear witness of the Book of Mormon and other restored truths. I am better prepared to answer that question today than I was then.

Brian L. Smith is a stake institute administrator for Utah Valley at the Orem Institute of Religion.

Lost and Found: The Plain and Precious Things

TWO REVEALING EXERCISES

Turn to the topic "Holy Ghost" in the topical guide in the back of your Bible (p. 212). You may recall that under each topic heading in the guide, the Old Testament references are listed first, then the New Testament, and then latter-day scripture follows. Under "Holy Ghost" we find no Old Testament references. What happened to the Holy Ghost in the Old Testament? Imagine, a member of the Godhead with little or no mention in the Old Testament text. Was the Holy Ghost known by another name in the Old Testament? Are we to believe that the Holy Ghost did not appear on earth until Christ ascended to heaven at the end of his earthly ministry, as the biblical text might lead us to believe? (see Acts 1–2). Latter-day scripture makes it abundantly clear that the third member of the Godhead has been manifest in every dispensation.

The Book of Mormon text covers the years 600 B.C. to A.D. 421. Much of its history happened within the Old Testament time period. We find evidence of the Holy Ghost very early in the text. Nephi was led by the Spirit to acquire the plates of brass from Laban (see 1 Nephi 4:6). Soon after this event, Nephi testified that his father, Lehi, spoke by the power of the Holy Ghost (see 1 Nephi 10:17). He additionally testified that the Holy Ghost had inspired individuals earlier than 600 B.C. and would continue to do so in the future (see 1 Nephi 10:19), and that he himself had been given authority by the Holy Ghost (see 1 Nephi 10:22.). Jacob testified of Christ by the power of the Holy Ghost (see Jacob 7:12, 17). Even the apostate Sherem was bold enough to ask for a sign by the Holy Ghost. Ironically, he received the sign, and before he died he testified that Jesus is the Christ and then confessed that the power of the Holy Ghost was real (see Jacob 7:13–20). Alma and Amulek were filled with the Holy Ghost as they taught the people (see Alma 8:30). Amulek warned the people to stop contending against the Holy Ghost (see Alma 34:38). From these selected references, we find that the Book of Mormon documents that the Holy Ghost was present in Old Testament times.

After Christ's visit to America, a new dispensation opened among the Nephites. The Book of Mormon refers to the Holy Ghost over twenty additional times after his visit. Other latter-day scripture documents earlier appearances, even from the time of Adam, where the Holy Ghost influenced the righteous (see Moses 5:9, 14, 58; 6:8).

Certainly, the Holy Ghost qualifies as one of the plain and precious parts of the plan of salvation. The Holy Ghost is the bearer of all truth in all dispensations. True doctrines of salvation can only be understood if witnessed by and learned through the Spirit (see D&C 50:11–24). When one testified that Jesus was the Christ anciently, it was by the power of the Holy Ghost, as it is in modern times (see Moroni 10:4–5, 7). Whenever the gospel is on the earth, the Holy Ghost is ever ready to witness, testify, reveal, teach, comfort, and sanctify those who are faithful. Mormon explained that when a society resists and eventually denies the existence of the Holy Ghost, they become ripe in iniquity, and they will perish (see Mormon 1:14; Moroni 8:28–29.)

Next, find the topic "Satan" in the topical guide (p. 447). Identify all the references to Satan in the Old Testament. There are only three (1 Chronicles, Job, and Psalms). Significant references to him by any other name are also conspicuously missing. What happened to Satan? If a people relied solely on the Old Testament for their religious beliefs, they might conclude that there is no such being as the devil. Although many theologians believe Satan was somehow related to the serpent in the garden and tempted Eve, the biblical text is weak on his identification.

The New Testament would lead one to believe that Jesus was inundated with people who were possessed by the devil, not to mention his own encounter with Satan after his forty-day fast. Did Satan suddenly burst onto the scene? Latter-day scripture restores many important details concerning Satan's history and his evil methods. By identifying and understanding his methods, we can better resist him. Book of Mormon prophets warned the people of their day, and of ours, to resist his evil power and influence. The Nephites were well aware of his influence. Early in the text, Nephi identifies the mists of darkness in his vision as the temptations of the devil (see 1 Nephi 12:17). In the Nephite scriptures, we learn that Satan tempted and deceived the Lamanites, Nephites, Jaredites, the wicked, and all apostates. He was a fallen angel, the founder of the great and abominable church, and preparator of hell, who delights in our misery, founded secret combinations, pacifies and flatters people, has a hold on

Lost and Found: The Plain and Precious Things 235

people's hearts, desires to sift us as wheat, is the master of sin, is the author of all sin, has the spirit of contention, is the father of all lies, will not support his children, is an enemy to God and the Saints, and seeks to destroy the souls of all men.[1]

The two previous examples demonstrate how the Old Testament has lost significant details important to the plan of salvation. Are we to believe that for four thousand years of biblical history neither the Holy Ghost nor the devil influenced anyone? Latter-day Saints know that the Holy Ghost inspired worthy Saints anciently and continues to do so in modern times. We know through modern scripture that Satan has tempted man through all dispensations. Yet, a significant part of the biblical text seems to ignore them. Could Satan's strategy be to remain anonymous and unrecognized? Can Satan influence more people by remaining unrecognized? (see 2 Nephi 28:22). (Undercover agents who do the most damage are those who are never discovered.)

In Moses 1, we read of an encounter Moses had with Satan. Eventually, Moses rejected Satan's advances and commanded him to depart. This defeat was lost from scripture until it was restored by the Prophet Joseph Smith. It was lost because of the wickedness of the people (see Moses 1:23). Was it "lost" because Satan did not want his defeat to be known among men? Did Satan play a part in the corruption of the scriptural text that documented his methods and defeats?

PLAIN AND PRECIOUS THINGS LOST . . . HOW?

Nephi learned from an angel that the "great and abominable church" would do serious damage to the inspired teachings and writings of the Twelve Apostles (see 1 Nephi 13:24–29). That "church," founded by the devil (1 Nephi 13:6), would bring about the intentional manipulation of the Bible. This manipulation included doctrinal biases that would produce evil results. It was a process that Satan was very interested in. He knew that the final results would propel his abominable efforts in corrupting mankind. Elder Bruce R. McConkie stated: "The devil wages war against the scriptures. He hates them, perverts their plain meanings, and destroys them when he can. He entices those who heed his temptings to delete and discard, to change and corrupt, to alter and amend, thus taking away the key which will aid in making men 'wise unto salvation.'"[2]

We learn from the angel that the modification of scripture was incremental. Nephi first describes how they had taken away plain and precious parts from the *gospel,* next they had taken away the *covenants* of the Lord, and finally, as a result of the previous efforts, plain and precious parts would actually be modified or *taken out* of the biblical text (see 1 Nephi 13:26–28). It is also probable that precious parts were taken away from the gospel, without altering the words themselves. One can change the meaning of the fundamental doctrines of salvation by overemphasizing some scribal bias.

The first principles of the gospel were changed or ignored in this way. As a result, faith in Jesus Christ can be emphasized in such a way that no true worship, righteous effort, and repentance in any form is expected. Repentance can be trivialized, and indulgences can be bought and sold (see Mormon 8:32). For example, though baptism is mentioned over twenty times in the New Testament, and being born again is mentioned twice, many choose to emphasize being born again and claim baptism as optional. Though false doctrines can flourish in an overzealous apostate environment, the Holy Ghost cannot bear witness of false doctrines. Therefore, unless people come to Christ and the true doctrines of salvation, the Holy Ghost has limited influence. Indeed, Nephi identified that because of the "things which are taken away out of the gospel . . . an exceedingly great many [would] stumble" (1 Nephi 13:29, 32).

Because of the changes that were made in the Bible, many of the covenants of the Lord have been ignored or lost. Covenants can be misunderstood or ignored because of a lack of knowledge concerning the promises given to the prophets. True authority and the knowledge of how to perform ordinances when covenants are made were also lost. The first time the word *covenant* appears in the Bible is in Genesis 6:18 when the Lord tells Noah he will establish his covenant with Noah and his family. Over fifteen hundred years passed between the days of Adam and Noah! Imagine for fifteen hundred years the Lord making no covenants with the ancients. The Bible text would lead us to believe that it was not until the time of Abraham that any significant covenants were made between man and God. The JST Genesis account documents the continuity of covenant making by all the great patriarchs with God. Each of the prophets, including Adam, Enoch, Noah, Melchizedek, and Abraham received the same covenant (see JST Genesis 9:15, 17, 21–23; 14:26–28; 17:3–8, 11–12).

Finally, many plain and precious things were *taken out* of the book. This actual modification of the text was done both deliberately and by accident. A lack of apostolic supervision over the text would allow corrupt and careless scribes to make modifications when recopying the text. Joseph Smith stated: "I believe the Bible as it read when it came from the pen of the original writers. Ignorant translators, careless transcribers, or designing and corrupt priests have committed many errors."[3] Scribes had replaced prophets.

Once the understanding of gospel principles was lost and the covenants lost their sacred meaning, scribes sought to clarify, expand, or delete parts of the text. The original meanings were lost and scribe's opinions were substituted in place of correct doctrines. Through this process they altered the meanings but still gave the perception that the text was yet intact. This process left a body of modified scripture with "a form of godliness" but "the power thereof" was missing (JS–H 1:19). Because many truths do remain in the Bible, the Christian world accepts and defends this diluted text as the final word of God even to this day.

Plain and Precious Things Lost . . . When?

Many of the textual corruptions took place shortly after the original manuscripts were penned by the apostles and prophets—perhaps even by the end of the first century—and were certainly continued into the second and third centuries A.D. Unless one were able to find the original document penned by the apostle, no matter how good the translator, you could not confidently trust the translated text. Joseph Smith stated: "We believe the Bible to be the word of God as far as it is translated correctly" (Articles of Faith 1:8) Since the tampering was more than just "translating" parts of the text, we can correctly say, We believe the Bible as far as it has been "transmitted" correctly. Moroni tells us that they "transfigured the holy word of God" (Mormon 8:33). The alterations were made before the Bible was distributed among the nations of the Gentiles (see 1 Nephi 13:28–29). Joseph Smith explained, "Many important points touching the salvation of men, had been taken from the Bible, or lost before it was compiled."[4]

Both the Old Testament and New Testament were affected. Nephi may have been referring to the Old Testament when he referred to the covenants being lost and the New Testament when reporting parts taken from the gospel (see 1 Nephi 13:26–29). In Jeremiah's day, he spoke of scribes who, with their lying pens, had falsified the words of holy scripture (see Jeremiah 8:8). Even in Jesus' day, scriptural misinterpretation was a concern. Jesus once declared: "Wo unto you, lawyers! For ye have taken away the key of knowledge, the fulness of the scriptures; ye enter not in yourselves into the kingdom; and those who were entering in, ye hindered" (JST Luke 11:53). John the Revelator was concerned about his writings being tampered with. He gives a solemn warning that curses would come upon anyone who added to or took away from any part of his textual document (see Revelation 22:18–19). It is likely that the early Greek Christians incorporated their secular philosophy by mixing their views with scripture. Even if the earliest manuscripts predating A.D. 200 were available to us, they would still be suspect. Most of the earliest known New Testament texts available today, including Vaticanus, Sinaiticus, and Alexandrinus,[5] date to the fourth century A.D. They all represent altered forms of the original documents.

THE LOSS OF PLAIN AND PRECIOUS THINGS CONTINUES

We find in 1 Nephi 13–14 some of the clearest descriptions of the corrupt status of today's Bible manuscripts. Without these descriptions, even Latter-day Saints would likely not understand the damage that was done to the original manuscripts soon after they left the hands of the prophets and apostles. Without inspiration from the gift of the Holy Ghost and the key of knowledge from the fulness of the scriptures (see JST Luke 11:53), today's scholars struggle to discern the accuracy of the text.

The Christian world has become increasingly embarrassed by the Bible. Some religious scholars have encouraged many of their students to abandon the biblical text as being authentic. The cry of "A Bible! A Bible! We have got a Bible" (2 Nephi 29:3) has lost much of its intensity. Many approaches now treat the Bible merely as mythological literature worth studying but not worth believing. Brigham

Lost and Found: The Plain and Precious Things

Young once stated: "Take this book, the Bible, which I expect to see voted out of the so-called Christian world very soon, they are coming to it as fast as possible, I say we take this book for our guide, for our rule of action; we take it as the foundation of our faith."[6] Such groups as the Jesus Seminar[7] have discovered some of the shortcomings of the biblical text and, in so doing, have attempted to intellectualize away the truths that are still contained within its pages.

Is the Bible just good literature? Is it divinely inspired? It takes inspiration to recognize inspiration. Today many substitute knowledge and learning in the place of inspiration and revelation. Educated guesses are not revelation. Jacob taught: "To be learned is good if they hearken unto the counsels of God" (2 Nephi 9:29). The Holy Ghost is a most necessary component for understanding scripture. Without the Holy Ghost, churches become progressively doctrinally confused.

Plain and Precious Things . . . What Survives?

In spite of all of its weaknesses, the Bible has been one of the most influential standards on the earth since the days prophets began sharing the revealed word of God. The Bible has been criticized, cursed, and abused more than any other book in history. Intellectuals, ministers, scribes, and kings have attacked and compromised its doctrines since its origin. Fortunately, it still contains the truths that have inspired and built faith for centuries. Many martyrs died for want of reading the text or for even possessing some of its pages. Satan, in his fury, has fought to keep the scriptures from being read or published. The fewer scriptures that survived the better, and if any did, an attempt to tamper with the text was made to destroy as much truth as possible. Every effort was made to convince the people that it is a confused, outdated, irrelevant document that must be philosophically debunked.

Even in its weakened condition, the Bible has been a powerful force for good. Elder Bruce R. McConkie stated: "And yet, with all this, we cannot avoid the conclusion that a divine providence is directing all things as they should be. This means that the Bible, as it now is, contains that portion of the Lord's word that a rebellious, wicked, and apostate world is entitled and able to receive."[8]

The Bible helped prepare men for the day when new revelation would come, as promised in the text itself. The Book of Mormon was prepared by prophetic hands and was destined to become a companion to the Bible (see Ezekiel 37:16–19). It would help establish the truthfulness of the parts "translated correctly" in the Bible. It would come forth to prove "to the world that the holy scriptures [Bible] are true" (D&C 20:11). Mormon taught: "For behold, this [Book of Mormon] is written for the intent that ye may believe [the Bible]; and if ye believe that ye will believe this also; and if ye believe this ye will know concerning your fathers, and also the marvelous works which were wrought by the power of God among them" (Mormon 7:9). The Lord spoke to Moses concerning the last days: "And in a day when the children of men shall esteem my words as naught and take many of them from the book which thou shalt write, behold, I will raise up another like unto thee; and they shall be had again among the children of men—among as many as shall believe" (Moses 1:41). In addition to establishing the truthfulness of the Bible, the Book of Mormon is a sign of the restored Church in the last days and is a witness that Joseph Smith received revelation and was a prophet of God.

PLAIN AND PRECIOUS THINGS FOUND . . . WHERE?

The Book of Mormon is unequaled in its explanations of many of the doctrines of salvation. Elder Bruce R. McConkie once stated "that Lehi and Jacob excel Paul in teaching the Atonement; that Alma's sermons on faith and on being born again surpass anything in the Bible; that Nephi makes a better exposition of the scattering and gathering of Israel than do Isaiah, Jeremiah, and Ezekiel combined; that Mormon's words about faith, hope, and charity have a clarity, a breadth, and a power of expression that even Paul did not attain; and so on and so on."[9]

It is the most doctrinally correct book on earth. Joseph Smith taught: "I told the brethren that the Book of Mormon was the most correct of any book on earth, and the keystone of our religion, and a man would get nearer to God by abiding by its precepts, than by any other book."[10] It has divine approval (see D&C 17:6). Other scriptures revealed to the Prophet, including the Doctrine and Covenants, the Pearl of Great Price, and the Joseph Smith Translation of the Bible, also restore lost truths of the gospel. Each of these texts is a

Lost and Found: The Plain and Precious Things

witness of Christ. The Lord himself testified that "in the mouth of two or three witnesses every word may be established" (Matthew 18:16).

PLAIN AND PRECIOUS THINGS RESTORED . . . ONE FINAL EXAMPLE

The Book of Mormon helps us understand the relationship between the spirit world, death, and the Resurrection. Alma's explanation of the Resurrection is unsurpassed by anything in the Old or New Testaments. Although the Bible documents Christ's resurrection and contains some references to the resurrection of general mankind, we can turn to Alma for a clearer explanation of what awaits each person's spirit as we enter the spirit world and there reside, waiting for the Resurrection (see Alma 40:11–14). What is the nature of the Resurrection? In the Bible we are led to believe that we are raised up with different types of bodies, each an incorruptible "spiritual body" (see 1 Corinthians 15:40–44). This belief has led some to spiritualize away the physical nature of the Resurrection. Other New Testament references refer to Christ as the "resurrection and the life" with no mention of details beyond Christ's own resurrection (John 11:25). The Old Testament is silent with only an occasional allusion to the Resurrection (see Job 14:14; Isaiah 26:19). We are left without an explanation of how the body and spirit are involved in the process.

Is the Resurrection corporeal? What about gender? Do males come forth males? Alma taught that our spirits will be restored to our bodies, with each limb intact in its proper and perfect frame (see Alma 40:23; 2 Nephi 9:11–12). We regain the body that we laid in the grave at death, both "male and female."[11] Once resurrected, we cannot die again (see Alma 11:45). The resurrected Christ appeared on the American continent and showed himself to many who experienced firsthand a resurrected being (see 3 Nephi 11–26). The Book of Mormon informs us that many people came forth from the grave after Christ in the new world (see 3 Nephi 23:9–10). Without the Resurrection we would eventually be subject to Satan and become devils like him (see 2 Nephi 9:8–9). From the Nephite text we learn the correct doctrine concerning restoration, justice and mercy, the state of the spirit after death (before resurrection), that those who are baptized can come forth in the First Resurrection, that everyone will be resurrected (even the wicked), and Christ's indispensable role in bringing about the resurrection of all mankind.

PLAIN AND PRECIOUS THINGS . . . FOUND AND APPRECIATED

These are some of the plain and precious doctrines that have been restored by the Book of Mormon. We have the Prophet Joseph Smith to honor for opening the heavens once again and bringing upon us a shower of revelations. Joseph Smith saw the Bible through the eyes of a prophet. I certainly agree with Brigham Young when he declared: "Would he [Joseph] not take the Scriptures and make them so plain and simple that everybody could understand?"[12] We can better understand our potential destiny because of the latter-day doctrinal restoration that continues to flow through latter-day prophets. Each of us, including our families, can be personally involved in the restoration as we live worthy of the inspiration that opens to us the plain and precious things of God.

NOTES

1. For Book of Mormon references to Satan before the birth of Christ, see 1 Nephi 13:29; 22:15; Alma 8:9; 10:25; 27:12; Helaman 16:23. For book of Moses references, see 1:12, 20–22; 4:1, 3–4, 6–11; 5:18, 28; 6:15, 49; 7:37.

2. Bruce R. McConkie, *Doctrinal New Testament Commentary*, 3 vols. (Salt Lake City: Bookcraft, 1966–73), 1:624–25.

3. Joseph Smith, *Teachings of the Prophet Joseph Smith*, sel. Joseph Fielding Smith (Salt Lake City: Deseret Book, 1976), 327.

4. Smith, *Teachings of the Prophet Joseph Smith*, 10–11.

5. See Robert J. Matthews, "Establishing the Truth of the Bible," in Monte S. Nyman and Charles D. Tate Jr., eds., *The Book of Mormon: First Nephi, the Doctrinal Foundation* (Provo, Utah: Brigham Young University, 1988), 206.

6. Brigham Young, in *Journal of Discourses*, 26 vols. (London: Latter-day Saints' Book Depot, 1854–86), 13:236.

7. From 1981 to 1991, almost two hundred biblical scholars met every six months to debate the accuracy and authenticity of the four Gospels. They concluded that less than 18 percent of what is in the present-day Bible was said by Jesus. The seminar's participants concluded that only one sentence in the entire Gospel of Mark was said by Jesus. Many believe that their findings are much too arbitrary and severe. See Robert J. Matthews, "What the Book of Mormon Tells Us about the Bible," in Bruce A. Van Orden and Brent L. Top, eds., *Doctrines*

of the Book of Mormon: The 1991 Sperry Symposium (Salt Lake City: Deseret Book, 1992), 101–2.; Jeffery L. Sheler, "Cutting Loose the Holy Canon," *U.S. News and World Report,* 8 Nov. 1993, 75; *The Oregonian,* 2 Mar. 1987; *The Oregonian,* 9 Mar. 1991; Robert W. Funk, *The Five Gospels, Search for the Authentic Words of Jesus,* The Jesus Seminar (New York: Macmillan Publishing, 1993).

8. Mark L. McConkie, ed., *Doctrines of the Restoration: Sermons and Writings of Bruce R. McConkie* (Salt Lake City: Bookcraft, 1989), 280.

9. Bruce R. McConkie, Conference Report, Oct. 1983, 106; or *Ensign,* Nov. 1983, 73.

10. Joseph Smith, *Teachings of the Prophet Joseph Smith,* sel. Joseph Fielding Smith (Salt Lake City: Deseret Book, 1976), 194.

11. See Smith, *Teachings of the Prophet Joseph Smith,* 295–96. See also "The Family: A Proclamation to the World," *Ensign,* Nov. 1995, 102: "Gender is an essential characteristic of individual premortal, mortal, and eternal identity and purpose."

12. Brigham Young, *Discourses of Brigham Young,* sel. John A. Widtsoe (1941), 459.

CHAPTER NINETEEN

THE DOCTRINE OF AGENCY IN THE BOOK OF MORMON

BLAIR G. VAN DYKE

Elder Richard G. Scott has taught: "Your agency, the right to make choices, is not given so that you can get what you want. This divine gift is provided so that you will choose what your Father in Heaven wants for you. That way He can lead you to become all that He intends you to be. That path leads to glorious joy and happiness."[1]

The Bible lacks clarity and scope regarding the doctrine of agency (in fact, the word *agency* is not found in the Bible). This doctrinal haziness leads many good-intentioned people to confuse absolute freedom with agency. Hence, the notion of freedom without moral responsibility often lies at the heart of challenges to society, such as fatherlessness in the home, increasing divorce rates, immorality, crime, excessive debt, as well as gender, social, and age gaps, and defiance of authority, to mention a few.

The Book of Mormon restores much-needed clarity and scope regarding the doctrine of agency. This restoration greatly enhances one's ability to successfully cope with the challenges of the last days because it effectively defines, explains, and illustrates the relationships between choice, accountability, and consequences. This chapter will offer a definition of agency from the Book of Mormon and then explore three stages of our eternal experience, wherein a clear understanding of agency is essential to our progression toward exaltation and eternal lives.

DEFINITION OF AGENCY

Elder Boyd K. Packer taught that "the phrase '*free* agency' does not appear in scripture. The only agency spoken of there is *moral agency.*"[2]

Blair G. Van Dyke is an instructor of religion in the Utah Valley North Area of the Church Educational System.

A powerfully definitive description of agency is found in the sermon of Samuel the Lamanite as he preached upon a wall in the land of Zarahemla. He taught that "whosoever will believe might be saved, and that whosoever will not believe, a righteous judgment might come upon them; and also if they are condemned they bring upon themselves their own condemnation.

"And now remember, remember, my brethren, that whosoever perisheth, perisheth unto himself; and whosoever doeth iniquity, doeth it unto himself; for behold, ye are free; ye are permitted to act for yourselves; for behold, God hath given unto you a knowledge and he hath made you free.

"He hath given unto you that ye might know good from evil, and he hath given unto you that ye might choose life or death; and ye can do good and be restored unto that which is good, or have that which is good restored unto you; or ye can do evil, and have that which is evil restored unto you" (Helaman 14:29–31).

Hence, agency consists of a merging of three fundamental axioms: freedom to choose, knowledge of opposites such as good and evil, and a clear understanding of how personal choices must result in a restoration of goodness or evil in the life of the individual agent.

With this definition and description of agency as a context, it is possible to explore the use of agency in the three stages of our eternal experience. These stages are agency in the premortal life, agency in mortality, and finally, agency in postmortality. Each is clearly addressed in the Book of Mormon.

AGENCY IN THE PREMORTAL LIFE

Like Abraham, Moses, Joseph Smith, Joseph F. Smith, and others, Alma had a clear understanding of the premortal life. From his insights, we have doctrines restored that are generally missing from the Bible. These doctrinal perceptions describe God's dealings with his children before he sent them to earth to prove their loyalties and capacities for obedience. Many of Alma's insights regarding the premortal life are found in Alma 13. Whether this information was gained through personal revelations and visions or gleaned from writings on the plates of brass or other scriptural sources then available is unknown. Nevertheless, Alma 13 is evidence that the ancient Saints had detailed knowledge concerning the premortal life.

Alma explains that in the premortal life every individual who is a high priest in the Melchizedek Priesthood in this life merited that calling as a result of faithful obedience to laws and principles of the gospel set forth before the foundations of this world (see Alma 13:1–4).[3] These verses are a clear example that our use of agency in the premortal life had significant bearing. According to Alma, there are at least three fundamental criteria upon which the righteous use of agency is predicated. The three are faith in Jesus Christ and his Father's plan of happiness, choosing good over evil, and equity.

Faith in Jesus Christ

It has been supposed by some that since we enjoyed the presence of our glorified, perfected, and resurrected parents in the premortal life, faith was not necessary. While Alma does not delineate precisely how faith was exercised in such knowledge-rich and veil-free circumstances, he does restore the understanding to the latter-day reader that faith was absolutely essential prior to coming to this earth. Alma notes that certain individuals were given weighty responsibilities in that realm "on account of their exceeding faith" (Alma 13:3).

Alma's language in chapter 13 leaves no doubt as to the existence of a spectrum of faithfulness in the premortal life. He explains that those called to holy positions of trust were faithful, "while others would reject the Spirit of God on account of the hardness of their hearts and blindness of their minds, while, if it had not been for this they might have had as great privilege as their brethren" (Alma 13:4).[4] This spectrum was created by the use of agency.

Choosing Good over Evil

Our conceptions of the antemortal experience may be prone to images of a static environment, wherein few adaptations, challenges, and choices between good and evil were necessarily faced. Again, we lack details, but Alma's revelations restore knowledge that was generally lost to apostasy. He informs us that the premortal life was marvelously dynamic, an arena wherein options were constantly placed before the spirit children of the Father. These options were not solely limited to choosing between good, better, and best. Apparently, the choice of outright evil was a very real and potentially tantalizing possibility (see Alma 13:3). The clearest illustration of this possibility is the fact that Lucifer used his agency to rebel, become a devil, and persuade countless spirits to follow him.[5]

Equity

Furthermore, Alma explains that we were "left to choose good or evil" (Alma 13:3). Being left to choose implies autonomy coupled with a level of knowledge and maturity necessary to make difficult choices. We reached a point of independence of thought and action wherein being "left to choose" was appropriate and fair. In this regard, it is important to acknowledge that we have no evidence of there being "handicapped" or "disabled" spirits who lacked capacity to learn the essentials of spiritual obedience to their Father. Alma explains that "in the first place they were on the same standing with their brethren" (Alma 13:5). In the beginning, the playing field was level and fair for all of the Father's spirit children. We all had opportunity to acquire the prerequisite knowledge to thrive in the presence of the Father and receive blessings from him.

Elder Bruce R. McConkie taught that "when we pass from pre-existence to mortality, we bring with us the traits and talents there developed. True, we forget what went before because we are here being tested, but the capacities and abilities that then were ours are yet resident within us. Mozart is still a musician; Einstein retains his mathematical abilities; Michelangelo his artistic talent; Abraham, Moses, and the prophets their spiritual talents and abilities. Cain still lies and schemes. And all men with their infinitely varied talents and personalities pick up the course of progression where they left it off when they left the heavenly realms."[6]

Hence, it appears that the only mechanism of differentiation among God's sons and daughters in the premortal life was the personal use of agency. In this regard he is perfectly equitable, meaning that all privileges are available for all children on the grounds of obedience (see Alma 3:4).

Summary

The Book of Mormon restores doctrine relating to agency in the premortal life through the explication of at least three basic principles. First, it was imperative to exercise faith in Jesus Christ in the antemortal councils. Second, the premortal life was not a stagnant environment; rather, it was greatly varied and challenging. We were left to choose good or evil. The results of our choices determined the opportunities for service within the bounds of priesthood blessings.

And finally, a loving Father created an environment of perfect equity. This equity was established through teaching his children (all who would submit and learn) how to use their agency to do his will.

Agency in Mortality

Mortality picks up where the premortal life left off. While the spirit is coupled with a physical body and the mind is veiled from premortal memories, the Book of Mormon confirms, the axioms of agency remain unchanged. Hence, Lehi explained to his son Jacob that "men are free according to the flesh; and all things are given them which are expedient unto man. And they are free to choose liberty and eternal life, through the great Mediator of all men, or to choose captivity and death, according to the captivity and power of the devil; for he seeketh that all men might be miserable like unto himself" (2 Nephi 2:27). In a phrase, the setting has changed, but the principles have not.

This accentuates the importance of the doctrines restored through the coming forth of the Book of Mormon. Prior to its translation, the world had no clear conception of the doctrine of agency as constituted in the premortal life or mortality. All was lost to apostasy. Now, the Book of Mormon is available to bring to light a complete restoration of saving truths, while exposing those false doctrines that undercut the principles of agency.

As an example, consider Nephi's exposure of ten major lies propagated by Satan in the last days (see 2 Nephi 28). Nephi explains that these lies will go forth in our day when Satan rages "in the hearts of the children of men, and [stirs] them up to anger against that which is good" (2 Nephi 28:20). The word *rage* implies that Satan is pouring forth his efforts in undiluted doses to destroy the latter-day work with a particular effort to dissuade sincere seekers of truth.

Given this context, it is interesting that an apparent intent of nine of the ten lies is to eradicate the doctrines of agency that were espoused by two-thirds of all of Heavenly Father's children in the premortal life. An overview of these nine lies may be helpful to highlight how effectively the Book of Mormon exposes an integral part of Satan's plan.[7]

Satan's Latter-day Lie	Incongruity in Light of Doctrine of Agency
"Eat, drink, and be merry, for tomorrow we die" (2 Nephi 28:7).	No ultimate judgment; outcomes and actions are not generally related.
"Eat, drink, and be merry; nevertheless, fear God" (2 Nephi 28:8).	Acknowledging God relieves accountability.
"He will justify in committing a little sin" (2 Nephi 28:8).	God does not treat his children equitably.
"If it so be that we are guilty, God will beat us with a few stripes" (2 Nephi 28:8).	"Real" justice or punishment is a myth.
"[Regardless of actions,] we shall be saved in the kingdom of God" (2 Nephi 28:8).	God makes exceptions for his "chosen ones" so do what you will.
"Hide their counsels from the Lord; and their works shall be in the dark" (2 Nephi 28:9).	God is often unaware of my choices.
"All is well in Zion" (2 Nephi 28:21).	Bad choices have little bearing on the condition of the Saints.
"There is no hell" (2 Nephi 28:22).	God lies: there is no final punishment for the truly wicked.
"I am no devil" (2 Nephi 28:22).	There is no opposition in all things.

Herein Nephi partially uncovers Satan's plot to attack the doctrine of agency. At the same time, Nephi's writings provide an implied key of understanding to each reader of 2 Nephi 28. That key comes from inverting the devil's intentions, which reveal several doctrines espoused by the Father. For example, the phrase "Eat, drink, and be merry, for tomorrow we die" could profitably be rendered "Choose righteously in all you do, for tomorrow you may die." The inversion captures the true doctrine that springs out of agency—there will be an ultimate judgment, wherein choices will be accounted for and actions will be seen in the light in which they were taken. Similarly, the incongruity in 2 Nephi 28:9, which claims that it is possible to "seek deep to hide their counsels from the Lord; and their works shall be in the dark," is a key to understanding that God knows all things and that attempts to hide thoughts or actions from him is futile when considered with a clear understanding of the doctrines surrounding agency.

While Satan attempts to cloud and fog our intuitive desires to follow the Savior, the prophets consistently create opportunities wherein those same intuitive desires are played upon to enhance spiritual growth and understanding. Consider two examples from the Book of Mormon that illustrate this point.

Mosiah 2 through 6 contains the concluding sermons of King Benjamin's long ministry. Many of the doctrines and feelings shared during those days at the temple have direct bearing upon the doctrines of agency. Remembering that the three axioms of agency are freedom to choose, knowledge of good and evil, and an understanding that our choices will result in a restoration of happiness or misery, consider King Benjamin's words:

"And now I say unto you, my brethren, that after ye have known and have been taught all these things, if ye should transgress and go contrary to that which has been spoken, that ye do withdraw yourselves from the Spirit of the Lord, that it may have no place in you to guide you in wisdom's paths that ye may be blessed, prospered, and preserved—

"I say unto you, that the man that doeth this, the same cometh out in open rebellion against God; therefore he listeth to obey the evil spirit, and becometh an enemy to all righteousness" (Mosiah 2:36–37).

In this passage, the phrase "after ye have known and have been taught" implies an understanding of good and evil; the phrase "if ye should transgress and go contrary to that which has been spoken" implies freedom to choose; and the phrase "that ye do withdraw yourselves from the Spirit of the Lord" implies that a restoration of good or evil will take place according to choices made. The doctrine of agency is laced throughout this verse and throughout King Benjamin's sermons.

The second example of how prophets in the Book of Mormon consistently amplify the doctrines of agency in their teachings is found in Alma 5 and 6. Alma was facing a spiritual crisis throughout the church of God. Apostasy had crept into the Church, and Zarahemla was not immune from the difficulties. These chapters preserve Alma's sermon, aimed to recover the members of the Church in Zarahemla from the ways of the adversary that had infiltrated the Church.

The Doctrine of Agency in the Book of Mormon

As part of his Zarahemla discourse, Alma posed approximately thirty pressing questions to the Saints. Many of these questions find their foundation in the doctrines of agency. Therefore, a careful reading of these questions suggests that one of Alma's primary objectives, as he calls the people to repentance, was to stir up a remembrance of the doctrines of agency so familiar to the Saints. From Alma we may learn that helping the wayward come to grips, once again, with the realities of agency can be a powerful tool to persuade a return to the fold of the Church. Alma's teachings had just that effect (see Alma 7:3–4). Some examples from his sermon may serve to demonstrate this point.

Alma's Question	Relationship to Axioms of Agency
"Do ye imagine to yourselves that ye can lie unto the Lord in that day, and say—Lord, our works have been righteous works upon the face of the earth?" (Alma 5:17).	Restoration cannot be circumvented.
"Could ye say, if ye were called to die at this time . . . that your garments have been cleansed and made white through the blood of Christ, who will come to redeem his people from their sins?" (Alma 5:27).	Freedom to choose may be used to implement the Atonement and gain forgiveness.
"Can ye imagine yourselves brought before the tribunal of God with your souls filled with guilt and remorse, having a remembrance of all your guilt, yea, a perfect remembrance . . . that ye have set at defiance the commandments of God?" (Alma 5:18).	You knowledge of good and evil will make a perfect restoration of good for good and evil for evil completely equitable.
"Can ye think of being saved when you have yielded yourselves to become subjects to the devil?" (Alma 5:20).	Knowledge of good and evil combined with pending restoration make this thought an impossibility.
"Have ye received his image in your countenances?" (Alma 5:14).	Freedom to choose can result in great blessings.
"Do ye exercise faith in the redemption of him who created you?" (Alma 5:15).	Faith requires a knowledge of good and evil and freedom to choose good.

Summary

Agency in mortality employs the same principles that were in place in the premortal life. The essentials have not and will not change. In mortality, however, where the veil shields memory, Satan is "raging" and periods of apostasy have muddied the doctrinal waters. Fortunately, the restoration of truth and light is well under way, and the Book of Mormon is available to the world. That volume of scripture exposes the tactics of the adversary as he attempts to undercut the vital doctrine of agency by infusing false and damning ideas into the philosophies of men. Those who carefully read the Book of Mormon may find clear and coherent descriptions of the plan of salvation, including the tenets of agency that are essential to a full and meaningful experience in mortality.

AGENCY IN POSTMORTALITY

Men and women have always been moral agents. Death will not change that reality. This section includes two cardinal examples from the Book of Mormon that illustrate how agency transcends the grave. First, an overview of the plan of restoration from Alma 41. This will be followed by an analysis of Amulek's teachings to the Zoramites in Alma 34.

The Plan of Restoration

As mentioned earlier, restoration is a key element of agency. Alma notes that a plan of restoration is essential if Christ is to be just in his judgments (see Alma 41:2). Were it not so, wickedness *could* become happiness (see v. 10). Alma explains that "the meaning of the word restoration is to bring back again evil for evil, or carnal for carnal, or devilish for devilish—good for that which is good; righteous for that which is righteous; just for that which is just; merciful for that which is merciful.

"Therefore, my son, see that you are merciful unto your brethren; deal justly, judge righteously, and do good continually; and if ye do all these things then shall ye receive your reward; yea, ye shall have mercy restored unto you again; ye shall have justice restored unto you again; ye shall have a righteous judgment restored unto you again; and ye shall have good rewarded unto you again.

"For that which ye do send out shall return unto you again, and be restored; therefore, the word restoration more fully condemneth the sinner, and justifieth him not at all" (Alma 41:13–15; see also 29:4).

The plan of restoration explains the perfection of the Savior's mode of judgment: That which you meted out in mortality will become yours in immortality. As Elder Neal A. Maxwell put it: "Therefore, what we insistently desire, over time, is what we will eventually become and what we will receive in eternity."[8] This is flawlessly fair. Our choices under the laws of agency become the standard for our ultimate rewards and punishments, thus making it possible for *every* tongue to confess before God that his judgments are just (see Mosiah 16:1).

The Book of Mormon restores, in plain terms, the plan of restoration. Striving to clearly understand this plan can lead individuals to better and more fruitful judgments in daily life. Such a course would result in joy, happiness, and contentment.

The Discourse of Amulek

Ironically, a misconception regarding agency in postmortality comes from the misreading of a scripture in the Book of Mormon. Amulek was preaching with Alma on the hill Onidah to a group of Zoramites who were despised by their brethren and cast out of their synagogues because of their poverty. Amulek's intent was to bear down in pure testimony in hopes of reclaiming this group of Nephite apostates (see Alma 31:5). In this setting Amulek taught that "ye cannot say, when ye are brought to that awful crisis, that I will repent, that I will return to my God. Nay, ye cannot say this; for that same spirit which doth possess your bodies at the time that ye go out of this life, that same spirit will have power to possess your body in that eternal world" (Alma 34:34).

This scripture has been interpreted by some to mean that it is not possible to use our agency in the world of spirits in order to draw closer to our Heavenly Father and more fully follow Christ. For the faithful, such a doctrine would be a damnation, since no one but the Savior passes out of this life in a state fit to receive exaltation in the celestial realms of the Father.

In reality, the world of spirits is a place of great preparation where the axioms of agency are still firm and diligence and faithfulness are still essential. Just as premortal temperaments carried over into mortality, so our mortal dispositions bridge death and carry over to postearth life.

In the King Follett Discourse, Joseph Smith taught that "when you climb up a ladder, you must begin at the bottom, and ascend step by step, until you arrive at the top; and so it is with the principles of the Gospel—you must begin with the first, and go on until you learn all the principles of exaltation. But it will be a great while after you have passed through the veil before you will have learned them. It is not all to be comprehended in this world; it will be a great work to learn our salvation and exaltation even beyond the grave."[9]

Therefore, Amulek's sermon serves to justify the fact that agency is vigorously implemented in the world of spirits by the righteous and those of a willing heart. The "awful crisis" that Amulek refers to is death without a repentant and submissive disposition. Simply put, a person who has used agency to disobey God and set at naught the atonement of Jesus Christ in this life will not alter markedly in disposition simply by passing through a veil from mortality to immortality.

Hence, Amulek's words are not intended to address the ability of the Zoramites to learn and grow spiritually in postmortal existence; rather, his words address their willingness. If they were not willing to follow Christ and repent in this life, that same spirit or disposition will go with them to the next life. Therefore, there is no reason to believe that they will change.

But the opposite is also true and constitutes an exciting prospect for the righteous. There is every reason to believe that the Savior will continue transforming his penitent followers grace for grace, according to their use of agency, until a fulness of joy and exaltation is achieved.

Conclusion

Through the Book of Mormon, the doctrine of agency has been restored. Therefore, we know that all of Heavenly Father's children have always been, are, and always will be agents. The definitions, explanations, and illustrations regarding this eternal precept that are laced throughout the Book of Mormon provide a clarity and scope that is not found in the Bible. With this restored knowledge, we may know that absolute freedom—the freedom to do anything at any time and be happy—is nonexistent. In this light, the Book of Mormon serves as a guidebook in the last days. It points the reader to Christ and simultaneously exposes the strategies and schemes of Satan, who so often tries to twist and wrest the doctrines surrounding agency. President James E. Faust urges that we should "not only . . . avoid evil, not only . . . do good but, most importantly, . . . do the things of greatest worth. We are to focus on the inward things of the heart, which we know and value intuitively but often neglect for that which is trivial, superficial, and prideful."[10] Understanding the doctrine of agency as restored and taught in the Book of Mormon will promote a level of discretion in decision making heretofore unknown.

NOTES

1. Richard G. Scott, Conference Report, Apr. 1996, 33; or *Ensign*, May 1996, 25.

2. Boyd K. Packer, Conference Report, Apr. 1992, 92; or *Ensign*, May 1992, 67.

3. See Joseph Smith, *Teachings of the Prophet Joseph Smith,* sel. Joseph Fielding Smith (Salt Lake City: Deseret Book, 1976), 365.

4. It is noteworthy that Alma's teachings, coupled with the teachings of the Apostle Paul, greatly influenced the young Prophet Joseph Smith, who explained in *Lectures on Faith* that "faith being the first principle in revealed religion, and the foundation of all righteousness, necessarily claims the first place in a course of lectures which are designed to unfold to the understanding the doctrine of Jesus Christ" ([Salt Lake City: Deseret Book, 1985], 1). As it is in this life, so it was in the premortal life.

5. Regarding our ability in the premortal life to choose evil and sin, Orson Pratt explained that "among the two-thirds who remained, it is highly probable, that, there were many who were not valiant in the war, but whose sins were of such a nature that they could be forgiven through faith in the future sufferings of the Only Begotten of the Father, and through their sincere repentance and reformation. We see no impropriety in Jesus offering himself as an acceptable offering and sacrifice before the Father to atone for the sins of His brethren, committed, not only in the second, but also in the first estate. . . . Now we may ask, Why was the Lamb, considered as 'slain from the foundation of the world?' If there were no persons who had sinned in their first estate, that could be benefitted by the sufferings of their elder brother, then we can see no reason for considering Him at that early period, as already slain: the very fact, that the atonement which was to be made in a

future world, was considered as already having been made, seems to show that there were those who had sinned, and who stood in need of the atonement" ("The Pre-existence of Man," *The Seer,* Apr. 1853, 54).

Additionally, John 9:1–2 illustrates an understanding among the Saints in the meridian that sin was possible in the premortal life. The scripture reads:

"And as Jesus passed by, he saw a man which was blind from his birth.

"And his disciples asked him, saying, Master, who did sin, this man, or his parents that he was born blind?" Commenting on this verse, Elder Bruce R. McConkie writes that "apparently the Jews had some understanding of the doctrine of pre-existence. Among their righteous forebears it had been taught plainly as a basic gospel truth. . . . It was a doctrine implicit in the whole plan of salvation as such was known to and understood by them. They had, for instance, no more occasion to prove the ante-mortal existence of spirits than they did to prove God was a personal Being. Both truths were assumed. . . .

"Jesus' disciples—probably as a direct result of his teachings—knew and believed that men were the spirit children of God in pre-existence and that in such prior estate they were subject to law and endowed with agency. Otherwise they never would have asked nor would there have been any sense or reason to a question which is predicated upon the assumption that men can sin before they are born into mortality." Bruce R. McConkie, *Doctrinal New Testament Commentary,* 3 vols. (Salt Lake City: Bookcraft, 1966–73), 1:480.

6. Bruce R. McConkie, *The Mortal Messiah: From Bethlehem to Calvary,* 4 vols. (Salt Lake City: Deseret Book, 1979), 1:25.

7. This material is an adaptation of information obtained from conversations with Ted L. Gibbons.

8. Neal A. Maxwell, Conference Report, Oct. 1996, 26; or *Ensign,* Nov. 1996, 21.

9. Smith, *Teachings of the Prophet Joseph Smith,* 348.

10. James E. Faust, Conference Report, Oct. 1997, 75; or *Ensign,* Nov. 1997, 53.

CHAPTER TWENTY

The Restoration of the Doctrine of Angels as Found in the Book of Mormon

Mary Jane Woodger

Elder Jeffrey R. Holland taught: "I am convinced that one of the profound themes of the Book of Mormon, one which may not yet have been developed enough, . . . is the role and prevalence and central participation of angels in the everlasting gospel story. . . .

"I believe we need to speak of and believe in and bear testimony to the ministry of angels more than we sometimes do. They constitute one of God's great methods of witnessing through the veil, and no document in all this world teaches that principle so clearly and so powerfully and so often as does the Book of Mormon."[1]

During his mortal ministry, Jesus Christ frequently spoke both literally and figuratively of angels (see Matthew 16:27; 18:10; Luke 15:10). In the Bible, angels participated in many of the important events related to the roots of Christianity (see John 20:12; Luke 1:13–19; 2:21), yet within centuries after the death of Christ, the concept that the heavens were closed was preached from the pulpits of Christendom. Christian leaders were educated with the premise "that revelation had ceased; that the voice of prophecy was forever silenced; that the ministration of angels was ended."[2] It was in the midst of this theological climate that Joseph Smith testified that he

---

Mary Jane Woodger is an assistant professor of Church history and doctrine at Brigham Young University.

was directed by an angel to bring forth a volume replete with passages depicting angelic visitations.

Not only did the restoration of all things include the restoration of angelic ministration but also the Restoration itself was brought about by heavenly messengers. Mormon testified that he knew the Restoration would come through the ministration of angels (see Moroni 7:30–32). Elder Bruce R. McConkie testified that "by the ministering of angels to men in modern times the Lord's great work of restoration is being accomplished."[3] This chapter examines the doctrine of angels as restored in the Book of Mormon and defines the role of heavenly messengers throughout the period when this sacred volume came forth. Angels' central participation and prevalence, their involvement in the Restoration, their ministry, and their eventual role in ushering in the Second Coming will be examined as revealed in this keystone of Latter-day Saint scripture.

THE BOOK OF MORMON DEFINES ANGELS

The word *angel* is found eighty-five times in the Book of Mormon; the plural *angels* is listed fifty-five times.[4] As used in this keystone of Latter-day Saint theology, an angel generally is any being who brings a message from God. Like those who receive their messages, angels are also "the offspring of God."[5] All heavenly messengers whose visits are recorded in the Book of Mormon are "those who do belong or have belonged to" the earth (D&C 130:5). Like mortals, angels are also "pressing forward along the course of progression and salvation, all in their respective spheres."[6]

Specifically, the term *angel* describes five different classes of beings who appear in human form, though their spirits may or may not be housed in a physical body. One angel classification is unembodied, or premortal, spirit children of our Heavenly Father who have not yet been born on the earth but will obtain tabernacles of flesh and bone in the future. For instance, Nephi is guided by a "spirit" through a vision of the Savior's mortal ministry by a being he identifies as "the Spirit of the Lord" (1 Nephi 11:11). Using the general definition above, Nephi's escort can accurately be called an angel, because he brought such an unprecedented message from heaven. Gospel scholars have identified this being as either the premortal

Jehovah or the Holy Ghost.[7] In either case, this angelic messenger from God the Father was unembodied.

Another kind of angel who appears without a physical body is the disembodied, or spirits of "just men made perfect" (D&C 76:69). Though it is impossible to tell in the Book of Mormon whether specific angels are premortal or postmortal, it is accurate to say that all spirits appearing to the American ancients before the appearance of Christ on this continent were either disembodied or unembodied spirits (see 1 Nephi 3:29; Mosiah 4:11; Alma 8:14–18; Helaman 13:7).

Those angels cited after 3 Nephi could have bodies. One kind of angel with a corporeal body is a translated being (see Alma 45:19). The Three Nephites, when translated, became "as the angels of God" (3 Nephi 28:30). Mormon tells us he had seen the apostolic trio but was unsure if they were "mortal or immortal, from the day of their transfiguration" (v. 17). Though they were "caught up into the heavens" (v. 36) at one point, they continue to "minister unto all the people" (v. 18) as translated beings. Joseph Smith enriched our understanding, informing us that such translated beings can minister "unto many planets."[8]

Another type of angel, also housed in a body of flesh and bone, is the resurrected being. These agents of our Father in Heaven have appeared since the resurrection of the Savior in the meridian of time. For instance, when the Book of Mormon prophet Moroni appeared to the boy prophet Joseph Smith, he had a tangible body, glorified through the resurrection process (see JS–H 1:30–32). Moroni "being dead [was] raised again therefrom."[9]

Righteous mortals who deliver messages from our Father in Heaven can also correctly be called angels. Nephi tells us that after a son or daughter of God receives the Holy Ghost he or she can "speak with the tongue of angels" (2 Nephi 31:13; 32:2).[10] Moreover, the very word in Hebrew, *mal'āk*, used for angel also means "messenger."

The Central Participation and Prevalence of Angels in the Restoration of the Gospel

One of the most important angelic appearances of all dispensations was that of Moroni on 21 September 1823. His appearance was an affirmation of the Resurrection—a tangible, corporeal witness that there is much more beyond the grave than many nineteenth century people understood. The Angel Moroni revealed the Book of Mormon, the keystone of Latter-day Saint theology.[11] As recorded in this sacred volume, the gospel was revealed to these ancient people in the same way it was revealed to Joseph Smith—by ministering angels. Truth was revealed to chosen servants of the Lord (Nephi, King Benjamin, Alma the Younger, Samuel the Lamanite, Amulek, etc.) by heavenly messengers. Elder Holland calls the appearance of these angels the "fairness doctrine."[12] He explains that in fairness, the Lord made allowances, blessing these people for their faith in an atonement that had not yet happened and in a Savior yet unborn. The Book of Mormon states clearly that the Lord does not prize the souls of any dispensation more than another.

It is as Alma asked his son Corianton, "Is it not as easy at this time for the Lord to send his angel to declare these glad tidings unto us as unto our children, or as after the time of his coming?" (Alma 39:19). Throughout the Book of Mormon the Lord answers Alma's question with a resounding, "Yes!" He sends angels to all peoples who exhibit sufficient faith. The Book of Mormon story itself begins with an angelic visitation, and even Sherem, the first Book of Mormon anti-Christ, eventually admits to the ministering of angels (see Jacob 7:17). In addition, the Angel Moroni fulfilled the Lord's promises as he effected the restoration of the Book of Mormon, which is now going forth to the descendants of America's ancient prophets (see JS–H 1:34).

Sensing the significance of Moroni's work, Elder Orson Hyde called him "the guardian angel of America." Elder Hyde tells us Moroni's ministry has even included the influencing of Columbus and George Washington.[13] As important as Moroni's responsibilities are, however, he does not stand alone as the angel of the Restoration. In truth the "angel of the restoration was *a composite angel*."[14] Fifty-nine angelic appearances to Joseph Smith, including some Book of Mormon personalities (Alma; twelve Nephite apostles, including the Three Nephites; Nephi; Enos; and Mormon), have been recorded.[15] Other angels besides Moroni had to come to ordain Joseph with apostolic authority to administer ordinances. As Elder Orson Pratt tells us, Moroni went "as far as he was authorised" in revealing the stick of Ephraim.[16] Without other angels, Moroni's contribution would have been ineffectual. These other "divers angels" came to

The Restoration of the Doctrine of Angels

restore authority with their keys and priesthood (see D&C 128:20–21; 27:5–13; 88:103).

Angels' Restoration of the Priesthood

An eternal priesthood organization exists among the heavenly hosts.[17] On this earth, priesthood was first restored on 15 May 1829 when John the Baptist reestablished the Aaronic Priesthood and with it the key of the ministering of angels (see D&C 13; JS–H 1:68–72). What does it mean that an Aaronic Priesthood holder can have the keys of the ministering of angels? Elder Dallin H. Oaks enlightens us on this subject: "Those who hold the Aaronic Priesthood open the door for all Church members who worthily partake of the sacrament to enjoy the companionship of the Spirit of the Lord and the ministering of angels."[18] In other words, the restoration of the ministering of angels is not only for worthy young men; but through the ordinance of the sacrament, all worthy Church members are blessed by the ministering of angels.

Other angels who brought priesthood keys, including three who restored the Melchizedek Priesthood, are also mentioned in scriptural works (for example, Gabriel, who is Noah, and Raphael; see D&C 27:12–13; 128:21). The recorded visits of these angels does not mark the end of their heavenly ministry. Angelic ministrations will continue until the Second Coming, when the Lord will appear with concourses of angels (see D&C 45:44).

Elder Holland suggests that there are "personal ministering angels who are with us and around us, empowered to help us."[19] These messengers come from God's presence in the eternal world to deliver messages that teach the human family eternal truths (see Mosiah 3). They minister to the Lord's chosen vessels (see Moroni 7:31–32), call us to repentance (see Moroni 7:31), bear glad tidings (see Mosiah 3:3), save us from perilous circumstances (see 1 Nephi 3:29–31), fulfill covenants made to the Fathers (see Moroni 7:32), assist in the gathering of Israel (see Matthew 24:31), and play a key role in the destruction of the wicked.

Angels Teach Eternal Truths

When angels appear, they "do not pose as ornamental fixtures"; they bring messages.[20] According to Nephi and Moroni, the Holy

Ghost is a key participant in all aspects of angelic ministry (see 2 Nephi 32:3; Moroni 7:31–32). Just as the third member of the Godhead does not speak for himself, neither do angels when teaching God's children. The ministries of all messengers, including Moses, Elijah, Peter, James, and John, are directed by the Holy Ghost (see D&C 110). Angels never speak for themselves. Nephi suggests that through the Holy Spirit these angels "speak the words of Christ," having great power and authority (2 Nephi 32:3; see also 33:1). This is seen clearly in Moroni's appearance to the Prophet Joseph Smith (see JS–H 1:36–41). In addition to his own words, Moroni was directed to quote scripture to tutor the Prophet Joseph Smith. Under the Holy Ghost's direction, Moroni and all other angels become ministers of Christ and are subject to his command (see Moroni 7:30).

ANGELS MINISTER TO THE LORD'S CHOSEN VESSELS

A verb often associated with an angel's visit is *minister* (see 1 Nephi 16:38; Jacob 7:17; Omni 1:25). In the Book of Mormon, *minister* is used ten times in association with angelic visits. In scriptural context this verb implies conversation. An angel's ministry or work is to teach those on earth (see Helaman 5:39). Joseph Smith called his four years of tutoring with Moroni "interviews" (see JS–H 1:43–54). Angelic pedagogy is never described as a one-sided lecture; the dialogue includes questions and answers. One such ministry is reported in 1 Nephi 11–14. The spirit visiting Nephi asks several questions, including "What beholdest thou?" (11:14) and "Knowest thou the meaning of the tree which thy father saw?" (11:21). In this selection, as Nephi answers his interviewer, it is clear that a messenger carries out his ministry by conversing with men, women, and children. What a chat such a conversation must be!

Such dialogue does not start out as ours do in as, for example, sharing news with a neighbor over the back fence. When the resurrected Christ appeared to those assembled in the upper room, we are told, they were "terrified and affrighted" (Luke 24:37). This seems to be a natural response to the appearance of angels.[21] When Joseph Smith attempted to take the gold plates while improperly thinking about their monetary value, Moroni touched him with "a shock that affected the whole body."[22] Alma the Younger and the sons of Mosiah fell to the earth out of "fear" when an angel visited them (see Alma

The Restoration of the Doctrine of Angels

36:7). It is no wonder such fear fills the human heart, for the effect of an angel's voice can be one of thunder that can cause the whole earth to shake (see Mosiah 27:11).

The timing of such visits can also be dynamic. Often angels appear to those who are asleep. King Benjamin told his people that he was sleeping peacefully when an angel demanded, "Awake, and hear the words which I shall tell thee" (Mosiah 3:3).

Many examples of this can be found in the Book of Mormon. We find that after many Lamanites had seen and conversed with angels, they became righteous and gained momentum in following the commandments of Jesus Christ (see Alma 19:34–35). The teachings of an angel to a servant of the Lord can be life changing. For instance, though Amulek was an untrained missionary, he had a "stunning grasp of theology." His knowledge was far beyond his experience because "he had been tutored by an angel."[23] We can also see the visit of the Angel Moroni as a turning point in Joseph Smith's life. After Moroni's interviews with him, Joseph's life was never to be the same. Not only was Moroni's visit life changing for Joseph but it also provided for the restoration of the Book of Mormon, opening eternal vistas to all who believe an angel conversed with the prophet of the Restoration. Angels will also visit during times of crisis, strengthening those they visit. Elder Bruce R. McConkie suggested it may have been the mighty angel Michael who strengthened Jesus Christ during his greatest moment of crisis, the Atonement[24] (see Luke 22:43). As worldwide crisis deepens with the second coming of the Lord drawing nigh, Latter-day Saints may need to be strengthened by angels even daily, as Nephi was before the advent of Christ's first appearance in America (see 3 Nephi 7:18).

From these examples found in the Book of Mormon, we see that angels most often minister to those the Lord selects as his chosen vessels, because they are of "strong faith and a firm mind" (Moroni 7:30). Faith is a key ingredient in receiving angelic ministration. For example, right before Moroni's visit, Joseph Smith was "endeavoring to exercise faith in the precious promises of Scripture."[25] In Joseph Smith's case, as in so many others, faith does precede the miracle of an angel's appearance. Along with faith, as Moroni tells us, a firm mind is a vital prerequisite (see Moroni 7:30). Despite what the world preaches, those receiving heavenly visitors are not hysterical, overly imaginative people with mystic gifts who froth at the mouth.[26] Those who entertain angels must be the most sane, stable, and intelligent souls who grace the earth.

Angels are often called upon to warn and protect. The greatest warning they give is the command to repent. One great scriptural example of an individual who was called to repentance by an angel is Alma the Younger. His father and other faithful Nephites had fasted and prayed for a change in this potential prophet (see Mosiah 27:14). This passage in the Book of Mormon restores another great truth of the doctrine of angels. Prayers in behalf of loved ones are efficacious, at times even bringing down the very angels of heaven. What a comfort this restored truth can be for parents who pray for a wayward child!

Other Book of Mormon prophets were also tutored by angels. As Samuel the Lamanite called the Nephites to repentance with incredible power, he testified that he had been instructed by an angel (see Helaman 13:1–7). In like manner, in one of Alma the Younger's moments of great despair, an angel comforts him and then tells him to return to Ammonihah and find a missionary companion who has also been called by a heavenly messenger to cry repentance unto the people (see Alma 8:15; 10:7).

In addition, it is important to remember that early in the story of the Book of Mormon, an angel also calls Laman and Lemuel to repentance (see 1 Nephi 3:28–29). Nephi reminds his wayward brothers that they had "seen an angel, . . . heard his voice from time to time; and he hath spoken unto [them] in a still small voice," but because they were "past feeling, . . . [they] could not feel his words" (1 Nephi 17:45). Commenting on this passage, Elder Oaks explained that "most angelic communications are felt or heard rather than seen."[27]

Heavenly messengers may also execute judgment. Eventually, they will have a commission to cleanse the earth of evil doctrines and practices (see D&C 86:5). While these angels of destruction wait to be sent (see D&C 77:9), ministering angels will continue to call the world to repentance (see D&C 43:25). Those who repent will begin to see the fulfillment of promises made to their fathers long ago.

Angels Help Fulfill the Promises Made to the Fathers

Early in the Book of Mormon, Nephi was asked an important question by an angel: "Rememberest thou the covenants of the Father unto the house of Israel?" (1 Nephi 14:8). One of the chief responsibilities of angelic ministers is "to do the work of the covenants," in other words, "to assist the Father and the Son in the fulfillment of their promises to Abraham and his seed."[28] The angels who bestowed keys and powers on Joseph Smith can be seen as extending the Abrahamic covenant. These angelic fathers (Adam, Abel, Noah, Abraham, Moses, etc.[29]) returned to a remnant of the house of Israel, not only giving oral instruction to Joseph Smith but also bringing back a volume of written instruction for their progeny.

The coming of angels is also a testimony that the dead care for the living. The disembodied are concerned for us, look over us, bless us, and instruct us because they are interested in preparing families on both sides of the veil for an eventual sacred family reunion. Indeed, the Restoration itself binds prophets and righteous men and women into one great family.[30] In the heavens, angels are part of a family (see Ephesians 3:15). They are organized into family units whose individuals are concerned with those branches of relationship that exist on the earth. Deceased members of immediate families may become angels. The visitation of a family member looking after a loved one from the other side of the veil is not uncommon. President Joseph F. Smith informs us that often those angels who come to us are not strangers but are "from the ranks of our kindred, friends, and fellow-beings and fellow-servants" and can include "our fathers and mothers, brothers, sisters and friends who have passed away from this earth, having been faithful, and worthy to enjoy these rights and privileges, [who] may have a mission given them to visit their relatives and friends upon the earth again, bringing from the divine Presence messages of love, of warning, or reproof and instruction, to those whom they had learned to love in the flesh."[31] President Smith herein explained that circles of concern do not diminish with death. Instead, death enlarges our family ties.

Joseph of Egypt envisioned dying as merely going "unto my fathers" (JST Genesis 50:24). On the same occasion, he pronounced that the Lord would raise up a choice seer who would bring a knowledge of covenants made with the fathers to his descendants, remembering generation to generation (see vv. 24–37). The title page of the Book of Mormon tells us that one of its purposes is "to show unto the remnant of the House of Israel what great things the Lord hath done for their fathers; and that they may know the covenants of the Lord, that they are not cast off forever." These covenants were brought back by angels at the time of the Restoration.

As God commissions his angels to come to earth representing him, there is a coming together of two worlds, a covenant in which those on both sides of the veil are joined through the Atonement. Elder Bruce R. McConkie concurs: "Angelic ministrants [come] from former days to confer upon mortals their rights and prerogatives, and the restitution of all things spoken by the mouths of all the holy prophets since the world began . . .—all bringing back again their ancient powers and glories."[32] Part of the glory and power that angels restore to Abraham's seed is to gather them to The Church of Jesus Christ of Latter-day Saints (see Revelation 14:6; 3 Nephi 20:27).

When Moses appeared in the Kirtland Temple, he restored the keys necessary to gather the family of Israel (see D&C 110:11). Gathering was not only at the heart of Moses' ministration, it is at the heart of angelic work. Elder Orson Hyde prophesied that after the Saints have done all in their power to gather the remnants of the house of Israel, the Lord will send the armies of heaven to aid them.[33] Furthermore, those living on this earth when the Lord comes, who have not yet been gathered, will be brought by angels in a "final gathering of the elect."[34] Then all the promises and covenants made to and with the fathers will be fulfilled, including the eventual covenant of the return of the Savior.

Angels Will Prepare the Way of the Lord

Angels were employed throughout the Book of Mormon to declare Christ's first coming (see Helaman 13:7). The Lord will prepare the Saints of this dispensation for his second coming in the same way as the ministry of angels continues today (see Moroni 7:29). Elder Holland declares, "Perhaps more of us, including our students, could literally, or at least figuratively, behold the angels around us if we would but awaken from our stupor and hear the voice of the Spirit as those angels try to speak."[35]

President George Q. Cannon stated that we will not see angels

The Restoration of the Doctrine of Angels

"until we can learn to control those evil influences that are now invisible . . . and obey the counsels of those appointed to preside over us."[36] Elder Bruce R. McConkie declared to the Saints : "I can entertain angels . . . and so can you."[37] Certainly the Lord expects us to have experiences with angels; otherwise he would not have given us a test for recognizing them (see D&C 129:4).

Heavenly visitations may occur more than we think. Due to the sacred nature of angelic experiences, the telling of their ministrations is not the stuff testimony meetings should be made of. The fact that such events are not publicized does not mean they do not happen. In truth, in order for the Lord to claim a church, angels must be part of its members' lives. The ministering of angels has always been the heritage of the faithful. This status will continue "so long as time shall last, . . . or there shall be one [person] upon the face thereof to be saved" (Moroni 7:36). The presence of angels constitutes a sign that the gospel has been restored.[38] Indeed, the "divinity of any organization" depends on this principle: if angels do not minister to us, we are not the Lord's people, and his kingdom is not with us (Moroni 7:27–38).[39] Angelic ministration is one of the signs that The Church of Jesus Christ of Latter-day Saints is the true Church, because angels are around us, empowering, looking over, blessing, and teaching. Men and women of strong faith receive the ministration of angels to strengthen, comfort, and assist them with their life's work and the challenges they face.[40] Angels, whether seen or merely felt, are still ministering in hours of need.[41]

Conclusion

God's angels, who are disembodied, unembodied, translated, resurrected, or mortal beings, will continue to visit Latter-day Saints as they wrestle with critical problems. Angels will appear to chosen vessels of the Lord, who will then testify to the world to confirm the truthfulness of the Book of Mormon (see D&C 20:10). Glorious promises will be fulfilled as angels and Saints are gathered together in family units, fulfilling the promises made to Abraham of old. As the millennial dawn draws nigh, the ministry of angels will become increasingly important in the lives of Latter-day Saints on both sides of the veil as they prepare for the second coming of the Lord.[42] And, when the conflict ends, the faithful will realize, as did Elisha, that "they [angels] that be with us are more than they that be with them" (2 Kings 6:16).

NOTES

1. Jeffrey R. Holland, *"A Standard unto My People"* (address to religious educators at a symposium on the Book of Mormon, Brigham Young University, 9 Aug. 1994), 11, 13.

2. B. H. Roberts, *New Witnesses for God,* 3 vols. in 1 (Salt Lake City: Deseret News, 1911), 1:207.

3. Bruce R. McConkie, *Mormon Doctrine,* 2d ed. (Salt Lake City: Bookcraft, 1966), 503.

4. See George Reynolds, *A Complete Concordance of the Book of Mormon* (Salt Lake City: Deseret Book, 1957), 37–38.

5. Daniel H. Ludlow, ed., *Encyclopedia of Mormonism,* 5 vols. (New York: Macmillan Publishing), 1:40.

6. McConkie, *Mormon Doctrine,* 35.

7. See Joseph F. McConkie and Robert L. Millet, *Doctrinal Commentary on the Book of Mormon,* 3 vols. (Salt Lake City: Bookcraft, 1987–91), 1:76–77. Millet and McConkie state: "The expression 'spirit of the Lord' is used some forty times in the Book of Mormon, and almost without exception it has reference to the Holy Ghost or to the Light of Christ. If, indeed, here the Holy Ghost was Nephi's guide and teacher, this occasion is of tremendous significance, for it is the only scriptural occasion wherein the Holy Ghost makes a personal appearance to man" (76–77). Elder McConkie states: "We are left to our own interpretive powers to determine whether the messenger is the Spirit of Christ or the Holy Ghost" (McConkie, *Mormon Doctrine,* 752).

8. Joseph Smith, *Teachings of the Prophet Joseph Smith,* comp. Joseph Fielding Smith (Salt Lake City: Deseret Book, 1976), 170.

9. Joseph Smith, *The Elders Journal,* July 1838, 43.

10. See also McConkie, *Mormon Doctrine,* 35–36.

11. See Ezra Taft Benson, Conference Report, Oct. 1986, 3–7; or *Ensign,* Nov. 1986, 4–7.

12. Holland, *"A Standard unto My People,"* 10.

13. Orson Hyde, "Celebration of the Fourth of July," in *Journal of Discourses,* 26 vols. (London: Latter-day Saints' Book Depot, 1854–86), 6:368–69.

14. McConkie, *Mormon Doctrine,* 635.

15. See H. Donl Peterson, *Moroni—Ancient Prophet, Modern Messenger* (Bountiful: Horizon Publishers, 1983), 132–34.

16. Orson Pratt, *Divine Authority,* no. 1 (Liverpool: K. James Printer, 1848), 15.

17. See Smith, *Teachings of the Prophet Joseph Smith*, 157, 208.

18. Dallin H. Oaks, Conference Report, Oct. 1998, 51; or *Ensign*, Nov. 1998, 39.

19. Holland, *"A Standard unto My People,"* 11. Nevertheless, not every person on earth has a guardian angel assigned to him or her, as some falsely assumed. See Bruce R. McConkie, *Mormon Doctrine*, 2d ed. (Salt Lake City: Bookcraft, 1966), 341–42.

20. Hugh Nibley, "The Book of Mormon: Forty Years After," in John W. Welch, ed., *The Prophetic Book of Mormon, The Collected Works of Hugh Nibley: Volume 8, The Book of Mormon*, 13 vols. (Salt Lake City: Deseret Book, 1986–94), 8:549.

21. Hugh W. Nibley, *Teachings of the Book of Mormon, Semester 1*, Transcripts of 29 Lectures (Provo, Utah: Foundation for Ancient Research and Mormon Studies, 1993), 463.

22. Joseph Smith, "The Wentworth Letter," in James R. Clark, comp, *Messages of the First Presidency of The Church of Jesus Christ of Latter-day Saints*, 6 vols. (Salt Lake City: Bookcraft, 1965–75), 1:137.

23. Jeffrey R. Holland, *Christ and the New Covenant* (Salt Lake City: Deseret Book, 1997), 124.

24. See Bruce R. McConkie, Conference Report, Apr. 1985, 10; or *Ensign*, May 1985, 9.

25. Joseph Smith, "Wentworth Letter," in Clark, *Messages of the First Presidency*, 1:137.

26. See Hugh W. Nibley, *Teachings of the Book of Mormon, Semester 4*, Transcripts of 27 Lectures (Provo, Utah: Foundation for Ancient Research and Mormon Studies, 1993), 281.

27. Oaks, Conference Report, Oct. 1998, 51; or *Ensign*, Nov. 1998, 39.

28. Merrill J. Bateman, *Aspects of the Holy Ghost's Mission as Taught in the Book of Mormon* (Provo, Utah: Foundation for Ancient Research and Mormon Studies, 1996), 3.

29. See Peterson, *Moroni—Ancient Prophet, Modern Messenger*, 132–33.

30. See Joseph F. McConkie, "The Preparation of Prophets," in ed. H. Donl Peterson and Charles D. Tate Jr., *The Pearl of Great Price: Revelations from God* (Provo, Utah: Brigham Young University, 1989), 86.

31. Joseph F. Smith, *Gospel Doctrine*, 5th ed. (Salt Lake City: Deseret Book, 1939), 435–36.

32. Bruce R. McConkie, *The Millennial Messiah: The Second Coming of the Son of Man* (Salt Lake City: Deseret Book, 1982), 401.

33. See Orson Hyde, in *Journal of Discourses*, 2:68–69.

34. McConkie, *Millennial Messiah*, 314.

35. Holland, *"A Standard unto My People,"* 12.

36. George Q. Cannon, *Gospel Truth,* sel. Jerreld L. Newquist, 2 vols. (1957–74), 1:71.

37. Bruce R. McConkie, "The Rock of Salvation," *Improvement Era,* Dec. 1969, 85.

38. See McConkie, *Mormon Doctrine,* 635–36.

39. Ibid., 503.

40. See Bateman, *Aspects of the Holy Ghost's Mission,* 3.

41. See John A. Widtsoe, *Evidences and Reconciliations,* arr. G. Homer Durham, 3 vols. in 1 (Salt Lake City: Bookcraft, 1960), 402.

42. See Holland, *"A Standard unto My People,"* 12.

INDEX

Aaronic Priesthood, restoration of, 58
Abinadi: on repentance, 41–42; on condescension of God, 75; on Christ as Father, 76–77; on heirs of kingdom of God, 84; on seed of the Messiah, 210–11; as type and shadow of Christ, 201–2, 213
Abraham, 103, 105; seed of, 138; covenant with, 213, 228, 265
Abuses, 175, 177; drug, 178
Accountability, 28–30; of children, 56; concept of, 67–70; age of, 68; personal, 157
Adam and Eve: fall of, 5, 13, 154; probation of, 31
Addiction, 175; Internet, 177
Agency, 54–55, 130; and the plan of salvation, 58; freedom and, 162; doctrine of, 244; moral, 244, 252
Adversary, avoiding deception of, 53. *See also* Satan
Alcohol, addiction to, 178
Alma: instructions to Corianton, 24–25, 33–34, 189, 260; on code of member conduct, 45; on Redeemer, 75; counsel to Shiblon, 150; and spiritual rebirth, 159; instructions to Helaman, 184; conversion of, 214; and Fatherhood of God, 223; on agency, 250–51
Alma the Younger, 141, 166

Amalickiah, 163
America, visits of Christ to ancient, 3, 64–65, 229
Aminidab, 142
Ammon, 166
Amulek, 81, 195, 220, 253–54
Angels, 257–58; unembodied, 258–59; in the Book of Mormon, 260; ministering of, 261
Anti-Christs, 152–53, 260
Anti-Nephi-Lehies, 167, 181–82
Apostasy, 97, 118, 248–50
Ascension, 77
Assurance and validation, process of, 21
Atonement, the: and the Fall, 5; infinite, 6; need for, 14; merciful effects of, 33; King Benjamin, 64; and salvation of children, 68; physical anguish of, 76; redemptive power of, of Christ, 80–81, 84; and Zion, 105; role of, 111; teaching in the Book of Mormon regarding, 148; blessings of, 150–51; and presence of God, 155
Authority: divine, 43–44; keys of priesthood, 44; loss of true, 236

Bachman, Milton, 39
Ballard, Melvin J., 223–24
Baptism: as a covenant, 42, 138; by immersion, 42–43; infant, 63;

271

manner of, 67; of Christ, 78, 221; unto repentance, 193
Baruch, 113–14
Battles, 180
Behavior, assessing, 25
Belief: synonym for faith, 16
Benson, Ezra Taft: on the Fall, 31; on Columbus, 122; on godly sorrow, 189
Bible: Book of Mormon as witness of truth of, viii; Joseph Smith Translation of, 12, 62, 119–20, 240–41; and premortality and foreordination, 130; and repentance, 189; accuracy of, 232, 237–38; references to the Holy Ghost in, 233
Blood, atoning, 82
Body, immortality of, 9
Bondage: spiritual, 176–79; deliverance from, 184; relief from, in the scriptures, 185
Book of Mormon, the: as foundation of The Church, vii–viii; purposes of, viii, 123; message of, 1, 140; as keystone, 3; and the plan of salvation, 11; and process of faith, 22; translation of, 38–39, 62; and salvation of children, 68; testament of Christ as Son of God, 74, 77, 218; as second witness, 90; Nephites and, 92; and spiritual gathering, 93; and redemptive power of Christ, 97–98, 150; as tool for gathering, 107; and foreordination, 117, 120–21, 130; restores truths, 135, 248; study of, 136; as witness of Jesus Christ, 142–43, 217; and hope, 146; and the Atonement, 148; on founding lives on Christ, 149; and teaching correct principles, 172; violence and terror in, 174; warfare in, 178, 180; on repentance, 198–99; as witness of God the Father, 217–19; purpose of, 219–20; and doctrine of God the Father, 221; doctrine of the Godhead in, 230; evidences Joseph Smith's divine calling, 230; warns of the devil, 234–35; and doctrines of salvation, 240; and doctrine of agency, 247; and plan of restoration, 253; and angels, 258–59
Brother of Jared, 18
Bushman, Richard, 39

Cannon, George Q., 266–67
Captivity, spiritual, 179
Celestial kingdom, 15, 70–71; candidates for, 196
Chains, symbolism of, 175–77
Change, permanent, 166, 194
Charity, 192
Children: salvation of, 6, 62, 68, 142; love of parent to, 34; and learning, 55–56; accountability of, 56, 67; baptism of, 62–63, 70; innocence of, 64–65; parents' responsibility toward, 134, 136, 140, 168, 170; and addictions of parents, 178; involvement of parents with, 180; concern of the Father for, 225
Choice: consequences of mortal, 24; personal, 245; between good and evil, 246
Christianity, and disbelief in premortality, 130
Church, great and abominable, 235
Church of Christ: need for establishment of, 43–44; conduct of members of, 45
Church of Jesus Christ of Latter-day Saints, The: Book of Mormon as foundation of, vii–viii; and baptism of children, 70; mission of, 197; angels and gathering to, 266–67
Commandments: keeping the, 185, 191; Abinadi and the Ten, 203–4

Index

Commitment, 181
Compliance, 169
Compulsion, 162–63, 165–66, 176; force and, 169
Conflict, morality of, 174
Consecration, law of, 45
Conversion, 162–63
Corianton, Alma's instructions to, 24–25, 33–34
Covenant(s), 42, 226; gathering, 92; Christ to fulfill promises of, 107–8; salvation as, 135; knowledge of, 138; power of, 139–40; new and everlasting, 142; faithfulness to, 158; Abrahamic, 213; children of the, 226
Cowdery, Oliver: and the validity of the Book of Mormon, vii; and the translation of the Book of Mormon, 38–39, 64; and baptism by immersion, 42; revelation to, 56; appearance of John the Baptist to, 58; on baptism, 67; knowledge of, lost, 236
Creation, spiritual, 120
Cross, suffering of Christ on the, 208

Dead, work for the, 66
Death: infinite nature of, 6; spiritual, 6–7, 13, 84, 154; physical, 6–7, 84, 154; second, 156, 177; chains of, 175–77; redemption from, 221; state of the spirit after, 241
Deception, avoiding, 53
Defenses, spiritual, 182
Deliverance, 18–19, 184
Destruction, angels of, 264
Devil, 6; as enemy of God, 51; casting out, 208. *See also* Adversary; Lucifer; Satan
Disciples, 226
Discipline, doctrine and, 24
Disobedience, 59

Doctrine: "very points" of, in Book of Mormon, 7; and discipline, 24; restoration of, 62
Doctrine and Covenants, 240–41
Drug abuse, 178
Dummelow, J. R., 89

Earth: celestialization of, 103–4, 108–9; new, 111; creation of the, 127
Enduring to the end, 19, 21–22
Enos, 141
Equity, 247
Eternal life, 15, 82; as fruit of faith, 21–22; Savior to give, 210–11
Evil: forces of, 175; disposition to do, 192
Exaltation, 15; covenant of, 58; principles of, 254; fulness of, 254
Eyring, Henry B.: and the power of covenants, 139–40

Faith: doctrine of, 13; justification by, 14; and repentance, 15; as principle of power, 17–18; fruits of, 18–19; and knowledge, 19–20; as divine attribute, 20; Book of Mormon and process of, 22; King Benjamin on, 41; salvation through, 82; and eternal heritage, 131; in God and hope, 135, 137; sufficient unto salvation, 144, 159–60; unto repentance, 192; in Christ, 194, 246; and miracles, 263
Faithfulness, 19, 125, 178
Fall, the: in the Book of Mormon, 5; effects of, on mankind, 5–6, 13, 31; redemption from, 81, 154
Families, LDS: model for, 137; hope for, 141; and the last days, 146; angels and, 265
Family home evening, 182
Father, mortal Christ as Eternal, 76, 212
Faust, James E., 255
First Vision, the, 218, 222

Force, 169
Foreknowledge of God, 74, 125
Foreordination, doctrine of, 117, 120; biblical teachings on, 130; of Mary, 223. *See also* Premortality
Forgiveness, 188; complete, 35n. 5
Fornication, 25
Free agency, 162
Freedom, 54; and agency, 162, 245; absolute, 254–55

Gadianton robbers, 168
Garden of Gethsemane, 208
Gathering: doctrine of, 87–88, 96; Book of Mormon and spiritual, 93–94; physical, to lands of promise, 94; chronology of, 94–95; Book of Mormon as tool for, 107
Gentiles, 4; Israel to be scattered among, 105; establishment of the, 226–27
Gifts, spiritual, 19
God (the Father), 218–19; nature of, viii, 118; faith in, 14; nourishment by good word of, 17; as embodiment of faith, 20; relationship with, 54; becoming like, 55; communication with, 59; and importance of first coming of Christ, 73–74; foreknowledge of, 74, 125; Christ Only Begotten of, 76; concept of, 130; faith in the existence of, 141; presence of, 155; obedience of Christ to, 170; mortality of Son of, 207; doctrine of, in Book of Mormon, 221, 230; bearing witness of the Son, 222; Christ speaks directly to, 225–26; doing the will of, 227
Godhead, 119, 218, 221
Good and evil: knowing, 49–50, 245–46, 250; and light of Christ, 57–58

Gospel: restoration of, 37; essential principles of, 41, 254; covenants and ordinances of, 138; new and everlasting covenant of the, 142; Savior defines, 227; principles of, changed, 236
Grace, 137, 151; doctrine of, 152; and salvation, 159
Groberg, John H., 52–53

Hafen, Bruce C., 151–52
Harris, Martin, 63
Heaven, kingdom of, 225
Heavenly Father: and salvation, 142
Helaman, 149, 156, 167–68
Hell: temporary, 28; chains of, 175–77
Heritage, eternal, 131
Hinckley, Gordon B., 140
Holland, Jeffrey R.: on restoration, 30; on angels, 257, 261, 266; and fairness doctrine, 260
Holy Ghost: listening to the voice of the, 27; denying the, 156; bestowal of, 194; gift of the, 221–22; sustaining power of, 224; evidence of, in the Book of Mormon, 233; inspiration of, and translation, 238; and angelic ministry, 261–62
Home teachers, 139–40
Hope: absence of, 6–7; and faith, 15–16; light of, 87; Book of Mormon restores, 134–35; in Jesus Christ, 137
House of Israel: Christ visits, 4; restoration of, 88, 110, 219–20; gathering of, 90–91, 93, 102, 228; covenants with, 98, 228; Book of Mormon written to, 135–36; blessings to the, 158; deliverance of, 206
Humanism, 151–54
Hunter, Howard W., 145, 160
Hyde, Orson, 260

Identity, eternal, 126, 130

Index 275

Idolatry, 203
Ignorance, those who die in, 70–71
Immorality, 177
Immortality, 9, 25
Individualism, 157
Integrity, 44
Intelligence, 126
Interpreters, 40
Isaiah, 91, 205
Israelites: Christ visits, 4, 229; scattering and gathering of, 87–88; land of the American, 225

Jacob (son of Lehi), and the Fall, 5–6; and covenant to gather Israel, 93; on the Atonement, 153
Jeremiah, 125
Jerusalem, New, 11–12, 94
Jessee, Dean, 39
Jesus Christ: testimony of the Book of Mormon, vii; appearances of, 3–4, 64–65; redemptive power of, 6, 81; faith in, 13; as Savior, 28, 142–43; mercy of, 32; doctrine of, 42; following, 51–52; light of, 57–58; covenant relationship with, 57–58; first coming of, to the Jews, 73; mother of, 74; birth of, 75; mission of, 75–76, 84–85; infinite and eternal nature of, 76; ministry of, 78–80, 204–5, 208; spiritual gathering to, 94; second coming of, 107–8; to fulfill promises in the flesh, 109–10; premortal existence of, 121; foreordained mission of, 123; hope in, 137; binding to, through covenant, 138–39; divinity of mission of, 144–45; founding lives on, 149; atoning sacrifice of, 151; discipleship to, 170; will of, 170–71; our sins and agony of, 191; reconciliation to, 192; coming unto, 196–98;
Abinadi as type and shadow of, 201–2; condescension of, 205–7; as both Son and Father, 212; seed of, 214; Sonship of, 219; and angels, 257, 266. *See also* Messiah; Savior
Jesus Seminar, 239
Jews, first coming of Christ to, 73
John the Baptist: visitation of, 42, 58; and baptism of Christ, 78; ministry of, 221
Joseph (of Egypt), 111–12, 265–66
Judgment, 10, 156; final, 28, 30–31, 249; between good and evil, 49–50; of heavenly messengers, 264
Justice, Jesus' mercy and, 32, 84–85, 241

Kac, Arthur W., 90
Keys: of priesthood authority, 44
Keystone, 3
Kimball, Spencer W., 159
King Anti-Nephi-Lehi, 159, 189
King Benjamin, 41, 82, 263; on the Atonement, 64; on salvation through Christ, 149; and repentance, 190–91
King Follett Discourse, 254
King Noah, 183, 202–3
King Orihah, 136
Kirtland Temple, 266
Knowledge: faith and, 19–20; covenants and, 138
Korihor, 14–15, 74, 152–53

Laban, 179
Laman and Lemuel, 134, 176, 178–79
Lamanites: Nephites and, 163–64; conversion of, 168
Last days, 146
Latter-day Saints: Book of Mormon restores hope to, 134–35; strengthening of, by angels, 263
Law: and freedom, 54; salvation of

those who die without, 66, 70; moral, 83–84
Leadership, participatory, 180
Lee, Harold B.: on faith, 21; on nature of scriptures, 50; on premortality, 128
Legalism, 151–53
Lehi, 175; on the Messiah, 80; and covenants, 109; on redemption, 149
Lewis, C. S., 153
Lewittes, Mendell, 90
Lost tribes, 98; Christ appears to, 3
Love: increase of, 33–34; pure, of Christ, 194
Lucifer, plan of, 8. *See also* Adversary; Devil; Satan

Manuscript, lost, 63–64
Marriage, 138
Mary (the mother of Jesus Christ): Nephi assured of role of, 74–75; foreordination of, 223
Matthews, Robert J., on translation of the Bible, 68, 71
Maxwell, Neal A., 117; on restoration of truths, 119; on premortality, 128–29; on hope, 146; on immortality, 253
McConkie, Bruce R.: on the Book of Mormon and the Bible, 2; on faith, 20; on the book of life, 29–30; on agency, 54; on salvation of children, 65; on accountability, 68; on the gathering, 91, 94–95; on millennial Christ, 108; on premortal existence, 121–22, 247; on Columbus, 122; on foreordination of Christ, 123; on intelligences, 126; on spirits of men, 127–28; on eternal realities of religion, 145; on the second death, 177; on second chance for salvation, 196, 199; on war against scriptures, 235–36; on the Bible, 239; on angels, 258, 263, 266–67
McKay, David O., 30, 162, 165; on the ideal society, 169
Media, 182
Melchizedek, 12; Priesthood, 246, 261
Mercy, 32; and justice, 84–85; repentance and, 85
Messiah: mission of the mortal, 73–74; coming of the, 201; teachings about, 204; mortality of, 207; ministry of, 209–10; seed of the, 212; testifying of Jesus as the, 217
Military, 174
Millennium, 94, 102, 108
Millett, Robert L.: on mercy and justice, 32; on salvation, 63
Ministry, lay, 44
Missionary work, 167; abandonment of, 25; Alma on, 45–46; of Alma and sons of Mosiah, 111
Mission of Christ, 84–85
Model: plan of salvation, 104–5; for families in Zion, 137
Morality, 24
Mormon, 15; on good and evil, 51; on salvation of children, 76–66; on the gathering, 95–96; on redemption, 155–56; on judgment, 157–58; on repentance, 189–90
Moroni, 163–65, 260; on becoming sons of God, 33; mentoring of Joseph Smith, 37–38, 46; on prayer, 172; on the Book of Mormon, 175; defenses of, 182
Mortality: purpose of, 58; agency in, 248–52
Moses: prophecies of, 87; law of, 204; appearance of, 266
Mosiah, book of: on missionary work, 45–46; sons of, 166
Mount of Transfiguration, 222

Index

Nehor, 199
Nelson, Russell M., 91
Nephi, 17; on the Bible, 60–61; on Christ's baptism, 79; on judgment of the Son of God, 82–83; on Isaiah's ensign, 91–92; on gathering, 92–93, 110; and following commandments of God, 137; on salvation, 149, 158–59, 178–79; on ministry of Son of God, 220; and the Godhead, 221–22
Nephites: visit of Christ to, 3–4, 224; and the Book of Mormon, 92; Savior's ministry to, 111; and Lamanites, 163–64; Three, 227–28
New Jerusalem, 11–12; Zion as, 106; Moroni prophesies of, 111–12; and salvation, 112; and faith in God, 191

Oaks, Dallin H.: on justice, 32–33; on revelation, 71; on keeping the commandments, 153
Obedience, 19, 169; compulsion to, 171; and love, 172
Ordinances, 42; administration of, 71; Book of Mormon and, of the gospel, 138
Outer darkness, 28

Packer, Boyd K.: on sin, 25; on true doctrine, 27; and the plan of salvation, 101–3; on values, 170; on obedience, 171; on moral agency, 244
Pahoran, 165
Pain, relief from, in the scriptures, 185
Parents: and teaching of children, 55–56, 134, 136, 168; conversion of, 169–70; addictions of, 178; involvement of, with children, 180; and wayward children, 264
Payne, J. Barton, 91
Peace, 111, 167

Pearl of Great Price, 240–41
Perfection, unity of the Godhead in, 229
Plagues, 203
Plan of Salvation, 11, 58, 190, 228; Joseph Smith integral to, 106; Zion as, 115; access to, 195; Holy Ghost as part of, 234; details of, lost in Bible, 235
Postmortality, 28–29; agency in, 252–54
Power of God, 206
Pratt, Orson: on the Book of Mormon, 2; on belief, 14; on second death, 156; on Moroni, 260
Prayer, 59
Premortality, 118–20, 128–30, 228; agency in, 245–46
Pride, 25
Priesthood: keys of, authority, 44; restoration of Aaronic, 58; angels and restoration of the, 261
Principles, teaching correct, 172
Priorities, 182
Prison, spirit, 31
Probation, 31–32
Procrastination, 194–96
Prodigal, 34
Promised land, 185
Promises, fulfillment of, 109–10, 115
Prophecy, 74, 203
Prophets: testimony of ancient, viii; living, 53–59; unique role of, 89–90; and spiritual growth, 250
Publications, prurient, 182
Purpose, Father and Son one in, 229

Rathbone, Tim, 39–40
Rebirth, 42–43
Redeemer, Jesus Christ as, 148
Redemption: and salvation, 80–81, 84; and restoration of scattered Israel, 110; necessity of, 148; through Christ, 150; Mormon on, 155–56

Reliance, 16
Remorse, 198
Repentance: faith and, 15; sincere, 25–26; necessity of, 32–33; Abinadi on, 41–42; and accountability, 67; and redemption, 81, 150; and mercy, 85; and salvation, 159–60; and the Book of Mormon, 187; process of, 188; James E. Talmage on, 190; procrastinating the day of, 194–96; in mortality, 196; angels command to, 264
Reproof, 33
Resolution, 198
Responsibilities, 137; moral, 244
Restoration: law of, 9–10, 241; plan of, 29, 252–53; blueprint for, 38–39; sign of the, 46; of doctrine, 62; and repentance, 198; latter-day doctrinal, 242; of good and evil, 250; angels in the, 259–60
Resurrection: appearances of Christ after, 3–4, 64, 241; law of, 9; definition of, 29; physical-spiritual restoration of, 30; First, 31, 241; and Christ's healing ministry, 85–86; universal, 155, 220; Bible documents Christ's, 241; angels and, 259
Revelation, new, 240
Reynolds, George, 39
Right and wrong: knowing, 49–50; and light of Christ, 57–58; discerning between, 59; in the Book of Mormon, 178
Righteousness, 44, 136; Christ to fulfill all, 79; insufficiency of, 153; enduring in, 227
Robinson, Stephen E., 118
Romney, Marion G., 127, 189

Sacrament, 138, 143–44, 193, 226
Sacred Grove, 218
Salvation, 21; from sin, 31; covenant of, 58, 135; of children, 63–65; of those who die without law, 66; through redemption, 81–82, 211; through faith, 82–83, 144; plan of, 101, 105; latter-day work of, 111; grace and, 137; binding link of, 138; through covenants, 142; humanist approach to, 154; of self, 191; no second chance for, 196; through the Son of God, 220; Book of Mormon and the doctrines of, 240
Salvationism, 154, 159
Samuel the Lamanite: on first coming of Christ, 78, 220–21; redemption and, 80–81; on righteousness, 155; and agency, 245
Satan, 234; plan of, 11, 162; and agency, 54–55; and compulsion, 176; Book of Mormon warns of, 234–35; subjection to, 241; lies of, 248–49. *See also* Adversary; Devil; Lucifer
Savior: false notion of alternate, 7–8; Jesus Christ as, 28; mortal, 74–75, 207; judgment and death of, 210; postresurrection appearance of, 224
Scattering, gathering and, 87–88, 96
Scott, Richard G., 146, 244
Scriptures: and guidelines for behavior, 50; devil wages war against, 235; modification of, 236; misinterpretation of, 238; Holy Ghost needed to understand, 239
Second Coming, the, 102
Seers, 53–59, 89–90
Self-will, 181
Sheep: other, 4–5; lost, 98
Sherem, 153
Shule, 136
Signs and wonders, 19
Sin: resurrection and, 31; original, 63; redemption from, 82–83, 150; overcoming repetitive, 181;

recognition of, 190–91; remission of, 193; offering for, 211
Smith, Alvin (Joseph Smith's brother), 63, 70
Smith, Alvin (Joseph Smith's son), 63
Smith, Emma, 40
Smith, Hyrum, 67
Smith, Joseph, Jr.: on the Book of Mormon, 2, 240; and translation of Bible, 12, 62; on faith as principle of power, 17; on testimony, 20, 22; on principle of revelation, 27; tutoring of, 37, 46; translation of Book of Mormon, 38–39; and baptism by immersion, 42–44; and need for establishment of Church of Christ, 44–45; and good and evil, 51; and revelation on Spirit of Jesus Christ, 57–58; appearance of John the Baptist to, 58; on prayer, 59–60; and age of accountability, 68–69; and revelations for the Restoration, 71; on the gathering, 95; and covenants, 109; on building up Zion, 114; on premortality, 120; on intelligence of spirits, 126–27; on power of the devil, 177; on repentance, 198; First Vision of, 218; and foreordination, 223; on the Godhead, 228–29, 230; on the Bible, 237–38; and King Follett Discourse, 254; and angels, 257–58, 262; on translated beings, 259
Smith, Joseph F., 149
Smith, Joseph Fielding, 105; on premortality, 128–29; on immorality, 176–77; on the spirit world, 195–96; on divine investiture of authority, 229
Smith, William, 63
Social services, 182

Sons of perdition, 156
Sorrow, godly, 188
Spirit(s): following the, 26–27; gifts of the, 27; postmortal, world, 28; repentance in the, world, 195–96; world of, 253–54; unembodied, 258–59; disembodied, 265
Suffering, relief from, 183
Symbolism, 143–44

Talmage, James E., 190
Taylor, John, 29, 68
Teachers, home and visiting, 139–40
Teancum, 164
Temple, 105–6
Temptation, 77, 175, 178; burying, 181–82; helplessness toward, 183; overcoming, 184
Terrestrial kingdom, 196
Testing, 128
Three Nephites, 227–28
Transgression, moral, 24
Translated beings, 259
Translation of the Book of Mormon, 38; sequence in, 39, 62–64; process of, 62
Tree of life, 109
Trust, 16–17
Truth, divine, 171
Truths, Book of Mormon restores, 135

Unbaptized, fate of, 63
Urim and Thummim, 40

Validation, process of assurance and, 21
Vision: to Nephi, 121–22
Visitations, angelic, 258, 267
Visiting teachers, 139–40

Walvoord, J. F., 90
War, 162, 164; in the Book of Mormon, 178, 180
Weakness, overcoming, 184

Welch, Jack, 39–40
Whitmer, John, 39
Wicked, resurrection of the, 241–42
Wickedness, 83–84, 156
Widtsoe, John A., 157
Wilkinson, Ernest L., 165
Will of the Lord, 179
Witness: Book of Mormon as second, 90
Wonders, signs and, 19
Woodruff, Wilford: on latter-day Zion, 113
Word, converting power of the, 168–69
Word of Wisdom, 177

Works: grace and, 151; salvation and good, 158
Worth, things of greatest, 255

Young, Brigham: on the Spirit of the Lord, 60; on Zion, 104, 114; on the Bible, 238–39

Zarahemla, 164
Zenos, allegory of, 96
Zerahemnah, 163
Zion: latter-day, 102, 104; establishment of, 111–14; as plan of salvation, 115
Zions, gathering to multiple, 93